BLINKERS ARE *NOT* OPTIONAL

THE LEADERS WE HAVE VS.
THE LEADERSHIP WE NEED

DAVID MILSTONE, Ed.D.

For Mom and Dad
For Sherri, Alexandra, and Matthew
For all the leaders, young and old,
whom I have been privileged
to work with and learn from

Leadership is in free fall,
but it's not too late to correct its course.

CONTENTS

INTRODUCTION

Does it seem to you that there is a significant shortage of effective leadership these days? It certainly does to me. Has it always been this way, or are we witnessing a decline in effective leadership and leaders who demonstrate honesty and integrity?

As social media and technology have evolved, a great deal of attention has been brought to the public's view of the actions of people in leadership positions. Unfortunately, much of this attention has spotlighted negative leadership,

- Doctors, politicians, professional athletes, entertainment moguls, religious clergy, and other trusted leaders have committed acts of sexual misconduct.

- CEOs of bankrupt organizations have received multimillion-dollar severance packages as their employees lost their jobs.

- College administrators have accepted bribes from parents to ensure admission for their children.

- U.S. immigration policy has been developed that intentionally separated immigrant children from immigrant parents trying to enter the country.

- Elected officials have knowingly and divisively shared blatant mistruths with the public they were elected to serve.

The public trust in politicians is at near historic lows. As of August 2020, according to a Pew Research Center survey, only 20 percent of Americans say they trust the government in Washington to "do the right thing most of the time."[1] Is it any wonder that the more often people hear about local, national, and global news, the less they trust their leaders?

In 2007, Lee Iacocca, former CEO of the Chrysler Corporation, wrote the book *Where Have All the Leaders Gone?*[2] The country was in conflict due to President George W. Bush's decision to enter the United States into war with Iraq. Iacocca implied that the war, which was responsible for the deaths of 4,400 U.S. soldiers and civilians,[3] and more than one million Iraqi soldiers and civilian deaths,[4] only occurred because of the personal agenda of the president and a few of his cabinet members. Believing that the United States should never engage in a war without proof of a risk to our security or that of an ally, Iacocca's book was a call for the return of strong, thoughtful, and ethical leadership. This book is a much needed second call.

A decade after Iacocca's book, we witnessed Donald J. Trump, a celebrity businessman with no previous political experience, elected to the position of president of the United States. Regardless of one's political affiliation, most agree that the style of leadership demonstrated by President Trump had not existed at the POTUS level in our collective lifetimes. His actions united a portion of the United States that had previously been ignored. This group, known as his "base," became part of an increasingly polarized U.S. society. President Trump's leadership style created a firestorm, resulting in congressional inquiries pertaining to his actions, routine fact-checking of his statements, a pandemic response that shifted from decisions based on science and medical expertise to decisions based on economic factors and an upcoming election, and numerous legal challenges sent to district courts and the Supreme Court alleging that his actions violated the Constitution and laws of the United States.

Our country has become politically divided to an extraordinary degree over issues such as the COVID-19 pandemic, voter rights, immigration, universal health coverage, gun control, and global warming. Political party leaders seem to disagree on almost everything and political science experts argue that the divisions between people in the United States have not been as drastically pronounced since the Civil War.

As a result of the vast divisions within the country and perhaps demonstrating a referendum on the president himself, the 2020 presidential election resulted in a record number of ballots (155 million) submitted in person and via the mail-in option, which was offered due to the election occurring in the middle of the worst pandemic since 1918. Despite unproven allegations and court appeals by the incumbent president that the election process was somehow "rigged," and the election "stolen," the country elected Joe Biden, who received more than 81 million votes to become the new president in 2021. This was a record high vote count for an elected president, and almost seven million votes more than the incumbent president received. From a leadership perspective, the citizens of the country sent a message that they were engaged and expected the new leadership to do better than the outgoing leadership.

This book responds to a national, regional, and local leadership trend that seems to parallel that of the Burger King slogan, "Have it your way." More and more leaders have bypassed the *rules of leadership* and let convenience be their guide. The rules once considered to be leadership expectations, such as learning how to increase organizational effectiveness and caring about the development of employees, are severely lacking in many U.S. organizations today.

According to a 2017 Gallup report:[5]

- Only 30 percent of employees and 35 percent of managers are engaged in their jobs.

- Lack of engagement costs the United States almost $400 billion annually in productivity.

- Only 18 percent of managers demonstrate the talent required for managing others, and organizations fail to choose the candidate with the right talent for a manager job 82 percent of the time.

To show a parallel to what has occurred in the field of leadership, let us look at another important part of society, namely, transportation, and specifically the use of automobiles. Drivers learn the "rules of the road" when they get their learner's permit and begin to drive. They learn about using the blinker (turn signal) when changing lanes, yielding to oncoming traffic, and keeping a safe distance from the car in front of them. These rules are not self-evident until one studies the training manual and takes to the road. Good drivers learn and practice them, but unfortunately, many drivers consider them within the Burger King "have it your way" framework, and as a result, these rules of the road have become seemingly optional to many people. For this reason, we have lots of accidents on the roads and a heck of a lot of road rage. It seems so simple—to reduce accidents and angry people, drivers need to remember that using blinkers, yielding, and refraining from tailgating are not optional. In a similar way, leaders need to learn and practice the "how-to's" of becoming effective leaders. Those, too, are not optional. By doing so, our organizations will prosper, our workers will find value and satisfaction in their work, and maybe our drivers will become a bit more civil.

Many current leaders take the "I am perfect just the way I am" approach as opposed to putting in the effort, as research argues is the way to be successful. This book argues for a different path for the leaders of tomorrow. In so many ways, at a time when the need for effective leadership has grown, effective leadership has deteriorated and needs to be fixed. Too often we are finding that the leaders we have, do not possess or demonstrate traits and skills that we need them to have. As a result, until we change our expectations and behaviors in this regard, we will continue to hire and elect individuals to leadership positions who are quite like what we have now—largely ineffective.

In the chapters that follow, we will look at the state of leaders in this country and around the world, replace old leadership questions with new ones, and offer a new paradigm from which to search for and find the leadership we need for the future.

As we begin, I invite you to recall the leaders you have worked for or with. How many would you consider effective? How many would you want to work with again?

CHAPTER I

The Current State of Leadership

As the data demonstrates, far too many of today's leaders are ineffective, ill-suited for their positions, and in many cases, do harm to their employees, teammates, and organizations. Leadership is free falling, but it does not have to be this way.

Who among us has not heard the mantra, "people leave managers, not companies," which has become the rallying cry behind the need to improve conditions in organizations nearly everywhere? Until recently, businesses believed that employee satisfaction and retention hinged on salaries, but according to Payscale, only 25 percent of employees leave their job because they want more money.[6] While salary, job title, work hours, and vacation days are certainly important to most of us, the data demonstrates what we have long believed - that most of the workers who voluntarily leave their jobs do so because of their bosses—their leaders.

A Gallup study conducted in October 2013 indicated that "one in two employees had left their job to get away from their manager at some point in their career."[7] DDI, a global leadership consulting organization, reaffirmed in their 2019 Frontline Leader Project that "people leave managers." Their study showed that 57 percent of the employees left, and an additional 32 percent considered leaving their jobs because of their manager. Even more disturbing, 14 percent had left multiple jobs for this reason.[8]

We know that people leave jobs for a wide variety of reasons:

- Looking for growth opportunities or jobs at other organizations,

- Wanting to try a different vocation or field of interest,

- Spouse gets a promotion in a different geographical area,

- Illness or retirement.

Even with all these reasons considered, it is critical to understand that good workers leave jobs and organizations most often and *primarily* due to bad bosses.

Based on our collective experiences, we know that *effective* leaders find ways to support the growth and development of their employees. As previously stated, however, we also know that *ineffective* leaders often cause good employees to quit their jobs. With this knowledge, I sought to supplement the data produced by Gallup and the Pew Research Center with a personal experiment. I wanted to learn the percentage of employees in my networks who found their past supervisors/leaders to be effective. To that end, I conducted a Facebook/LinkedIn poll in March 2021.[9] I asked respondents to consider and share whether their past supervisors/leaders had been 1) excellent/good, 2) fair/between-good-and-not-good, or 3) not-good/poor. The responses were eye-opening.

In total, the survey respondents considered a total of 1,412 supervisors/leaders and rated **only 37 percent** of them as "excellent/good." Conversely, 63 percent of respondents assessed their supervisors to be less than "good." Several respondents indicated that they were uncomfortable sharing online ratings about their past leaders due to concerns that their supervisors might somehow identify their posts and retaliate against them, which is telling. A few respondents also communicated off-line to indicate that they believed *none* of their past supervisors were "excellent or good." Whether these numbers match your experiences or not, I would be willing to bet that you find them discouraging and unacceptable, as do I.

It is important to note that the results of the Facebook/LinkedIn survey cannot be generalized to all supervisors, given the small sample size. These responses certainly were in line, however, with studies done by national agencies such as Gallup and Pew and suggest that most leaders are not effective, and some even toxic, which as you know, is the primary reason that good employees leave their jobs.

Three clarifying statements are needed before we continue. First, while all supervisors are leaders, not all leaders are supervisors. A great majority of leaders do supervise others in a formal, organizationally sanctioned sense. They hire their staff, train them, and formally evaluate their efforts. Some other leaders are responsible for a program or project that involves others, or work with volunteers, but are not considered formal supervisors. They may carry the title of "advisor," but certainly need to take a leadership role.

Second, some organizational members demonstrate leadership from more of an informal position. You likely have heard of "leading from the middle" in which employees gain a great deal of influence and can take on a leadership role as a situation warrants it. An example from professional sports would be a pitcher on a Major League Baseball team who takes it upon himself, during a team slump, to offer inspiration or strategy based on his years of experience or simply because he is trusted. Leaders from the middle can also come from grassroots efforts, exemplified by Alexandria Ocasio-Cortez, a congresswoman currently representing New York. Ms. Ocasio-Cortez has helped raise a deep, grassroots effort, along with Vermont Senator Bernie Sanders, pertaining to a Green New Deal that focuses on climate action. All leaders can have a large amount of influence on the productivity, growth, development, and success of their organizations in virtually all professional fields. The formal leaders' roles, however, differ from those of the informal leaders, so to help simplify a very complex topic, this book looks primarily at positional leadership, which gives an individual their leadership status by the nature of their position.

The third clarification pertains to the role of "leader" versus the role of "manager." In this case, all leaders are managers, but not all managers are leaders. The roles of each are unique, and in practice most formal/positional leaders have a job description that includes management functions as well as leadership functions. Management functions pertain to the daily administrative operations such as budgets, hiring, planning, running staff meetings, and so on, and leadership functions pertain to providing vision, inspiring possibilities, creating an environment conducive to effecting change, helping to tap the motivations of employees, and so on. Can you imagine a Chief Executive Officer (CEO) who focuses only on maintaining the status quo or one who creates vision without a plan on how to achieve it? Probably not, because both are necessary. Management functions are a separate and important component of organizational effectiveness, as are leadership functions. Both management and leadership are necessary for the growth and development of an organization or of a smaller entity, such as an organizational subunit, like a committee, team, or department. The often-asked question of which is more important - management skills or leadership skills - is not a fair one. It depends on the result you desire, right? In terms of this book and developing more effective leaders, our answer needs to be "both."

As we delve into the factors that surround the current status of leadership, we should be aware that there is no lack of available educational materials about leadership. In fact, there is a wealth of information available to help leaders develop their skills. A search on Amazon.com in January 2021 indicated that there were more than 70,000 books currently for sale which focus on the topic of leadership.[10] Some books focus on the "how-to" methods of increasing leadership effectiveness. Others target the crucible moments in which ordinary people were faced with extraordinary challenges. A smaller number of books discuss the theories that explain leadership and the connection between leadership and organizational success.

With all the literature available to leaders, my survey data begs the question—why are so few leaders and supervisors deemed "excellent/good" and what can be done, individually and collectively, to increase the percentage who achieve success?

Before looking directly at some reasons that so many leaders are ineffective, I'd like to expand on a topic from the introduction and share a personal experience that has helped me to classify leaders into three categories and focus on why effective leadership matters.

Highway Leadership

While driving down the highway on a colorful fall day, I observed a vehicle move from the middle lane to the right lane without using a turn signal. It may have been a sign of my age, but under my breath, I sarcastically said, "Oh, I must have forgotten that Mercedes drivers are exempt from needing to use blinkers." A short while later, a different vehicle entered traffic from the right side on-ramp and flew past the yield sign without slowing down at all – in fact, I believe they sped up as they merged into the highway traffic. Not too much later, I saw another car in the left lane tailgating the car in front of it. What does the Registry of Motor Vehicles say about the space between cars?[11] I believe they use a three-second rule that requires enough space between cars to count to "three one-thousand," or something like that, right? This one was not even close – or, well, you know what I mean. For people who drive on a regular basis, seeing these traffic violations is nothing new. In fact, some would say that they have unfortunately become the norm.

As I see it, there are three general types of drivers on the roads today. The first type of driver makes the effort to be constantly aware of their driving. They consider the comfort of their passengers and pay attention to how their vehicle interacts with the other vehicles on the road. We will call these the *Progressive Drivers.*

A second type of driver seems oblivious to the vehicles around them. They do what they deem necessary to get to their destination. They are used to hovering close to the car in front of them and do not seem to notice that their passenger is holding onto the strap above their window while trying to not show fear. We can call these the *Win at All Cost Drivers.*

A third type simply drives as they always have. They do not give their driving habits much thought. It has worked for all the years leading up to now, so why fix something that is not broken? We will call these the *Same-Ole, Same-Ole Drivers*.

Leadership can be viewed in much the same way that we view these three categories of drivers. The first category of leaders (Progressive Drivers) understands that successful transportation is about meeting the needs of those in the car as well as others on the road. They pay attention, listen carefully, and enjoy the ride. Progressive Drivers take responsibility for mistakes they make and keep their priorities clear, as their number one priority is to get everyone in the car safely to their intended destination.

The second category of leaders (Win at All Cost Drivers) sets their sights on the desired destination and does whatever is necessary to get there. They may be aggressive at times, prefer to micro-manage their passengers, and believe that anyone who sees the road differently than they do is wrong. The Win at All Cost Drivers may get to the finish line first on a regular basis, but they often upset their passengers and neighboring vehicles, so many people may not want to ride with them for very long.

The third category of leaders (Same-Ole, Same-Ole Drivers) does not give driving much thought and spends the time driving their cars the same way they always have. They have driven these roads for so long that they feel they can run on autopilot. The gas tank gets filled on Fridays, the tire pressure and washer fluid are checked once a month, and the oil is changed every six months. These routines have worked for decades, so they see no need to change anything.

Just as driving styles matter to most people (and most insurance companies), years of research have demonstrated that leadership matters a great deal to the success of employees and organizations. In terms of leadership, many readers will likely agree that the example of the Progressive Drivers parallels what we refer to as *Effective Leaders*. The individuals who practice effective leadership:

- Create an atmosphere of honesty and trust
- Achieve success by setting clear goals, developing a strategy to achieve the goals, and evaluating the results of their efforts
- Celebrate accomplishments
- Offer employees positive and constructive feedback as well as opportunities for growth and development
- Actively support employees' career goals

In return for spending between 33 to 50 percent of their lives at work, according to a survey by the Society for Human Resource Management (SHRM), employees expect the following from their leaders:[12]

- To be treated with respect
- To receive equitable pay
- To develop trust between employees and leaders
- To have reasonable job security
- To be given opportunities to apply their skills to their work

Business magnate Richard Branson, founder of the Virgin Group, nicely linked what effective leaders do and what employees expect from them when he said, "Train people well enough so they can leave, but treat them well enough so they don't want to."[13]

Some organizations accomplish this linkage of expectations and leadership effectiveness so well that their employees nominate them as one of the "Best Places to Work" on an annual basis through programs run by *Fortune, Forbes, Glassdoor*, etc. Unfortunately, however, the Gallup and Pew research and my personal Facebook/LinkedIn survey suggest that a great many employees have not had the experience of working for an organization that they believe to be a "best place" or even a *good* place to work, in large part due to their leaders.

To see where many leaders, managers, and organizations fall short, we can learn a lot from the Win at All Cost Drivers. Most readers will likely agree that the examples of the Win at All Cost Drivers in many ways parallel what we refer to as *Ineffective Leaders*. The individuals who practice ineffective leadership tend to:

- Micromanage staff to ensure that tasks are done *their* way
- Believe that employees work *for* them, not *with* them
- Establish an "every-person-for-themselves" approach to achieving goals
- Often take credit for successes, regardless of who was responsible for them
- Create an atmosphere of mistrust and lack of support
- Create an environment in which risk-taking is only valued when it is successful—otherwise, it leads to reprimands or terminations
- Block productivity due to employee frustration

In practice, the results of ineffective leaders' actions may sometimes achieve short-term productivity, but quite often they cause employees to become dissatisfied. These workers then bring their negative attitudes to work with them each day. They lose their excitement about their work and often share their negativity with others in their organization. As mentioned, this ineffective leadership style very often leads to employees quitting their jobs.

The TV show, *Saturday Night Live* portrayed this negativity through characters called "Wendy Whiner and Doug Whiner."[14] Wendy and Doug had the uncanny ability to find the negative in virtually everything. When it was sunny outside, Wendy reminded everyone that by the time they got out of work, it would probably be dark and cold. When employees received raises, Doug would remind them that after taxes and the increase in health-care costs, they would be lucky to afford to buy dessert with their lunch.

Negativity in the workplace is one of the greatest enemies of productivity and creativity. No one wants to work with negative people and when they must, they end up counting down the hours until they leave for the day, for a vacation, or for good.

Circular Toxicity

At their worst, ineffective leaders can create more than just an uncomfortable place of work, but a *toxic* environment in which many of the best employees feel compelled to leave. Each time that occurs, an employee's departure leaves the organization or department with one less top-notch employee. At the same time, other workers may want to leave the toxic environment, but for a variety of reasons, they cannot or do not.

Why would anyone choose to remain in a toxic work environment? One reason an employee might stay is that their choices may be limited, for example, due to being new or having less-developed skills at this point in their career. Other employees may need to remain in the region due to geographic considerations for their families. Some employees do not leave because they do not see or feel the toxicity in the environment—it has become invisible to them. In these cases, sadly, the toxicity of their workplace has become their expected *norm*. Their environment is so negative that these staff members *expect* the environment to be negative and soul-sucking because that is how they have come to see all workplaces. This circumstance is somewhat like one partner not leaving an unhealthy relationship—it often takes someone from outside the environment to see what is going on.

If these circumstances were not hard enough, sometimes an employee remains in a toxic environment because they are waiting their turn to take the lead in the organization. Often, these employees will have a path to the leadership role due to union rules, seniority, or political favors, and may then perpetuate the circumstances that created the toxic environment.

In addition to the devastating effect a toxic environment can have on its workers, such an environment will also be unattractive to external candidates. Skilled candidates who are unhappy with their workplace have the choice of moving to a different organization—one that is vibrant and exciting. In this all-too-common toxic environment scenario, the skilled employees leave, the remaining employees (often less-skilled or geographically bound) become the nucleus of the organization, and positions vacated by the frustrated workers attract only mediocre candidates due to the organization's reputation for toxicity. If this sounds like a negative, vicious cycle, that is because it closely resembles one. I call this *circular toxicity*. Stated more simply, the characteristics of ineffective leaders, workplaces, and circular toxicity can be highlighted as follows:

Ineffective Leadership

- A lack of concern for employee development
- Micromanagement of direct reports
- Lack of employee involvement in decision-making
- Finger pointing/playing the "blame game"
- Low level of emotional intelligence demonstrated by the leader

Dysfunctional Workplace

- Employees are frustrated and lose excitement about their work
- Negativity permeates the workplace
- Employees sabotage the efforts of their colleagues and supervisor(s)
- Lower levels of innovation, creativity, and productivity
- "Clock-watching" becomes the norm
- Skilled employees often quit their jobs

Circular Toxicity

- Skilled employees have left their jobs

- Less-skilled employees stay (not able to get jobs elsewhere)

- Some skilled, but dissatisfied employees remain because they are geographically bound (feel "stuck" there)

- Some employees become blind to the dysfunctions of the workplace (rudeness, apathy, lack of collegiality), thus unknowingly perpetuating the dysfunctions

- Less-skilled candidates are the only external applicants for advertised jobs due to the organization's diminished reputation

- Productivity of the workplace remains low

- Ineffective leadership and dysfunctions of the workplace continue

A recent Accountemps study of 450 employees working in office environments in the United States showed that 59 percent had first-hand experience with an overbearing boss/micromanager. Of those with a micromanager, 68 percent of employees said it decreased their morale and 55 percent said it hurt their productivity.[15] In another study, BetterUp Labs surveyed 2,285 U.S. workers about their workplaces. Nine out of ten employees indicated they would trade $20,000 or more from their annual salary to be in a workplace that offered them work with a sense of meaning and a supportive supervisor who cared about their growth and development.[16]

The Changing Perception of Leadership

In the next chapter, we will explore many of the reasons that today's leaders are ineffective and how we can alter this as we move forward. To better understand the current views of leadership, we will first look back at how leadership has changed shape over the years.

Many people have asked the question, "Are leaders born or made?" In the earlier days of leadership, most leaders were chosen from physical characteristics they received at birth. As an example, the Russell Crowe type of leader in gladiator movies was selected based on being male, strong, tall, and bearded. His on-stage character clearly was not selected for leadership for having effective active listening skills, as demonstrated by his routine use of grunts. Most of us have never seen a movie about a war or battle prior to the nineteenth century in which the leaders were short, thin, bald, clean shaven, laid-back, and spectacled, unless they were soon to be the loser of that fight or perhaps lunch for the leader's pet lion.

Along with the belief that leaders at that time were "born leaders" or sons of leaders, it was the leader's role to *direct* the efforts of their teams and groups. The leader did not focus on the team members as anything more than bodies needed to accomplish *his* goal. In other words, the focus of leadership was on the leader himself. Unfortunately, it is not uncommon to find a leader operating in this way today.

In more recent times, it became clear that different types of people could assume leadership positions, since most leadership did not only require traits from birth, but also a skill set that could be learned by virtually anyone with the desire to do so. Along with this significant shift in thinking that allowed others to join the leadership ranks, the *focus* of leadership efforts also changed—from developing the individual leader to developing *all* team members.

So how do we define "leadership" today? In leadership classes, seminars, and workshops, it is common for the presenter to ask their audience to define "leadership." Google the question, and you will learn that there are as many definitions of leadership as there are leaders.

Warren Bennis was the founding chairman of the Leadership Institute at the University of Southern California and the author of 25 books on leadership, including the best-selling *On Becoming a Leader*.

Margaret Thatcher was the British Prime Minister from 1979-1990. Here is how they each defined leadership:

- **Warren Bennis:** "Leadership is the capacity to translate vision into reality." "Leaders keep their eyes on the horizon, not just on the bottom line."[17]

- **Margaret Thatcher:** "Don't follow the crowd; let the crowd follow you."[18] To her, leadership meant having followers.

These Bennis and Thatcher quotes highlight intended products of good leadership but follow the old concept of leadership that focused solely on the development of the leader. Current leadership authors and theorists have moved to a different definition of leadership that includes not only the desired group outcomes, but a focus on the development of team members. Here are a few:

- **Peter Northouse:** "Leadership is a process whereby an individual influences a group of individuals to achieve a common goal."[19]

- **James Kouzes and Barry Posner:** "Leadership is the art of mobilizing others to want to struggle for shared aspirations."[20]

- **John Maxwell:** "Leadership is influence – nothing more, nothing less."[21]

Perhaps this shift is seen most clearly in the definitions of leadership from Jack Welch, previous Chairman and CEO of General Electric (and author of *Straight from the Gut*), and Sheryl Sandberg, COO of Facebook (and author of *Lean In*):

- **Jack Welch:** "Before you are a leader, success is all about growing yourself. When you become a leader, success is all about growing others."[22]

- **Sheryl Sandberg:** "Leadership is about making others better as a result of your presence and making sure that impact lasts in your absence."[23]

Shep Hyken is a leading authority on customer service and author of *Shepard Virtual Training*. Hyken emphasizes the "Employee Golden Rule," which argues that making the employee the central point of focus results in treating the customers well. He identified Herb Kelleher, President of Southwest Airlines, as a great example of one who "walks the talk."[24]

Today, the leaders of most organizations preach the belief that if they treat their employees *right*, the employees will treat their customers *right*. In translation, however, many organizations fail to help their leaders understand what they mean by treating someone "right." Treating them "right" could mean that they plan to teach their employees to do things the organization's way, or the supervisor's way. Ideally, treating them "right" from a leadership perspective means helping employees develop skills that allow them to determine (and meet) the needs of the customer. The hypothetical example that follows helps to demonstrate the confusion in the expectations of a leader with respect to following the Employee Golden Rule mantra:

> Frank is the second-shift supervisor and oversees the work of five employees, including Susan. Susan is required to submit a weekly sales report each Friday before leaving the office. She is normally punctual and consistent in meeting this requirement, but the past week was particularly challenging. Two of her four colleagues called in sick, and Susan needed to spend time helping the remaining employees to get the shelves stocked, change sale prices, and create inventory assessments. She stayed late on Friday to get these jobs done and left Frank a note saying that she would do the sales report over the weekend from home and give it to him on Monday morning.
>
> Upon arriving at her office on Monday, Frank was waiting for her. "Susan, I'm disappointed in you," he said. "You failed to get me the sales report on Friday, so I didn't have the information I needed for my Monday morning divisional

meeting. I thought you had better sense than that. Why didn't you just stay until the report was done? When I trained you, that's what I told you to do if you had a busy week."

Despite knowing that Susan had a rough week, stayed late on Friday, and worked over the weekend, the unspoken message from Frank was that she serves in her role to meet the needs of her supervisor. Since Frank did not ask about her decision-making process, it apparently did not matter to him why she chose to act as she did, only that the result differed from what Frank expected her to do.

Certainly, there are some circumstances under which an employee simply needs to do what has been prescribed, such as calling 911 when there is an emergency. There are also some organizations in which employee decision-making is not typically considered appropriate, such as the military, where officers are expected to problem-solve and the enlisted folks are expected to follow the orders. This Frank and Susan scenario, however, demonstrates an example of a supervisor focusing on himself and not on his employee.

Frank had several options to choose from if he wanted to be team-member focused. Arguably the easiest option was for him to ask Susan about the thought process that led to her decision. *Asking* rather than *telling* is often an important distinction between effective and ineffective leadership. In this instance, perhaps Susan had to bring her elderly mother from the hospital to a nursing home after work on Friday. Without asking for more information, what was Frank's leadership purpose? Was it to make sure Susan did exactly what he had trained her to do, or to demonstrate concern for her situation and help her develop problem-solving skills that could assist her in the future?

Frank was not exercising effective leadership when he turned Susan's professional decision into a personal one. In this case, his response, "I am disappointed in you" is paternalistic behavior. Susan believed she made the best decision she could make at the time and Frank's follow-up could have been much more supportive and developmental. His personalized response of disappointment implies that the focus of Susan's work should be knowing and acting on exactly what Frank wants, as opposed to using her own problem-solving and critical-thinking skills. You may be asking, "What's the difference?" Let us explore this further.

If you were Susan, would you feel that Frank was more concerned about you not following his directive, or more so about helping you consider the options available to you to avoid a similar conflict next time?

Probably the former, right? Your action was not personal, but his response probably felt personal. How likely would you be to feel a sense of loyalty to Frank, and possibly the organization, after receiving this response from him? If the goal is to teach you, the employee, to not use your mind and judgement, but to follow the leader's directive, what happens the next time you are caught in a situation in which the leader has not instructed you how to act? Wouldn't you then be dependent on the leader to resolve your next challenge as opposed to learning how to effectively problem-solve on your own?

Alternatively, if Frank asked you to share your thought process about what happened, demonstrated concern about your well-being, understood the challenging situation you were in, and took time to explore *with you* the other possible responses to missing the Friday deadline, would you feel respected, and that Frank cared about your growth and development? Which response would likely result in you feeling a greater sense of loyalty to him and the organization? Also, after which of these scenarios would you be most likely to bring your best attitude to the next client or customer that requested help after your meeting with Frank ended?

In the next chapter, we will look at many of the reasons that leaders are judged to be ineffective, which we know can lead to dysfunctional organizations, and in some instances, circular toxicity.

CHAPTER II

Why Are So Many of Today's Leaders Ineffective?

This chapter looks at ten reasons that too many of today's leaders are ineffective. They are not in order of importance, nor alphabetically listed. Each example identifies a problem we see on a regular basis (The Leaders We Have) and shares strategies to strengthen leadership regarding the issue/category (The Leadership We Need.) There are certainly other reasons that today's leaders are ineffective, but these ten will get us started.

1. The "Anyone can do that job" Theory

2. Fit Matters

3. Lazy Leaders Ignore History at Their Own Peril

4. Staff Training and Development Resources are Often the First Cut

5. Employee Orientation Programs are Undervalued

6. Affirmative Action is Often Misunderstood

7. Moving the Problem is Rarely the Solution

8. The Relationship Between the CEO/President and the Board of Directors

9. The Rise of Narcissistic Leaders

10. Unethical Role Models Abound

1. The "Anyone can do that job" Theory

Many of us have heard that others believe our work is so simple or obvious that "anyone can do it." Or maybe you have heard someone say, "It's not rocket science." These expressions can make a person's skin crawl. Some professions seem to be more associated with this "anyone can do it" label than others, such as, bank tellers, store cashiers, sanitation workers, fast-food restaurant employees, and Uber and Lyft drivers, to name a few examples. Anyone doing these jobs, however, knows that they are not simple, and they require certain skill sets to be effective.

For those of you who are crossword buffs, a common crossword puzzle clue is, "Someone who offers TLC" (tender loving care). The answer is usually "RN" (Registered Nurse). Anyone familiar with the health profession knows that registered nurses are some of the most highly skilled and trained professionals. The crossword clue may subconsciously imply to readers that doctors offer real medical care and RNs only offer TLC, but one trip to the hospital would alter that misconception. What hurts us most is when someone we respect believes that our professional job is something that "anyone can do." Others certainly may know something about our job but knowing something about a job and believing that any breathing individual can successfully do the job is quite different.

In addition to damaging a person's pride, this "anyone can do it" label makes it more likely that the skills needed to perform a job will be undervalued and possibly missed or ignored by interviewers, clients, and supervisors. As an example, if anyone can be a "house cleaner," then are all house cleaners born with the knowledge of how to remove a blood stain from a couch or mud from an expensive rug? Or is that a skill they learn and develop? Further, does it make sense to assume that anyone with a pulse can *lead* a team of house cleaners? If so, it stands to reason that the house cleaner who has been doing it longer than anyone else should be promoted to be responsible for the work of others, right? Occasionally, yes, but as a rule, absolutely not. The reason is because the skill set needed to *lead* a group of house cleaners is entirely different from the skill set needed to *be* a house cleaner.

While it is true that having house cleaning skills may help one who is involved in teaching a new employee, can an individual supervise a house cleaner without well-developed teaching and supervising skills? Therein lies this leadership problem—if those hiring the leader of the house cleaners fails to understand that "leading" is a skill that is separate from the task of house cleaning itself, they are likely to hire a leader/supervisor who has experience with house cleaning skills, but not necessarily the skills needed to supervise and lead. You may ask, "so what?" Well, what happens when someone is a poor leader? Perhaps they micromanage the staff, set unreasonable expectations, care little about the employees, and ultimately become the reason that good employees leave the organization.

As an example, Sheldon Cooper, the genius physicist from the television show *Big Bang Theory,* would be the first one to tell you that he knows numerous facts about most subjects.[25] However, his character demonstrates that he clearly lacks the communication skills and other interpersonal skills most people want and need from their leader. What would an average day with Sheldon as your supervisor look and feel like? Unfortunately, many workers in many professions live with this situation as we speak. Here is a real-life example:

> Michelle, a business owner, needed to decide whether to pro-
> mote Larry or Gail to the vacant supervisor position in the
> technology division. Gail had very strong technical skills but
> no experience supervising or leading others and was not a
> strong communicator. Larry, on the other hand, had good
> technical skills, currently supervised a group of employees,
> and was a highly competent communicator. Michelle decided
> to promote Gail because she felt she had the best technical
> skills, thus should lead the department. A year down the road,
> the department had lost some of its previous productivity,

and gaps in employee development had become obvious. If the vacant position was exclusively a technical one, Michelle's choice may have been successful, but as technical skills and supervision/leadership skills are entirely different skill sets, Larry may well have been the better fit for this leadership position.

When filling leadership positions, many onlookers may assume that employees who know their jobs can become successful leaders simply by telling employees what to do, how to do it, and what will happen if they do not do so. Too often, leaders give little thought to what they can do to support and encourage their staff, help them strengthen their skill sets, and change direction when necessary. As mentioned earlier, the old model of leadership focused on the leader, but the effective leader for today and tomorrow needs to see the development of team members as equally important to their own development.

It is important to emphasize here that effective leadership does not focus on the team members to the *exclusion* of the leader. If the leader of a group of carpenters has never been a carpenter, the employees may not initially respond well to receiving feedback on their technical skills from this leader. Leaders with "credibility" stand a much better chance of gaining acceptance from employees. Having credibility means that those reporting to you know you understand their jobs and that your feedback will be valuable because your words come from a position of knowledge and experience. This is not to say that every leader must have done every job that they supervise in their organization, but there is much to be said for a leader taking the time to learn about their employees' jobs. Here are three real-life examples:

- Following an organization restructuring, Shauna was asked to have a department report to her which had previously reported to another supervisor. She had not supervised that department in the past, nor did she know much about the skill sets of its employees. Shauna asked for information she could read to better understand what those employees did daily. As she absorbed information about the new department, Shauna developed questions and spoke with colleagues from similar organizations who had substantial knowledge of that type of work. She also asked the most senior-level employee in the new department to meet, for the purpose of "tapping her vast knowledge" about the functions associated with the department. Shauna ultimately earned the appreciation of the employees in her new department by establishing credibility. She could now "speak their language" and better understand many of their challenges. Furthermore, Shauna gained respect by not assuming that anyone could easily figure out what they did and how they did it.

- John was the assistant director at his organization for more than 20 years when the director decided to leave. A search process was established for the position and John intentionally chose to not apply. Three months later, Daniel was selected to be the new director. On the first day at his new job, Daniel approached John and asked if he had been a candidate for the position, given his many years of experience at the organization. John shared that he had chosen not to apply for the director position and told Daniel that while he loves the work he performs, he had no interest in becoming a supervisor. John explained that he enjoyed working with his colleagues and loved the fact that he was only responsible for himself.

When he was younger and working for another organization, John supervised staff and was not effective in leading the group in the ways expected of him. John had applied to work at his present organization 20 years ago, in part, because he noted that the assistant director did not supervise anyone. As the days and months went by, Daniel found John to be a great assistant director and felt fortunate that he had stayed on in this role.

Four years later, Daniel accepted a promotional opportunity at another organization and announced to his boss (the executive leader) and colleagues his intent to leave his position. The executive leader approached John and told him that due to budget challenges, he would need John to assume the now-vacated director position and they would eliminate the assistant director position. John shared with the executive leader his previous experience as a supervisor and his desire to remain in his current position. He even offered to take on more responsibilities if that would be helpful. Dismissing John's explanation, the executive leader informed John that he needed to make a choice—either take on the director role or leave the organization. Faced with this uncomfortable and difficult decision, John accepted the director position. He hated being the director for two years and was eventually terminated from the position by the executive leader for not effectively meeting the responsibilities of the position.

This scenario represents the danger in the "anyone can do it" way of thinking, which seems to occur far too often in the workplace. John had been happy and was doing his job well, but the executive officer needed to save money and simply assumed that John could step up and handle the director role, which included supervising other employees. He failed to consider John's concerns about his unsuccessful past experiences and to understand the fact that effective leadership is not innate, but rather a learned skill. As a result, the organization lost John, who was a good employee for more than 24 years. Additionally, during the last two years of his employment, things didn't go well, which caused a ripple effect of confusion and low morale for the staff, and ultimately had a negative impact on the organization's customers. The executive leader was then forced to conduct a time-consuming and costly search for a new director, knowing that the selected person would face an uphill challenge from the start.

- Samantha was the vice president of a large, complex division comprised of several disparate university departments. After a long and successful tenure, she announced to the president and her colleagues that she would be retiring at the end of the year. Peter was the Assistant to the President and was tasked with reviewing the job description and revising it, as necessary. He was also responsible for putting together a search committee and several interview teams to meet with candidates. Though Peter previously had little interaction with Samantha's division, he set out to meet the president's assignment.

  Peter made a few job description revisions with the Human Resources department, which worked to get the advertisement posted on the appropriate job sites. One of the changes Peter made was that the candidates no longer needed prior experience in any of the departments associated with the position. At a meeting with the search committee, when asked by members of the division why he made this change, Peter argued that a leader for this division did not need to have direct experience in the work of the departments. He also confidentially informed the committee that a potential candidate was a local ex-politician who had a lot to offer the university. This potential candidate did not have experience directly related to any of the departments in the division. In this division, many of the department heads were required to have specialized knowledge that pertained to their work. Peter explained that he believed the ex-politician had a lot of experience and it would not be a problem because "anyone with management skills should be able to step in and do this job."

  The committee was frustrated with Peter's assessment that "anyone could do the job" and held a strong belief that a successful candidate would need to be seen as "credible" by the staff to successfully supervise and support their efforts. The committee brought their concerns to the university president, who understood their concerns, but felt it was too late to alter the hiring process. Fortunately, the ex-politician chose not to submit his application, so the conflict was avoided, but by luck as opposed to intentionality.

In this example, the president assigned a person with little knowledge of the divisional functions to coordinate finding a replacement for Samantha, the leader of the division. As a result of the changes to the job posting, which included the decision to not require any previous experience in the functions of the division, Peter's actions were received as disrespectful by the search committee and the employees in the divisional departments. The employees also wondered if his actions were previously known by the president, so their trust in the executive leader of the organization was also injured. By directly stating his belief that "anyone with management skills could do the job," Peter sent a message that successful leadership in one venue would logically translate into successful leadership in another. Although it is widely believed that many skills are transferable to other venues and some experiences closely parallel other job tasks, those were not the messages received by the search committee and employees. This single incident caused the working relationships between members of the division and the assistant to the president to be strained in the years that followed.

2. Fit Matters

Just as leaders come in all shapes and sizes, leadership positions are not one-size-fits-all opportunities. In one environment, an aspiring leader may excel, but the same person may not fare well in a different environment. Why is this?

Environmental Fit

Like anyone else, leaders and aspiring leaders have strengths and areas that they need to further develop. Often, the success of a leader is contingent upon finding an environment where the needs are a good match with the candidate's strengths and style. There are several variables that need to be considered for one to decide that a leadership position could be a good fit for "the right" candidate. Failing to take the time to do so often leads to a mismatch of the candidate and the position and/or the organization. When that occurs, the leader is not likely to remain at the organization for very long. The leader may dislike the community/culture, not be able to effectively demonstrate their skills, and may be viewed as less capable than their skills would normally demonstrate. Peter Northouse, author of *Leadership: Theory and Practice* refers to this as the "contingency theory of leadership."[26] According to Northouse, one key for successful leadership is to ensure a good fit between the candidate's skills and the organization's needs. The leader's ability to be successful is deemed to be "contingent" on that fit.

As discussed earlier, anytime a leader leaves an organization, a significant amount of unrest and turmoil can be expected to follow. Between the time one leader leaves and the new leader arrives, staff members may not receive the support they need, the clientele may become unhappy, and the senior leadership of the organization may need to spend valuable time re-doing what they did not do successfully the first time—finding the right fit. A hypothetical example follows:

> Norman served in the military for four tours before deciding that he wanted to support veterans and others in a higher education environment. He had enlisted at the age of 18 and proudly served in the Marine Corps. He had excellent success in the military, received several commendations, and was promoted three times. Norman had strong leadership skills and well-developed problem-solving, analytical, and

administrative skills. His primary area that needed improvement was his interpersonal communication skills. Norman aced his higher education job interview and was hired to be the coordinator of the campus Veteran Affairs office.

Six months into his new position, Norman and his supervisor met to discuss his performance to date, as was the normal procedure for new employees. According to the feedback received from students who were veterans, Norman had performed well, particularly with those who were self-motivated and knew the path they wished to take. Norman was less effective with veteran-students who needed help developing a path for their success. Norman tried his best to help these non-self-directed students, but was less comfortable assisting them, and often needed to refer them to other campus advisors for support.

Certainly, many candidates with military experience may have been excellent fits for the Veteran Affairs position, but the college environment was not a comfortable fit for Norman, as he preferred a more concrete and directive type of environment rather than a flexible one, as found at this particular college.

Supervisor's Leadership Style Fit

The leadership style of the supervisor is a second variable to consider when exploring the fit of a position with a candidate's strengths and areas in need of growth. As mentioned, we know that leaders' styles may vary widely and while some can successfully supervise a wide variety of employees, others may be less successful in doing so. Far too often, candidates for leadership positions focus only on presenting themselves to the prospective organization and forget how important their relationship with their new supervisor will be. They try to impress the interviewers and respond to questions honestly but fail to inquire about their future supervisor and colleagues. A real-life example follows:

Debbie applied for a department-head position at an organization she heard about online. She enjoyed her interviews and knew from the interviewers' reactions that her responses had been well-received. Debbie was offered the position, immediately accepted it, and was anxious to get started. In the past, Debbie's supervisors always let her do her job without a lot of oversight because it was clear she was a hard worker and excelled in all that she did. With her new supervisor, Paula, she fully expected to have the same experience.

Paula was confident that as soon as Debbie was deemed ready, she would be able to use her creativity and knowledge to take her team to new heights. When it came time for her six-month performance review, Debbie informed Paula that she had applied for and was offered a position at another organization and was giving her two-week notice. Being very surprised by this sudden development, Paula asked Debbie why she was choosing to leave so soon. Debbie hesitated, but eventually told Paula that she felt smothered by constantly needing to get approval on things that she believed were unnecessary. Debbie explained that she needed to have the freedom to do her job using her own style, and it was obvious to her that Paula was not one to easily give up control of decisions that affected the department.

This fit confusion likely occurred because Debbie never asked about Paula's supervisory style prior to accepting the position, and Paula never took the opportunity to ask about how things were going during Debbie's first few weeks and months on the job. Had either person initiated such a discussion before Debbie accepted the job, the "fit" problem may have been avoidable. By doing so on her end, Debbie could have spared herself the trouble of looking for a new job, and if Paula had initiated a discussion, both she and the organization might still have had a strong leader on board —something that is not often in great supply.

Supervisors should not wait for their organizations to require them to conduct performance reviews to communicate about transitions. If leadership teams want to focus on the needs, well-being, and development of their employees, they need to take the initiative to ask questions about the "fit." How are their new employees adjusting to their jobs, the organization, the region, etc.? Are their family needs being met? Are there concerns that can be discussed before they become professional obstacles? This is particularly important for new employees that are from underrepresented populations. Has the new employee found a comfortable sense of community for their family members? Has the school system met their needs? Some supervisors believe asking those questions is too personal, and they are correct that they are personal. However, if you want the employee to be comfortable and stay, these are likely some of their primary concerns. The organization took the time to recruit and hire a great candidate – why would it become laissez-faire during the most critical time for a new employee?

Clientele Fit

A third variable with respect to a candidate's fit in a new position is the clientele with whom the hired leader will work. Has the candidate given thought to the population with whom they will work? Were there questions in the interviews that would give the organization insight as to whether the candidate understands the unique needs of the organization's clientele? Did the candidate seem genuinely excited to work with the people here or did the interview responses sound like the candidate would "make the best of it"? If the latter, and if the position involves working with clients daily, the candidate is not likely to come to work each day with a big smile on their face to "deal with them" or "make the best of it."

Co-Workers Fit

The fourth and final variable we will consider here pertaining to organizational fit involves co-workers. As an interview day is planned, will the candidate have an opportunity to meet with enough potential colleagues to get an idea of the degree to which they will click? As we know, when times get tough, colleagues are often the first people that stressed out employees seek for support. Conversely, will the candidate stand out like a sore thumb in this environment? Many organizations are family-like in nature. Not only do colleagues support and care for each other, but they can sometimes be at odds with other departments or specific people. When this occurs, the clientele can often feel the tension, and who wants to work in a tense environment?

3. Lazy Leaders Ignore History at Their Own Peril

Teddy Roosevelt believed, "the more you know about the past, the better prepared you are for the future,"[27] and George Santayana, a philosopher and novelist, argued, "those who do not learn history are condemned to repeat it."[28] Is there a leadership book or article anywhere in the world that suggests ignoring history will lead to more effective leadership? I have not seen or heard of one, but for some reason, we are seeing an emergence of leaders who confidently state that "history does not matter."

In one sense, it is certainly understandable when a new leader says, "I want us to only look forward." They may hope to avoid rehashing conflicts that previously brought discord to the organization. It is also understandable that a new leader wants to avoid the assignment of blame for past incidents so as to help the community heal from past trauma. This approach may be easier and faster than learning the history of the organization, the highlights and lowlights, and how it got from there to here, but skipping on learning from past experience generally fails to consider the current needs of the community members.

Two types of leaders are more apt to dismiss the use of history for acceptable reasons. The first involves an organization that is autocratic by design and intention, such as the military. In this environment, the leaders and members mutually agree that the leaders expect to give orders that are carried out. The members, or "rank and file" in this case, expect to take orders and not question the rationale for them or the history behind them. It is an expedient form of communication in an environment in which fast action saves lives.

The second environment that reasonably looks to the future and does not spend time looking back is a counseling center that emphasizes a behavioral approach. Some therapists use techniques that require their clients to spend a great deal of time talking about their personal history, but behavioral approaches commonly use "conditioning" to help clients learn new skills and behaviors. One example of this approach involves smoking cessation. Using a behavioral approach, the clinician does not seek to understand a client's childhood (history), but rather attempts to teach a new *learned behavior*. In this case, the patient may be encouraged to look at a picture of their child whenever they feel the urge to smoke. The behavior of not smoking is then linked to having more time to spend with their child as opposed to taking the risk of dying early from lung cancer.

Aside from these two examples, most leaders who choose the no-history approach likely do so because it appears to be much simpler, faster, less painful (for the leader) and/or because the leader is ill-equipped to deal with the conversation that emerges when folks recollect the rationale for previous failures. Other leaders use the no-history approach because they were not there when the issue began, and it is convenient to blame those who came before them. Sometimes, overly self-confident or arrogant leaders see themselves as more gifted than their predecessor and believe that they can handle whatever happens moving forward. Still other leaders use the no-history approach because they are part of the seemingly growing group of leaders called "narcissists," but that group deserves its own analysis, which will come shortly.

Regardless of why the past is ignored by some leaders, the risk to those affected by this no-history approach is unnecessarily high. The no-history approach may lead to an expedient, short-term solution to a problem, but usually at the cost of failing to solve the problem from a more permanent, long-term perspective.

In summary, it certainly *does* matter how organizations got to where they are, as chronicled by Jim Collins in *Good to Great*,[29] and by Thomas Peters and Robert Waterman, Jr. in *In Search of Excellence*.[30] If it did not matter, the stories of unique and complex challenges faced by leaders would not be so instructive to leaders today. Michael Useem, author of *The Leadership Moment*[31] and Mukul Pandya and Robbie Shell, authors of *Lasting Leadership*,[32] share opportunities to learn from the experiences of many acclaimed leaders. Their stories offer today's leaders a blueprint of their thinking so we may understand their challenges, possible solutions, failed attempts, and successes. History allows us to understand and celebrate past efforts towards developing new solutions. Moving forward without looking back often leads us to places we would rather not be.

4. Staff Training and Development Resources are Often the First Cut

A Deloitte 2020 report estimates that the global annual budget spending for leadership development and training is over $50 billion.[33] In ideal environments, all levels of employees have access to staff training and development opportunities. Since most organizations are complex, they have a multitude of different functions that are handled by people with different skill sets and experiential and academic preparation. As a result, organizations have a choice to make. They can either ensure that all newly hired employees come to their organization with well-developed skills (and be willing to pay higher salaries accordingly), or the organizations must find ways to support the growth and development of their employees in-house. In most organizations, a combination of these two methods is the reality.

Medium and large organizations are more likely to have specific staff members that are exclusively responsible for the skill development of their employees. In other words, rather than having the training and development of the employees as one of many job functions on which one or more employees focus their time, organizations often employ "Human Resources" or "Talent Development" professionals to focus exclusively on these areas. These professionals often offer in-house workshops and opportunities to purchase books, watch webinars, and attend regional or national seminars and conferences that are available in many fields of work. In some organizations, employees may also take classes outside of work hours, at a reduced cost or no cost.

The success of staff development depends on at least four things:

1. The talent development staff needs to be familiar with all positions in the organization and the skills needed to perform those jobs.

2. There needs to be good communication between the talent development staff and the supervisors/leaders of each department, so that the individual needs of employees are observed, known, and addressed.

3. The leaders must be skilled as supervisors to assess the skill levels of their employees.

4. Adequate financial resources must be allocated for staff development purposes.

A study by the Corporate Leadership Council indicated that despite the large number of resources allocated to staff development, their results, on average, accounted for only a two percent increase in employee production.[34] There are several possible reasons for this limited success:

- The organization may be without its Human Resources/Talent Development employees for a lengthy period of time.

- The supervisors/leaders may be too busy to contribute the necessary time for assessing the skills of their employees.

- An employee who is new to a position may not have the minimal level of skills needed to fulfill their job responsibilities (e.g., those involved in the hiring may have miscalculated the candidate's skill level based on interviews, etc.).

- The variety of new organization requirements pertaining to ever-changing laws and governmental mandates often become the responsibility of the Human Resources/Talent Development Office. The sheer volume often results in their considering staff training to be low on their "priorities" list.

- Financial resources may have been reduced due to fiscal challenges.

- Anyone can call themselves a consultant and some consultants are not effective.

When an organization experiences financial challenges, one of the first places its financial resources are reduced is often the area of staff development. In these situations, it is not unusual for organizations to restrict business travel to conferences and/or funding for external consultants, because these activities are often seen as "frills," or activities of the organization that are less important parts of its core mission. Staff development must be considered essential, however, because without effective staff development, leadership development is left to *luck* rather than intentionality.

5. Employee Orientation Programs are Undervalued

Most organizations have an orientation program for new employees. Some are more formalized, and others are handled informally. These onboarding programs need to occur, at least initially, for the organization to get new employees loaded into the payroll systems. In some cases, this process and the addition of a handout or lecture about employee benefits is all that a new employee receives.

Some organizations assign a "mentor" to each new employee. A mentor is normally someone who has been at the organization for many years and is perceived to have good interpersonal skills. Mentors can be extremely helpful to new employees who can benefit from professional support as well as personal connections to the community.

What does this have to do with the influx of ineffective leaders?

BambooHR surveyed 1,000 employed Americans and *nearly a third* said they left a job prior to their six-month mark due to poor onboarding.[35] For new employees in leadership/supervising positions, they are commonly left to their own devices to "wing it," which often does not end well.

Abraham Maslow, an American psychologist, professed that there is a hierarchy of human needs. He argued that basic needs such as food, water, warmth, rest, security, and safety must be met before psychological needs and self-actualization can be met.[36] In short, Maslow argued that before an employee can perform at their best, their basic needs must be met. In the case of a new employee, this might include knowing their compensation benefits and work hours, and understanding how to obtain a parking decal, use the office phone, and find the bathroom. Many organizational leaders also include understanding the organization's budget process, navigating the computer system, and knowing the names of the key people in the organization.

When a Human Resources/Talent Development office offers a *comprehensive* orientation for a new employee, the employee's basic needs can be quickly met, thus allowing the employee to feel valued and able to devote their full attention to their new job. When this function is not handled centrally, some combination of the supervisor, administrative assistant, and other colleagues must address these issues individually.

The involvement of the organization's executive leader in organization-wide orientation programs is meaningful, but rarely occurs. When the leadership of the organization is not involved, the message to the new employee seems to be, "You don't matter very much." Executive leaders who pay little regard to their employees' well-being risk perpetuating a culture of apathy and disengagement.

First impressions are critical, and the entire orientation of a new employee feels like a first impression. When the onboarding process is well-thought-out and has numerous human touches, the new employee is likely to instantly feel important and appreciated and begin their new experience with positivity. When this occurs, the message the new employee receives is to treat staff and clients with that same level of appreciation, as it is obviously part of the organization's culture and expectations.

Of course, it would be extremely challenging to try to develop a one-size-fits-all type of orientation program for all new employees, even within a small organization, due to the vastly different types of jobs that people do. As an example, higher education organizations have a unique organizational structure. Their staff functions much like staff members in other industries, but their faculty are an entirely different entity who operate as subject matter experts. They are one of the very few types of employees that can achieve tenure (lifetime employment) if they demonstrate a high level of competency in terms of teaching, research, and service.

Some faculty arrive on a campus with teaching methodology expertise and others may have little teaching experience, except for possibly serving as a teaching assistant in graduate school. As a result, newly hired faculty may need their orientation experience to fill whatever gaps their experiences have not provided them to date. These orientation programs cannot be optional, as they relate to the core of that industry's function.

Generally, all organizations need to assess and provide training as it pertains to the core functions that each organization provides.

What happens when this does not occur?

Anyone who has spent time in, or around higher education institutions knows it is abundantly clear when faculty are excellent teachers of their subject matter and conversely, when they are not. Why would university leadership allow their *primary reason for existing* to be subpar? What would you do if you found that your classroom professors were not teaching you effectively? Most of us would try to find other classes or another college or university where our needs would be better met. For these new faculty, there is a time-sensitive need to ensure they have a teaching style with which they and the organization are comfortable. For this reason, some institutions establish a Faculty Development or a Teaching and Learning Center that enlists faculty *experts* to mentor and guide new faculty. As with all professions, the question that needs to be asked is, "To what standard should new employees be able to master the core functions of their organization before they are allowed to perform these functions?"

6. Affirmative Action is Often Misunderstood

One of the most misunderstood hiring policies of the past century is affirmative action. President John F. Kennedy signed an executive order in 1961 which required government employers to "not discriminate against any employee or applicant for employment because of race, creed, color, or national origin" and to "take affirmative action to ensure that applicants are employed, and that employees are treated during employment, without regard to their race, creed, color or national origin."[37] In 1965, President Lyndon Johnson affirmed the federal government's commitment "to promote the full realization of equal opportunity through a positive, continuing program in each executive department and agency."[38] Affirmative action was expanded to include women as a protected class in 1967.

This executive order was designed to bring equity and equality to the workplace and greatly broaden the number of qualified candidates available to fill job vacancies. The idea was highly commendable, and today we see previously excluded groups listed on most job postings. In practice, however, in the years since the affirmative action law was enacted, some organizations have reaped the rewards of this executive order, but many others saw this as an order to simply not exclude populations, which is not the same as an order to include them equitably. Additionally, in the early days of the order, many organizations confused affirmative action with developing *quotas,* which are understood to be a set number of employees with specific traits defined by race, gender, sexual orientation, physical ability, veteran status, etc. As a result, some organizations gave priority to hiring members of these protected groups, regardless of employee readiness, until they had successfully met their quotas.

Some organizations also used a quota system as a strategy to attract diverse candidates for their leadership positions. Their thinking was that having diversity at the leadership level would send a message to potential candidates that diversity was valued in the organization. For this reason, while many highly qualified candidates from underrepresented populations were hired, some under-qualified candidates were also hired, because quotas refer to numbers and not qualifications.

When a supervisor is hired and does not perform well because they do not have the requisite leadership skills, it creates a large problem. Their lack of success negatively impacts their direct reports, their supervisors, and their clients. Additionally, a common result of quota hiring is that these newly hired leaders do not stay long at their organizations, and their departure feeds into unfounded stereotypes that candidates from certain underrepresented backgrounds are unsuited for certain types of leadership positions.

Affirmative action was never intended to be utilized as a quota system. Instead, these hiring efforts have always been intended to create a significant focus on the development of a diverse candidate pool of qualified candidates, which would facilitate the creation of a staff that better reflects the diversity in our society. As a complementary explanation, affirmative action was intended to bring awareness that continuing to recruit in the same ways that created homogeneous candidate pools was likely to produce the same results unless additional and different efforts were made.

It is also important to understand that affirmative action does not alter the types or number of skills expected from the underrepresented candidates in the process. Since it intends to create a process that more successfully reaches out to a diverse pool of candidates who are qualified for a position by experience and education, much of the work must be done *prior* to interviewing candidates. The marketing of available positions needs to include media sources that are commonly seen by the population the organization seeks to reach, including newspapers, journals, conferences, and websites. Additional efforts sometimes involve current employees serving as candidate-recruiters and, in some cases, hiring professional hiring consultants, who have access to qualified and sitting (already in similar positions at other organizations) underrepresented candidates to make these potential candidates aware of the opportunities.

In practice, after this expanded and more targeted process has occurred and applications have been received, if a candidate pool is not deemed to be diverse, the spirit of the affirmative action order should encourage the hiring authority, before moving the search forward, to determine if all appropriate efforts were made to create a diverse candidate pool. When it is determined that this has not occurred, the hiring authority should be encouraged to re-market the position, as opposed to continuing the process with a candidate pool that lacks reasonable diversity. Some organizations work hard to perform affirmative searches and due to their geography or inability to financially compete with similar organizations, fail to achieve this goal. Others may fail due to searches that are rushed due to perceived time pressures (to fill positions) and some due to executive leaders who may be satisfied with the status quo.

In simplified and practical terms, affirmative action is extremely important to the hiring process for two reasons:

- Affirmative action intentionally addresses issues of inequity and facilitates the ability of organizations to hire a staff that more closely reflects their clients and regional demographics.

- Affirmative action ensures that hired individuals have the skills needed to be successful in their new positions. From a leadership viewpoint, hiring any person who does not meet the requirements of a position, as deemed by the job description, leads to a situation in which the hired person may be set up to fail. This risk is heightened when a person from an underrepresented population who does not meet the requirements is hired, because if they are unsuccessful, it may make it more challenging to recruit and hire candidates from underrepresented populations in the future.

When we hire to fill a quota or for appearances sake, we set up the candidates to fail. When we limit our applicant pools and hires due to bias or prejudice, we continue an inequitable system and considerably reduce the potential number of candidates who could successfully fill leadership positions.

7. Moving the Problem is Rarely the Solution

Most of us have witnessed an underperforming employee be moved to a different department or assignment in hopes that it will solve the underperforming problem. When the underperforming employee is in a leadership role, it is especially important to first analyze why they were unsuccessful, as opposed to assuming that a fresh start will fix things. The practice of moving an underperforming person should remain a possibility, but one among many others worthy of consideration.

An analogy for this can be found in professional sports. It is not uncommon for an athlete who underperforms to find greater success when they are traded to another team. Even though the talent is there, perhaps the athlete had "fit" challenges as was discussed earlier, or maybe there were family issues that split their attention between performing well and helping to meet their family's needs. They may have been dealing with marital challenges, or recently had a baby and were getting only two hours of sleep every night. Sometimes an athlete simply loses confidence in their abilities. A rough start can also lead to an athlete getting into what seems like an endless rut, but these things can change.

If this were not true, how do we explain the rise of an athlete like recently retired David Ortiz of the Boston Red Sox?[39] Prior to being traded to Boston, Ortiz was platooning with another player at first base for the Minnesota Twins. Shortly after moving to the Red Sox, he blossomed into a team leader and likely a future Hall of Fame inductee. However, before this gives anyone the idea that simply "trading" leaders will result in another David Ortiz story, it is important to understand that most traded athletes do not blossom into all-stars.

This is probably where the professional sports analogy ends. Most organizations do not "trade" employees (although I *was* once traded, but that's a story for another time) and there is normally no bench for organization employees who deserve less playing time. But the problem is clear—any person leading other employees can do considerable damage to a working team if they do not possess the skills and emotional intelligence needed to be an effective leader.

So, what can you do about an ineffective leader?

- *Leave them alone* and hope they will improve with time. However, crossing your fingers is not usually considered an effective problem-solving technique.

- *Move them to another job or department* to give them a fresh start and opportunity to contribute. Moving them is the easy route to take. No one needs to do any extra work, such as developing a coaching plan for the leader. However, not many leaders/supervisors want to take a pay cut or will be motivated to do well with an organization that has demoted them.

- *Fire the employee* and seek to hire or promote a new supervisor. There may be political reasons that the leader cannot simply be relieved of their job, however, such as being a friend of a board member, or the son or daughter of the owner. Further, the underperforming leader may be at a unionized organization and due to their tenure, cannot be dismissed or moved against their will, except for "cause." In this case, cause may mean something very significant such as sexual harassment, a physical altercation, embezzlement, etc. There may also be a legal reason they cannot be fired. If the person is considered a disabled person under the law, certain accommodations may be required first. If the person has developed a serious problem with alcohol or other drugs, an external agency such as OCR (the Office for Civil Rights) may require that your organization take steps to support the employee and give them the opportunity to change.

So, if it is not easy to fire your way out of a problem, and moving an underperforming or poor leader from one place to another is unlikely to resolve the situation, and you are not comfortable playing the wait and-see-game, what alternatives are left?

This question is challenging even when we assume that the organization wants what is best for the employee and that the employee cares about being successful in their work. Of course, the options may become even more limited if the employee sees nothing wrong and does not want any action to occur and/or if the organization has a history of treating employees like easily replaceable bodies.

Three possible avenues can be used to address this situation in which a leader is underperforming and ineffective. The first is to consider an internal move, but not to another leadership position. Does the employee have an interest in another area of the organization where their skills can be better utilized? If no such position exists, would the organization benefit from creating such a position for a couple of years? Perhaps the organization has already been considering the addition of a new service or function for which the ineffective leader has both expertise and genuine interest.

A second avenue could be to meet with the ineffective leader to discuss their long-term professional goals. Ideally, the employee is aware that their performance has fallen short of the organization's expectations and that a change is needed. If there is a supervisor in the organization whom the employee trusts and who is genuinely interested in helping the employee find their passion in life, that may be the best place to start. If not, perhaps someone in Human Resources/Talent Development or an external Employee Assistance Program (an organization hired to support employees through difficult circumstances) can explore career interests with the employee.

When the organization helps an employee to successfully find a new job, everyone wins. The ineffective leader gets support towards a new and exciting career path, and the organization knows it helped a good person find a better fit for their talents. Further, the other employees see that the organization cares to resolve the organizational problem and that it treats employees as valued members of its professional family, which leads to organizational loyalty and employee retention. This option may include the organization offering flexibility for the employee while they job search - in terms of using an office and providing career support in return for a letter of resignation that allows the organization to move forward with a search process to replace the leader.

A third possibility worth considering goes along with the organization's staff development program that hopefully already exists for all employees. Organizations may stop short of enacting a creative, personalized, and robust professional development plan for an unsuccessful leader because it takes time, personnel investment, and financial resources to undertake such an option. Remember though, that the rationale for exploring options is to relieve the organization from a situation that negatively impacts numerous employees and very likely, colleagues and customers, every day it is left unresolved. From a return on investment (ROI) viewpoint, is it better to expend more resources to plug the hole in the ship by helping the leader gain the skills they lack, or is it better to risk losing good employees and gaining a reputation for being a place with low standards and circular toxicity?

8. The Relationship Between the CEO/President and the Board of Directors

Boards of directors or trustees are, in most cases, responsible for the oversight of fiduciary and legal matters related to an organization. One of their most important roles is the hiring, evaluation, and termination of the CEO or president (for simplicity, to be referred to as the Executive Leader, or EL from this point). The board generally establishes the mission and sets direction for the organization, meets with the EL, and votes on significant organization issues. The board represents, as coined by Harry S. Truman, "where the buck stops."[40]

Some boards are composed of volunteers while others have compensated members. Many boards of state-run entities are appointed by the governor of that state. These members typically have very similar political interests as the governor and often, these appointees are already connected to the political world. At private organizations, board members often fill their own board vacancies, in collaboration with the executive leadership of the organization. Some of these appointments are made to add members of like-minded thinking and some are made to include individuals with experience and knowledge that they believe is currently missing from the board.

As part of the board's oversight of the organization, board members are normally expected to "contribute their expertise, time, talent and resources," as stated in the YMCA of America board materials, for example.[41] Most boards formally meet with the organization's leadership on a quarterly basis and contribute financially to the organization, particularly when the organization is a non-profit agency or educational organization. As a result of these involvements, board members have a personal stake, thus a strong commitment to assuring the success of their organizations.

That said, a significant leadership problem exists when a governing board gets too close to, or stays too far away from, the organization's executive leader. The former may cause the EL to leave and the latter may cause everyone else to leave.

Too often, a board is unaware of problems caused by the EL's actions until significant damage to the organization and/or employee morale has occurred. Board members walk a tightrope at times. They have certain responsibilities pertaining to oversight of the organization, but the day-to-day efforts are left in the hands of the organization's executive leader, or their designee. Most ELs do not want to be micromanaged by their board but welcome a collegial and advisory relationship. The tensions associated with finding an acceptable balance for all parties can cause executive leaders to leave an organization, so a good amount of attention is normally devoted to this issue. There are industry standards and "best practices" to help guide both ELs and boards, but each relationship is unique and must be cultivated to be effective.

The tightrope between taking responsibility for but not micromanaging the EL makes it challenging for board members to be aware of the pulse of employees, and to be proactive regarding problem-solving. If the organization were made up of only a few employees, it would be easy for the board to focus almost exclusively on the product of the organization. However, organizations normally consist of numerous employees, who realistically are the ones collectively responsible for the organization's product. As a result, it is vital that the executive leader be evaluated not only on the organization's productivity, but also on the ability to create and support an environment in which employees thrive. Unfortunately, some board members may believe that if their organization is meeting its physical and monetary goals, then the employees are fine. That is a lazy and dangerous assumption. It is very possible for an organization to produce great short-term results while alienating its employees. The result of such a combination is likely to be long-term crises.

Many questions keep board members awake at night. How can they know why vice presidents or other employees of the organization choose to leave? What is considered acceptable interaction between the board members and organization employees? Finding a way for a board to know if their ship is sailing along or slowly sinking is essential to maintaining strong leadership. If their communication is exclusively with the executive leader, there is a risk that the board may be unaware of problems until they are past the point of resolution. Board members sometimes learn of personnel problems after an EL's direct report or another key employee has left the organization, or an undesirable climate has already been established.

One of the check-and-balance forms of communication between the EL and the board that exists at many organizations is an employee-union affiliation. The topic of unions can be quite controversial in organizations. The purpose of unions is to ensure that employees' rights are respected and that they are not inadvertently taken advantage of, exploited, or treated poorly by the executive leadership.

While very few executive leaders assume their positions with the intention to treat employees poorly or create a toxic environment, it is clear from the research that for some ELs, this is exactly the outcome of their efforts. As a result, during the four or five times per year that the board meets with the EL and their executive staff, establishing a subcommittee to meet with union leadership (or where a union does not exist, a core group of employees) can be extremely helpful towards giving board members insights regarding important productivity-related issues and organizational climate. In other words, a board would be wise to not assume that "no news is good news." They should periodically ask probing questions of employees other than the EL or their executive staff to get a feel for how things are working (or not). Unfortunately, this seldom occurs.

In addition to establishing communications with union leadership, the board should also meet with various groups that make up the different components of the organization. Some groups may be internal, such as middle-management representatives and/or employees of color, and some groups may be external, such as community leaders and/or organization constituents. A major goal for the board in holding these meetings should be to receive "no surprises." If an effective balance exists between the board's awareness of organizational challenges and the EL not feeling micromanaged, the challenges raised by these organizational groups should already be familiar to the board. Conversely, surprise topics would indicate a communication gap.

As previously mentioned, one of the essential roles of a board is to hire, evaluate, and if appropriate, to fire the executive leader. The successful functioning of an organization is often predicated by the degree to which the board handles these functions. The hiring process must create the greatest likelihood that the person the board selects to lead the organization will be the person they *intend to* hire. The word "intend" refers to two things here:

- The hiring process should help find and select the candidate who best meets the needs of *all* constituencies –the board, EL team, employees, customers, community, etc.

- The hiring process needs to give the board the best possible information about each candidate to reduce the chance that a candidate will demonstrate their leadership style, values, and skills differently on the job than they demonstrated during the hiring interviews.

Pertaining to the second intention, most of us believe we can distinguish genuine interest, understanding, and empathy from an interview candidate - until one fools us. The tried-and-true way to escape this possible trap is to include in the hiring process a variety of checks and balances and different looks at each candidate. It should no longer be acceptable to simply have a search committee narrow down the candidate pool and set up final interviews with the executive leader candidates. In practice, this means the board needs to, at a minimum, take actions from the following list:

- Involve more than just board members and executive leader team members in content interviews

- Include a candidate presentation to the community on a predetermined topic to view their industry knowledge as well as teaching and coaching skills

- Intentionally select participants to join candidates for a meal during which they may assess the candidate's human-relation skills

- Conduct reference checks personally rather than outsourcing this function

- Verify the candidate's stated accomplishments with appropriate people from the candidate's recent organizations

- Investigate and analyze any discrepancies in the evaluations a candidate receives from different constituency groups

These steps can serve to provide some security that "who you see is who you will get." Additional information pertaining to employee hiring will be addressed in Chapter V.

9. The Rise of Narcissistic Leaders

Former President Trump was often referred to as a "narcissistic leader." Particularly during his presidency, this led to a sharp increase in requests for information about narcissistic leadership. In addition to understanding this leadership style, people have long sought knowledge of how to best predict the actions of a narcissistic leader and how to successfully function when they work with one. This has been extremely challenging for many.

The term "narcissist" carries a negative connotation. Most people who get labeled with this personality style are not well-regarded. However, Michael Maccoby, author of *The Productive Narcissist*, argues that narcissistic leaders can play a positive, short-term role, which helps to explain why some narcissistic leaders are intentionally hired or elected.[42]

Narcissistic leaders, according to HRZone, "are those concerned only with their own self-actualization, social standing, and place in the world - they are self-absorbed and take actions to improve these factors, even if it's at the expense of other people."[43] This type of leader exhibits the characteristics of arrogance, dominance, and hostility. According to Maccoby, "Freud told us that narcissists are emotionally isolated and highly distrustful. They are usually poor listeners and lack empathy. Perceived threats to a narcissist can trigger rage and achievements can feed feelings of grandiosity."[44]

While research in this area is somewhat scant, many leaders today are perceived as having at least some narcissistic tendencies—even some of the better-known leaders. An executive at Oracle described his narcissistic CEO, Larry Ellison, by saying, "The difference between God and Larry is that God does not believe he is Larry."[45]

On the positive and productive side of narcissism, Maccoby noted that "Productive narcissists have the audacity to push through the massive transformations that society periodically undertakes. They are not only risk takers willing to get the job done, but also charmers who can convert the masses with their rhetoric."[46]

For those of you who have experience working with a narcissistic leader, you also know that they scale low on emotional intelligence factors such as self-awareness and the ability to control their emotions and impulses. They seek power and glory, see things only through their own lens, and are quick to refute alternative ways of viewing a situation. Narcissistic leaders most often surround themselves with people who will agree with them, and they are quick to dismiss or distance themselves from others who express disagreement. They are prone to see anyone blocking their success as their enemy and can easily become paranoid. Does this sound familiar? If so, I bet that Bob Woodward, journalist, and author of *Rage,* would agree with you.

As fast as a narcissistic leader may achieve success, due to a willingness to take on difficult or unpopular tasks, they are also quick to fall after their breakthrough has occurred and the next step calls for interpersonal skills, such as teamwork, empathy, and listening. For this reason, we see a lot of narcissistic leaders as short-term leaders, especially when they supervise others. Quite often, we see narcissistic leaders hired to "clean house," meaning they have marching orders to fire an array of employees, either due to budget challenges, corporate mergers, re-organizations, or when an organization's culture needs to drastically change.

As is argued by Maccoby, narcissists can be helpful when intentionally hired to perform specific goals. In other circumstances, however, they can be extremely destructive to an organization, so it is essential to know when a candidate fits this leadership style. Many narcissistic candidates hired into leadership positions can initially camouflage their narcissistic tendencies and show themselves to be confident, knowledgeable, and gregarious. As a result, these personalities are often viewed positively at first. The simpler the hiring process (few people interviewing or spending time with the candidate), the more likely that a candidate will be able to fool the search committee and ultimately, the hiring authority. Conversely, the broader the hiring process, the more likely that a narcissistic candidate will show glimpses (or more) of their narcissistic tendencies.

Discounting the positive contributions that productive narcissists can bring to an organization in the short term, the long-term impact of narcissistic leaders is often like a cancer to an organization. While it is rare to experience a purely narcissistic leader, many leaders exhibit *some* of the behaviors attributed to narcissists. These are often unidentified until a good amount of damage has been done to the organization and in particular, to the employees who have close contact with these leaders.

If a narcissistic leader is unintentionally hired or elected, it normally does not take long for seasoned employees to quickly identify their narcissistic leader tendencies. Several of these employees typically leave the organization or are pushed out by the narcissistic leaders because they are seen as disagreeable, and in some cases, are seen by the leader as the "enemy." From 2015 to 2021, for example, it was common to hear former President Donald Trump refer to the media and Democrats who disagreed with him as "enemies of the people."[47]

Less experienced leaders and employees tend to be the most vulnerable to being negatively impacted by narcissists over long periods of time. They have had fewer leaders with whom they can compare the narcissistic leader, and even less experience trying to successfully work with them.

As stated, narcissistic leaders have many qualities that can initially be perceived as extremely helpful to an organization—such as being visionary, willing to battle roadblocks, extroverted, gregarious, and able to quickly change the climate of an organization or department. These qualities may temporarily blind hiring authorities, as well as board members, especially when the narcissistic leader is the executive leader.

The rise in narcissistic leaders and those with some narcissistic tendencies (I call them "mini-narcissists") is another reason that board members need to remain connected to both the newly hired executive leader and the executive staff of their organizations following the completion of an executive search. The early tenure of a new EL is traditionally a time they are given more independence, also known as the "honeymoon period." The cost of waiting too long, however, before getting a pulse on the impact of the new executive leader is extremely high.

What signals should you look for to avoid hiring a narcissistic leader?

One key place to look is the candidate's resume. Short stints at numerous organizations are often a clue that something happened to sour the candidate's time at these workplaces. Candidates may try to explain it by saying that they wanted to be closer to aging parents, that they followed their spouse's career moves, or that they were recruited from one place to the next. Reference calls to the candidate's prior workplaces may clear up this concern or produce others. As will be discussed more in Chapter V, reference calls for leadership positions should not be limited to the list of names provided by the candidate because of course, these people will be positive. If not, why would the candidate have selected them as references? With the permission of the candidate, calls can and should also be made to additional people from their previous workplaces. The bottom line, as usual, is to trust your instincts.

10. Unethical Role Models Abound

In the 19th century, British politician Lord Baron Acton coined the phrase, "Power corrupts; absolute power corrupts absolutely."[48] He believed that as a person's power (title, influence, etc.) increased, their moral sense decreased. While this is of course a broad generalization, there have certainly been numerous examples throughout history that support his belief.

What does this have to do with leadership today?

Seeing and hearing about unethical and abusive behavior by leaders makes it especially challenging for new leaders to understand why lying and cheating are not ways to help make their path to success easier. It is human nature to see a behavior by someone you admire and assume that if it is acceptable for them to engage in the behavior, it is fine for you to do the same.

Throughout history, numerous leaders across the world have abused their power, so while recalling examples of world incidents is heartbreaking and anger-inducing, it rarely surprises us. It seems that people have become virtually immune to being shocked by the seemingly constant stories of unethical behaviors of leaders. This is a scary and extremely sad reality. The following well-known examples of extraordinarily unethical leadership behavior from the 19th and 20th centuries were compiled by *ListSigma:*[49]

- **Leopold II of Belgium** – Succeeded his father as King from 1865-1909. Ran the country for his personal enrichment. Under his governmental regime, approximately 10 million Congolese people were killed.

- **Jozef Stalin** – General Secretary of the Communist Party of the Soviet Union from 1920-1953. Led a massive campaign of repression by the government, party, intelligence, and armed forces in which millions of "enemies of the working class" were imprisoned, executed, or exiled, without due process.

- **Benito Mussolini** – Prime Minister of Italy from 1922-1943. He was the founder of Italian Fascism and responsible for more than 500,000 deaths in Italy.

- **Adolf Hitler** – Chancellor of Germany from 1933-1945; ordered the invasion of Poland and was the central figure behind the

Holocaust, which was responsible for the genocide of 6 million Jews. In total, Hitler was responsible for the killing of 19 million civilians and prisoners of war.

- **Ante Pavelic** – Croatian fascist dictator who ruled the Ustase party. Took control in 1941 and created a system like fascist Italy and Nazi Germany. His brutal regime was responsible for the genocidal persecution of Jews, Serbs, and Romani.

- **Ho Chi Minh** – Vietnamese Communist revolutionary leader who was Prime Minister from 1945-1955 and President from 1949-1969. Prominent figure in the foundation of the Democratic Republic of Vietnam. As dictator of Vietnam, Minh was responsible for the killing of 2 million Vietnamese, not from war, but from murder and starvation.

- **Kim Il-Sung** – Supreme Leader of the Democratic People's Republic of North Korea from 1948-1994. His country became a socialist state riddled with economic crises and political instability. North Korea's economy collapsed in 1991, leading to widespread poverty and famine.

- **Mao Ze Dong** – founding father of the People's Republic of China. Ruled as Chairman of the Communist Party of China from 1949 to 1976. His effort to change China from an agrarian economy to an industrial power caused the deaths of 15 to 55 million people. In total, he was responsible for the deaths of 40 to 70 million people through prison labor, starvation, and execution.

- **Pol Pot** – Cambodian revolutionary leader who led the Khmer Rouge from 1963-1997. Presided over a totalitarian dictatorship and caused the deaths of 25 percent of the population of Cambodia.

- **Idi Amin** – President of Uganda from 1971-1979. His rule was characterized by political repression, abuse of human rights, extrajudicial killing, ethnic persecution, corruption, nepotism, and gross economic mismanagement, resulting in the deaths of almost 500,000 people.

- **Jean Kambanda** – Prime Minister from the start of the Rwandan Genocide in 1994, that killed almost 1 million Rwandans. During his regime, more than 2 million people were displaced and became refugees.

Lord Acton would also have undoubtedly felt justified in being pessimistic about leadership in the United States over the past 30 years, as examples of leaders abusing their authority and acting for personal gain are plentiful. Here are some of the best-known examples from the last three decades, the first four from K. M. Trust:[50]

- **Enron**'s massive accounting fraud that wiped out $78 billion in stock market value in 2001.

- **Tyco International** – Leaders of Tyco stole hundreds of millions of dollars out of the organization to fund their lavish lifestyles in 2002.

- **Bernard Madoff's** $65 billion Ponzi scheme that wiped out the life savings of numerous investors (many of whom he considered friends) in 2008.

- **Lehman Brothers** – Top executives caused this $600 billion investment bank to go bankrupt in 2008, causing a worldwide financial crisis.

- **Jerry Sandusky** – Assistant head football coach for Penn State, who was involved in 45 counts of sex abuse of children between 1994 and 2009 and sentenced to 30 to 60 years in prison. Head coach Joe Paterno, a national college coaching icon, knew of the situation at the time and "showed total and consistent disregard for the safety and welfare of Sandusky's victims."[51]

- **Larry Nassar** - USA Gymnastics national team doctor and osteopathic physician at the University of Michigan was accused of assaulting at least 150 young women and girls between 1992 and 2016. He was sentenced to 40 to 175 years in prison after pleading guilty to seven counts of sexual assault of minors.[52]

- **William Rick Singer** - owner of the Edge College Career Network and CEO of the Key Worldwide Foundation, who took bribes from 50 parents of college applicants (more than $25 million between 2011 and 2018) to inflate entrance exam test scores and bribe campus officials. He admitted to facilitating improper college admission for children in more than 750 families to institutions including Yale, Stanford, USC, Wake Forest, UCLA, University of San Diego, University of Texas, and Georgetown, and faces up to 65 years in prison.[53]

- **Harvey Weinstein** – A well-known and influential film producer, Weinstein was found responsible for sexually assaulting two women in the film industry and committing numerous sexual-related acts against five women between 2004 and 2013. He was sentenced to 23 years in prison.[54]

- **Tim Cook** - Apple CEO who intentionally slowed down older iPhones by using sub-standard batteries. In front of Congress in 2017, Cook characterized this as a "misunderstanding" and subsequently sold battery replacements for the iPhones for $29 as opposed to the normal price of $79.[55]

- **Martin Shkreli** - The former CEO of Turing Pharmaceuticals, who bought the marketing rights to the drug Daraprim in 2015. This drug is used to treat a serious parasite infection in people with HIV, people with compromised immune systems, and malaria, and has been on the market for 62 years. Overnight,

Shkreli raised the price from $13.50 to nearly $750 per pill. Called before Congress to explain, Shkreli invoked the Fifth Amendment, and then tweeted that the lawmakers who questioned his tactics were "imbeciles." Shkreli is currently in prison for seven years for an unrelated securities fraud violation.[56]

- **Donald Trump** – Starting prior to his taking office in 2017 and continuing throughout his presidency, former President Trump made public misogynistic comments, accused Mexican immigrants of being rapists, stated his desire to ban Muslims from coming to the United States, dismissed evidence of Russian acts against the United States, and became only the third U.S. president to ever be impeached by the House of Representatives—and the only one to be impeached on two occasions (but not removed from office by the Senate). The first impeachment alleged that he asked the Ukraine government to investigate a 2020 election rival, while withholding almost $400 million of congressionally approved aid and a request for an Oval Office meeting. The second impeachment alleged that he incited an insurrection that led to the storming of the Capital, the deaths of several people including police officers, injuries to 140 officers, and hundreds of arrests.

Further, over the course of his presidency, Donald Trump was accused of firing numerous employees who would not take actions he demanded, often due to the illegality and/or unethical nature of such actions. Several ongoing lawsuits from New York allege that Trump misrepresented the value of his real estate properties as he applied for bank loans and to avoid paying appropriate taxes.

On the topic of workplace ethics, Arthur Schwartz, professor of Leadership Studies, published an article in *Career and Workplace* listing the five most common unethical behaviors in the workplace:[57]

1. *Misusing organization time* – employees doing personal business while being paid by their organization

2. *Abusive behavior* – supervisors and employees mistreating and disrespecting others

3. *Employee theft* – one out of every 40 employees in 2012 was caught stealing from their employer (average of five and a half thefts and a total of $715 worth of items taken). According to the FBI, employee theft is the fastest growing crime in the United States today.

4. *Lying to employees* – one of every five employees report that their supervisor has lied to them in the past year.

5. *Violating organization internet policies* – At least 64 percent of employees were found to be surfing the web when they should have been working.

A Pew Research Center survey conducted in 2014 demonstrated that 84 percent of the 1,835 respondents considered *honesty* to be the most essential trait for any leader,[58] yet the previously mentioned article tells us that 20 percent of employers lied to their employees. When unethical behavior occurs in the workplace, particularly by leaders of the organization, this survey tells us that most employees will likely lose the most respected and admired trait in their leaders. As a result, some employees choose to leave the organization in search of a workplace where the community values are more in line with their own.

Fortunately, there appears to be at least one silver lining to this disturbing trend. To support the reporting of unethical behavior, the Whistleblower Protection Act (WPA) was signed into law in 1989 by President George H. W. Bush, "to protect Federal employees and applicants for employment who lawfully disclose information they reasonably believe evidences a violation of law or regulation, gross mismanagement, a gross waste of funds, an abuse of authority, or a substantial and specific danger to public health or safety."[59] The WPA was strengthened in 2012 when Congress added protections for federal employees who report fraud, waste, or abuse.

Since the advent of the WPA, many organizations not covered by this law have developed their own, similar practices to encourage their employees to come forward when they become aware of possible ethical violations. This protection is an important message to employees about the organization's expectations regarding workplace ethics. It is also a message to abusive leaders that they may no longer commit these acts with impunity.

The future of ethical and successful leadership depends on leaders responding to the top attribute that employees say they seek in their leaders – honesty. Some of the visible leaders mentioned previously did little to model honesty, like former President Donald Trump allegedly making more than 30,000 false or misleading claims over a four-year period in office, according to the *Washington Post*.[60]

For this moral and ethical challenge to be met, organizations need to commit to ethical leadership as an important personal attribute that impacts hiring, evaluations, terminations, and productivity. Ethical leadership needs to be a component of students' classes in all vocational fields, and of employee workshops in the form of case studies and discussion groups. Finally, all organizations need to demonstrably support and encourage employees to take responsibility for reporting acts of unethical behavior, and in particular, retaliatory actions that occur. Like expectations pertaining to discrimination, these ethics and retaliation values and policies need to be publicly shared via organization websites and discussed with new employees at onboarding sessions. If ethical leadership abuses are to be eradicated, organizations need to do more than provide an annual online ethics quiz, as is the current practice in many organizations.

CHAPTER III

Is This Person Leadership Material?

Born or Made? (Revisited)

In Chapter I, we visited the age-old question, "Are leaders born or made?" It was concluded that, although for many years people saw leaders as being *born* with traits that encouraged others to follow them, current leadership theorists now see leadership as being attainable by most people who have the desire to lead and possess well-developed leadership skills.

In addition to having attributes such as intelligence, perseverance, and self-confidence, which are associated with the list of traits one may be born with, there is a group of people who gain an almost automatic entry into this leadership world by a different kind of attribute—their last names. Often referred to as "legacy leaders," these people have inherited the title of leader by having a family member or relative by the same name who's known in the leadership world. Examples from U.S. politics include several prominent families such as: Adams, Bush, Clinton, and Kennedy. In the world of athletics, Ali, Bonds, Earnhardt, Hull, Manning, Unser, and Williams are names that connect us to a parent, child, or sibling whose name was synonymous with leadership and widespread recognition. This is certainly not to say that these legacy politicians and athletes may not have earned their way to achieve the celebrity status they have received. However, for each of these legacy people, their names have brought them added attention. Their names gave them recognition and opened doors more quickly.

The recent research about leadership argues that leadership effectiveness consists of more than just the attributes you were born with or the last name you own. While some traits may influence a person's success, those alone are now deemed insufficient. Today's leaders are identified as having a set of skills which can be learned, such as effective communication, coaching, empathy, critical thinking, problem solving, and time-management. The popular opinion is that leadership skill training can and should be made available to anyone with an interest in becoming a leader.

By opening the field of who may be able to assume a leadership role within the United States, we have made it possible to expand the leadership pool to include people of any gender, age, race, ethnicity, sexual orientation, or national origin. In doing so, we have essentially doubled or tripled the potential number of people who can seek leadership roles. Some vocations, which were previously identified as male-only, such as lawyers, doctors, engineers, police, firefighters, and politicians, are no longer societally restricted by gender. Similarly, some leadership vocations that were once considered to be exclusively female, such as teaching and nursing, are no longer societally restricted by gender.

In practice, however, this leadership skill-based epiphany that was destined to make leadership available to everyone has been slow to materialize in some professions. Although everyone can learn the necessary skills to be effective in most, if not all industries, societal sexism in the United States continues to limit women, in particular, from assuming a larger share of the leadership pie. Some statistics that support this argument follow:

- Of the Fortune 500 organizations in 2021 only eight percent (41) were led by female CEOs, which represents an all-time high.[61]

- The United States elected Kamala Harris as its first female vice president in 2020, yet still awaits the election of its first female president. Around the world, 60 countries have had female heads of state since 1960.[62]

- In the U.S. military, as of 2019, females comprised 14 percent of the enlisted and 16 percent of commissioned officers (compared to four percent in 1973), yet only two percent (19) of the 976 generals.[63]

- In higher education, as of 2019, female students comprised approximately 57 percent of the college student population,[64] yet only 30 percent of college presidents were female.[65] In public high schools in the United States during this time, 76 percent of the teachers were female, yet only 24 percent of district superintendents were female.[66]

- In January 2021, women held 143 seats in the U.S. Congress, comprising 27 percent of the 535 members. In the Senate, 24 percent of the 100 seats were represented by women and in the House of Representatives, 27 percent (119) of the 435 seats were represented by women.[67]

The question, "Are leaders born or made?" is still important because the research has demonstrated that most leaders are *made* through skill development as opposed to being *born* to lead. An appropriate follow-up question may be, "Can all people become leaders?" In the United States today, the research indicates that virtually all leadership positions can be held by any person with a combination of traits, such as intellect and ambition, and skills, such as self-reflection, control of emotions, empathy, supervisory techniques, and communication skills. The answer focuses on the attributes and skills that match the needs of the group or organization, but only if the playing field is equal.

As demonstrated earlier, we know that leadership in many vocational areas does not yet match the demographics of society. We can surmise that this imbalance is caused by existing sexism in U.S. society, as opposed to a lack of female leaders with the requisite attributes and skills. If we know that women can be effective as organization presidents, for example, are we subconsciously limiting our access to possible outstanding leaders by allowing candidate pools for these positions to remain unbalanced? Are there ways we are structuring the leadership positions or the places we are advertising them that subconsciously targets men more than women?

There is no one-size-fits-all solution to increasing the diversity of our candidate pools since organizations vary to such a large degree. That said, all organizations that can be led by a person of any gender should be encouraged to review their own data with these questions in mind.

As was discussed in the affirmative action section of the previous chapter, the efforts to improve hiring practices as they relate to the quantity and quality of candidates is often lost in the candidate recruitment efforts.

How can we encourage underrepresented but qualified people to become applicants?

If successful, this recruitment effort could result in increased numbers of both typical *and* atypical candidates. Stronger recruitment efforts can strengthen, for example, a presidential candidate pool in terms of gender as well as candidates from other underrepresented demographics such as race, age, national origin, sexual orientation, etc.

The next question following "Are leaders born or made?" and "Can all people become leaders?" questions would be:

Should we encourage everyone to try to become leaders?

Author Sherrilyn Kenyon coined the phrase, "Just because you can doesn't mean that you should."[68] This expression normally applies to ethical situations, such as taking advantage of a cashier who inadvertently gives you change for a $20 bill when you gave them a $10 bill. In this case, the expression is intended to mean something different. Not everyone who possesses leadership qualities and skills should take on the role of leader. It is not a "next step" or something one is owed. Being a leader is not easy. One must have the time, energy, and the passion for being a leader and frankly, anyone lacking these should probably refrain from taking on leadership challenges.

Having the title of director, manager, coordinator, captain, boss, etc. designates individuals as leaders. Herein lies one of the often-discussed problems regarding the practice of leadership. The title signifies the job, but it takes much more to characterize someone as an *effective* leader, which is really the ultimate goal of leadership.

There have been numerous high-profile leaders throughout history who met the common definition of a leader but were unsuccessful in their efforts to achieve established goals. Since we know from Chapter I that the number one reason employees leave their organizations is due to poor leadership, this book strives to clearly state what needs to change in terms of "the leaders we have now versus the leadership we need" moving forward. Here is a big one:

We need to focus on what it takes to identify individuals as potential leaders, but more importantly, as effective and ethical leaders.

We must stop assuming that everyone is ready to be an effective and ethical leader. We know what happens when we assume, right? The belief that anyone can be an effective leader (the "anyone can do it" mindset) has been proven to be incorrect time and time again. So how can we know if a person is "leadership material"?

Why Does the Candidate Want to be in this Leadership Role?

Anyone who has read at least one book about leadership likely knows that an important first step toward becoming an effective leader or assessing a potential leader is to ask *why* one wants to become a leader. In interviews, one of the early questions should seek to understand the candidate's knowledge about the leadership aspect of the position. That question should *not* be, "Why are you the best person to assume the role?" since the candidate has no way of knowing that answer without knowing the other candidates' strengths and areas for growth, and it is unlikely to elicit the type of information you seek. Besides, determining the best candidate is the committee's responsibility, right? The question, "Why do you want to be a leader?" or "Why are you interested in this particular leadership position?" can be asked in a variety of ways but needs to elicit *why* they want to take on a leadership role and how they view that role. From their response, you should get a glimpse into their motivation and passion, or conversely, possibly learn that they have little idea what they would be getting into.

When we ask the question "why," it is amazing how many people are stumped by it. This should be the first thing a candidate is able to address confidently and clearly. If you see the candidate furrow their eyebrows, that is likely an indication that they have not thought enough about why they want to lead, which could be an accident waiting to happen.

As an interviewer, understanding why a candidate wants to take on a position allows you to determine if they have a reasonable understanding of what the organization expects in terms of production requirements, as well as employee support and development. If the candidate responds to the question, "Why do you want to take on a leadership role in our organization?" by mentioning the organization's geographic location, the fact that the position will serve as a promotion from their current position, that they have all the requisite skills, or that they are ready for a new challenge, does that tell you anything about what you might expect from their leadership? If not, then you are not yet able to truly evaluate their leadership potential, so would need to ask additional questions or raise a caution flag. These responses may well be honest, but they say nothing about what to expect if they were to get the job and become *your* leader. What motivates them each day? How would they describe their leadership style? How would they respond to an employee who is not meeting their job requirements? Responses to questions like these may give you a window into how a candidate views employee development and their views on the role of leadership. After hearing their responses and before moving on, you really do need to be able to answer the question,

Would I want to be supervised by this candidate?

One of the most widely read authors on the topic of leadership is John Maxwell, with more than 20 million books sold and translated into 50 languages. In his book, *Developing the Leaders Around You: How to Help Others Reach Their Full Potential,* John Maxwell argues, "relational skills are the most important abilities in leadership."[69] In another of his best-known quotes, Maxwell states, "leadership is not about titles, positions, or flowcharts. It is about one life influencing another."[70]

Tom Brady, a well-known all-pro quarterback, was once asked what he thought about the disruptions to his team when Antonio Brown was let go by the Patriots due to allegations of misconduct. Brady said, "I think there are a lot of human elements, and as a player and as a person, I care deeply about my teammates...You want everyone to become the best they can possibly be. And you try to provide leadership and try to care for people...you invest not just your head but your heart, your soul."[71] Like Maxwell, Brady focuses his view of leadership not exclusively on the end result of an initiative, but to a large extent, on the people he leads.

The definitions of "leadership" in Chapter I imply that for effective leadership to occur, there is a process that includes:

- The leader

- The influenced individuals

- The common goals

Each component of the process must be considered and attended to for the leadership efforts to have a chance to be considered effective.

All organizations need to develop their own definition of leadership and determine how it will be measured in the workplace. Without coming to an agreed-upon definition of what we expect from an effective leader, we risk:

- Leaders focusing exclusively on themselves and their own development
- Potential leaders making decisions to take on leadership roles without consideration of their impact on the individuals they will lead
- The established goals not being effectively assessed
- Leaders assuming a one-size-fits-all style of leadership

Once the definition of "effective leadership" is established by an organization, the related behavioral expectations need to follow. These should be included in the job descriptions for each of the leadership positions. By doing this, new leaders can understand exactly what will be expected of them. Seeing only the words "responsible for supervision of staff" on a job description does not sufficiently share the specific expectations the organization has for how leaders will support and develop their employees. Yet, this is the current norm.

Self-Awareness

One of the very first stages of leadership development is self-awareness. Not surprisingly, it is also the first component of what is referred to as "emotional intelligence." Before a person can effectively support, understand, and lead others, they must first understand themselves. In an interview, there are questions you can ask that will directly measure this leadership component, such as:

- How do you respond to constructive criticism? Can you share an example of when you accepted criticism and used the feedback to make changes that helped you to be more effective?

- Have you asked anyone for feedback in the past?

- How do you respond to stressful situations? How will your colleagues and staff know when you are stressed?

- What does being a role model mean to you? How would you demonstrate this in practice?

- What does it mean for you to be responsible for other people in the organization?

- What makes you confident that you will be successful in a leadership role? Receiving the response, "I have been successful in the past" is not a particularly useful response.

If the candidate has not given enough thought to their own leadership style and how others perceive them, how can they be ready to effectively lead others? Leadership theorists would say that they cannot. So, are they leadership material? In this case, probably not (yet).

This chapter has argued the importance and justification for including specific, desirable, (and measurable) leadership skills and attributes in the job description. Most job descriptions related to leadership positions list only tasks (often as outcomes) that the employee is expected to accomplish and the fact that the employee "will provide leadership for a department or division." As stated, the job description needs to delineate this further. What is meant by "provide leadership?" Certainly, it is not limited to running staff meetings and making decisions, because that would sound much like the old version of leadership or management – to tell people what to do and hold them accountable if they do not do it. Effective interviewers seek specific examples of what a potential leader will do, to analyze during the interviews. In that way, they can help answer the question, "Is this person leadership material?"

CHAPTER IV

What Qualities and Skills Do Effective Leaders Need?

Leadership is a challenging endeavor. Many experienced leaders and leadership authors will agree that being an effective leader includes having a wide repertoire of human-relation and project-management skills and continually working to strengthen each one. In counseling, therapists use the term, "intentional counseling" to mean that the therapist is skilled in a variety of techniques, such that all are well-developed, and the therapist can determine which counseling style will work best with each client. Likewise, leadership involves an array of skills that need to be well-developed and called upon to problem-solve, support people, and accomplish tasks.

As human beings, we all have some skills and attributes that are well-developed and others that may be less developed. Leaders are first and foremost human beings, like everyone else, but to be effective leaders, they need a wide variety of skills to respond proactively and reactively to the challenges they will face.

Have you ever known someone who everyone thought to be a "natural leader?" There are some people who excel in leadership positions and seem to handle all aspects of the role effortlessly. Regardless of how easy these leaders make it look, there is no such thing as a "natural leader." Yes, some leaders are fortunate to be born with some of the *traits* that many people value in leaders—intelligence, confidence, creativity, ability to inspire, and an action-orientation, but there are also *skills* that leaders need to strengthen, in order to earn the designation "effective leader." These include crisis management, problem-solving, empathy, feedback, public speaking, and time management, to name a few.

While it is possible to develop a huge list of all the potential skills an effective leader may seek to develop, leaders are not a one-size-fits-all entity, so specific leadership skills should usually be prioritized according to the skills most needed in a specific profession or organization. For example, an effective elementary school teacher needs to be empathic, creative, inspiring, and have good teaching and conflict-resolution skills. An elementary school principal, on the other hand, may find those same skills helpful in their work, but must possess skills in the areas of organizational vision, analysis, budgeting, strategic planning, and community networking. Therefore, the most important leadership skills are normally the ones that are most pertinent to one's job.

In addition to demonstrating specific leadership skills, an overarching leadership philosophy also defines the ways a leader will act. The following represents the tenets of my personal leadership philosophy – you are encouraged to develop and share your own.

The Milstone Leadership Philosophy:

1. Effective leaders demonstrate respect for all people with whom they come into contact.

2. Effective leaders strive to meet the needs of all constituents involved in their sphere of responsibility.

3. Effective leaders treat all members equally when the playing field is even and equitably when it is not.

4. Effective leaders approach problems and challenges with a positive attitude.

5. Effective leaders involve team members in planning and decision-making whenever possible.

1. *Effective leaders demonstrate respect for all people with whom they come into contact.*

Perhaps the most important thing a leader can remember is that every person with whom they interact deserves respect, regardless of the purpose of the contact. Early in my career, a new department head spoke to my team and said, "Every member of this organization is essential to the success of our team. We may have different jobs and different titles, but every one of us contributes an essential service to this organization." His message seemed so simple at the time, but it has stayed with me throughout my career and frankly, throughout my life.

Related to the first tenet, an important aspect a leader needs to remember is that most employees and team members do not come to work each week primarily to make the executive leader look good. They do not see their paycheck as a symbol that they work for one person. They work for an organization, an industry, a cause. They come to work because they want to make a difference—a positive difference. The ultimate disrespect a leader can give to team members or employees is to assume that they are pawns that work for them.

An effective leader/supervisor ensures that the assigned work is getting done, that every employee has the opportunity to enhance their skills and their contributions, and that every employee gets evaluated on a regular basis. It does not mean that the employee exists to be a servant to that leader.

Poor leaders seem to exclusively focus internally and seek to utilize team members for meeting only the leader's objectives. Effective leaders simultaneously focus internally and externally. By doing so, the leader helps team members to meet their needs for involvement, recognition, and respect, while also targeting the leader's personal goals and objectives.

A common complaint from employees is that they feel like part of a class system in which upper-level administrators often walk by them without saying "hello" or even making eye contact. Leaders in large organizations are certainly not expected to remember the names of every employee, but it takes little effort to at least acknowledge someone, smile, and say "hello." It is such a small act, but it can make an incredible difference in the workplace. Just a simple acknowledgement sends a message that the employee is important. Conversely, ignoring an employee can send the message that they are not significant enough to acknowledge. Some people are especially good with names, and some are comfortable introducing themselves and asking for an employee's name. Ironically, this is one of the easiest ways for a leader to spread goodwill, yet far too many leaders walk past employees, seemingly in their own little world. How many times have you felt like a "little" person when a leader walked past you without acknowledging you? Or perhaps you mustered up the courage to say something, and were met with silence? That little insecure person lives in most of us to some degree, so when you are the leader, be sure to pay attention.

Some leaders treat some people within the organization well and treat others less well. It is not uncommon for some leaders to literally yell at the staff they supervise when something goes wrong. This happens most frequently to administrative assistants and other employees who may be at the lower end of the salary hierarchy. Not only is this type of behavior disrespectful, but it may well constitute the creation of a hostile workplace and in some cases, harassment or discrimination, which are legally unacceptable conditions. An effective leader never uses language or takes an action that would make an employee feel threatened or disparaged. When this occurs, it is unlikely to be a first-time or one-time incident, so following up appropriately is essential. If the employee being disrespected is comfortable sharing the incident directly with the supervisor, that may be a good approach, but when they are not comfortable doing so, they should be advised to bring the matter to their Human Resources office.

A common mistake many leaders make is publicly recognizing certain people but excluding others, especially at large group events. On one hand, any positive recognition for employees sends the message that their efforts are appreciated. Some leaders add something to the effect of "...and my thanks go to the many people who also helped make this happen." This recognition at least acknowledges that the leader knows that many people helped, but it is far better to mention specific employees or at least specific departments. In general, many employees tend to feel that their work is unnoticed by senior leaders, so taking time to acknowledge their efforts and importance energizes employees and encourages them to continue the type of behavior that gets recognized.

Have you ever been at a group event where the leader says, "I don't want to mention specific names because I am sure I will forget someone"? Then, they proceed to do just that and forget you or someone you know. Being excluded while others are included can be demoralizing and feel disrespectful. As a general practice, it is better to not mention anyone by name than to mention some while omitting others. While leaders are certainly human, audiences are quick to catch on to who is left out of leaders' acknowledgements.

Leaders who have more contact with certain employees or departments are more likely to see the outcomes and efforts of those individuals and groups more clearly. As is often the case when individuals are excluded from acknowledgements, the same is true for departments and services. Far too often, these same departments and services are overlooked and excluded from receiving the public kudos.

In any organization, it takes great teamwork from all departments and all employees or members to accomplish challenging goals. While some members and departments seem to get more of the glory when goals are accomplished, it is critical that leaders acknowledge the importance of each member and department in achieving common organizational goals. To only mention those closest to you (as the leader) sends a clear message that the only people who matter are those who interact more with the senior leaders. That may be true in an autocratic environment but is usually a "kiss of death" in a team-oriented organization. Omitting parts of the team is not only lazy, but in reality, many insightful leaders know that the most important members of their teams on a daily basis are rarely the senior leaders or department heads, but rather the entry-level and mid-level employees, administrative assistants, custodians, food-service workers, and others who are rarely acknowledged.

2. Effective leaders strive to meet the needs of all constituents involved in their sphere of responsibility.

Unsuccessful leaders may at times have a bit of tunnel vision in that they focus their efforts on projects that involve a small number of employees or volunteers. As mentioned, the leader has responsibility for certain outcomes, but they also need to be focused on ways that all employees or volunteers can meet their professional needs.

One such critical area, as mentioned earlier, is the professional development programs of the organization. Seeing the executive officer attending an optional staff development opportunity not only sends a message regarding the importance of ongoing development but gives the executive leader (EL) an opportunity to get to know more team members on a personal basis. In most cases, after the employees return to their departments, they make it a point to mention to their colleagues that the EL was at their session.

In the higher education world, for example, ELs may need to decide at the end of a long day between attending the racism awareness program on campus or going home to see their family. They often forget to see these decisions through the eyes of their constituents – their students. When they attend, even if they do not open their mouths, they are seen by students as leaders who are committed to their students. To students, this is probably the most important thing campus leaders should be doing. Conversely, when they do not attend, they may be seen as leaders who do not care about the students or their concerns. These choices for campus leaders are not always obvious or clear, but again, leaders can increase their perceived effectiveness by viewing decisions through the eyes of their teams (in this case, students) as opposed to exclusively through a personal lens.

There is a somewhat common belief that the higher the level of responsibility of an employee, the less supervision and support they should need from their supervisor. As a result, many leaders use staff meetings to focus only on how their direct reports can help to meet the needs of the leader. This occurs in many levels of management. While striving to meet the needs of the leaders is important, it is also important to designate time in staff meetings for all members to seek help and support from colleagues and their supervisor. New situations arise in organizations and new challenges are undertaken on a regular basis. A Chief Financial Officer (CFO), for example, may not need a lot of assistance determining the best way to analyze budget protocols, but they may want/need assistance and support following an organizational crisis, such as seeking ways to identify possible savings that could be used to balance the budget. Staff meetings should have multiple priorities and when we consider the amount of money it costs, for example, to have five department leaders in a room for two hours, it behooves the leader to ensure that the needs of the entire team are met. In addition to meeting the needs of the leader, this encourages teamwork, and helps to strengthen trust. These types of efforts also show comradery to the rest of the organization, which gives them a sense of security that the entire team is moving in the same direction.

At all levels of leadership, inexperienced leaders regularly view one-on-one meetings with employees they supervise as a checklist of items to cross off. They ask for updates on projects, inform the employee what they need from them, and share information from other departments that may impact the employee's planning. That can be productive, but what is missing? Related to this, many supervisors/leaders cancel their regularly scheduled one-on-one meeting with an employee when they are busy or when they feel their list of topics to discuss is short. Everyone likes to have time back, right? Yes, but what about questions the employee has, or updates on how *their* employees are progressing? What about taking time to review the employee's professional development goals that help to prepare the employee for a promotion? Again, for both the leader and the employee to be successful, each interaction needs to have a dual purpose – what the leader needs from the employee and what the employee needs from their leader.

When asked to describe their supervisory style, some leaders respond with something like, "I establish goals with each person and hold them accountable for meeting those goals." That sounds productive, but it also sounds a bit robotic. No two people are the same, so why would a supervisor focus only on the brush strokes that are similar to all? A common misunderstanding is that leaders must treat all employees the same. In some facets of their positions, employees *should* be treated the same – due dates, meeting times, professional expectations, etc., but when helping an employee with a problem, or providing professional support, an effective supervisor must understand that not all employees took the same path to get where they are today. Some had an easier road, some had to fight tooth and nail to get there. Some employees feel competent and some constantly feel as if they are in over their heads, whether they express it or not. Each employee deals with different challenges and each has a different view of what success means to them. One employee, for example, may prefer to have little oversight from the supervisor and may be most comfortable updating the supervisor only when problems arise that they need help to overcome. Another employee may be undertaking an endeavor that is very new to them and may appreciate having more supervisory support than they normally desire. Yet another employee may want more handholding than their supervisor deems appropriate or has the time to provide.

Effective leadership is anything but simple. There are leaders who try to simplify things to make their own jobs more manageable, but leaders who see supervision as peripheral to their position or expect to have lots of time to get their own goals met are often unnecessarily frustrated. Meeting the needs of their staff members is an important part of the leader's job, and that takes time – just like every other vital part of a leader's job. In most cases, leading a group - large or small - means getting the best output from those in your sphere of responsibility. When new leaders have only been responsible for themselves in the past and now need to focus attention on others, it can be a considerable adjustment. As the saying goes, however, "that is why they get paid the big bucks." It is challenging to be responsible for others and it takes commitment, energy, and a strong desire to meet the needs of your group of individuals – all of them.

3. Effective Leaders treat all members equally when the playing field is even and equitably when it is not.

As discussed in the previous tenet, leaders must always balance the need for consistency with the need to understand ways in which an uneven (or perhaps unfair) playing field requires different treatment of an employee or volunteer. This may sound familiar, but there are many leaders out there who firmly believe that no one deserves "special treatment," and anything that deviates from the norm is discriminating or giving someone an unfair advantage.

In some cases, an employee's need for unique or special accommodations is required by law through the Americans With Disabilities Act (ADA). For example, physical spaces must accommodate a person's wheelchair, parking must be made available near the entrances of buildings, offices in upper floors must have elevator access if a person using a wheelchair needs access to it, and elevators must have braille to assist a legally blind person. Those are some of the easy ones that even the most inflexible leaders do not seem to argue against. Assisting mobility-challenged individuals during fire alarms or real fires, keeping building supplies away from doorways so a wheelchair can pass, and building ramps and making curb-cuts are just a few of the lesser-known ways that leaders need to attend to disabled employees' physical needs.

Many of the challenges faced by disabled people today pertain to learning and communication challenges. While in high school or college, many students receive "reasonable accommodations" according to law, such as untimed exams, assigned note takers, signers, and specialized equipment. In the working world, these needs do not disappear. Candidates for jobs may apply and be hired for any position for which they are qualified with the addition of "reasonable accommodations."[72] While this is sometimes confusing, effective leaders understand the value that disabled people bring to any workplace. As a result, organizations can send clear messages of support to their communities by establishing accommodations prior to an employee or service-user expressing the need. These are messages that will be welcomed. Some organizations are exempt from some of the ADA laws, so they need to weigh the costs and benefits of accommodating individuals with physical, emotional, or learning challenges. Caution should be used, however, before intentionally excluding any population that has the skills and abilities to help an organization prosper.

Many times, the "uneven playing field" pertains to demographics, such as being a person of color in a primarily white organization, a female working in an environment that is predominantly male, or a person of the Jewish faith working for an organization that was founded based on Christian values. The playing field may also pertain to recovering alcoholics, women who are pregnant, or people from the LGBTQ+ community working in a conservative organization in which it does not feel safe to "be out." In each of these types of situations, organizational leaders can choose to take actions that serve to level the uneven and sometimes unfair field. These decisions will impact the way many employees and constituents feel about their organization. Additionally, serving as an active member of an organization's diversity committee may help an employee concerned about an inequity see you as a possible ally or advocate. Offering a social event for employees at which alcohol is not served sends a supportive message to a person in recovery. Likewise, having a symbol of support for the LGBTQ+ community, such as a pink triangle or rainbow flag, in a visible location can instantly impact how an employee feels every day. These seemingly small actions can be the difference between an employee feeling unwelcome or feeling like a part of a family. In which environment do you believe a leader is more likely to build trust, loyalty, and have employees that go the extra mile? Certainly, the one who says, "I see you and I respect and appreciate you."

4. Effective Leaders approach problems and challenges with a positive attitude.

You have likely heard the adage, "Do what you love, and you will never work a day in your life." It is an offshoot of what American author Ray Bradbury said, "Love what you do and do what you love."[73] Career centers encourage people to find their passions in working toward this goal. Encouraging a positive environment is a facet of this thinking as well.

Employees and volunteers want to enjoy their work rather than dread going to work each morning. Any place that expects more from employees than they can produce, does not routinely celebrate accomplishments, and seeks to find fault when something goes wrong, is a place that can and usually will suck the life out of its employees. Despite the obviousness of this statement, many organizations are viewed in this way, and the leadership plays a significant role in the development of that culture.

Alternatively, imagine working at an organization in which the employees are friendly, supportive of the work done by colleagues, able to learn from failed efforts without having fingers pointed at them, and enthusiastic about joining celebrations to acknowledge successes of employees, departments, and the organization as a whole. Why is this scenario not the norm? It does not cost much, if anything, to celebrate success and appreciate others.

On an episode of the television show, *Seinfeld*, Jerry's friend George Costanza has a job working for the New York Yankees. He tells his friends that the way he remains in the good graces of his supervisors is by waiting for them to walk by his office, and then looking like he is angry (by throwing a file on his desk and shaking his head). His assumption, as is validated on the show, is that people who are angry all the time must be working hard.[74]

Many of us may have seen this anger in a colleague and thought it was a sign of a passionate and hard-working colleague. However, this type of negativity and anger can only get someone so far. Can you imagine working with someone who was always angry? Imagine you are in a good mood and pass this angry person in the hallway. You say, "Hi ___, how are you doing?" You receive an eye roll and "You don't want to know." Does a regular occurrence of this make you want to spend more or less time working with that colleague?

Periodic demonstrations of emotion are not uncommon, and in fact make leaders appear more human. Too much negativity, however, may encourage teammates to not share bad news for fear of sparking the anger. Negativity also makes it uncomfortable to share good news. When someone is in a bad mood, most people choose to ignore them as opposed to sharing anything, good or bad, that may make them feel worse.

Positive thinking, according to the Mayo Clinic, "helps with stress management and can even improve your health." For those of you with leaders who are often negative, the Mayo Clinic offers, "If you tend to be pessimistic, don't despair – you can learn positive thinking skills."[75] So, positivity is good for the leader and good for the organization. As a general philosophy, positivity leads to more positivity. Positive people generally prefer to be around other optimistic, positive people. They feed off the energy that they each bring from this mindset. Further, customers and other onlookers are apt to view positivity from employees and leaders as a sign that the organization is productive and treats people well. This does not mean we should fake being optimistic, however, because honesty is one of the most important skills an effective leader possesses, according to their team members. Effective leaders see the advantages to having and developing positivity, and the importance in seeking this trait/skill in the employees they hire.

5. *Leaders involve team members in planning and decision-making whenever possible.*

We have all heard the adage that to understand another person, we must try to walk in their shoes. This is widely mentioned in counselor training programs and is equally true in leadership development. When leaders seek to employ ways to empower their team members and to increase their ownership in organizational decisions, the obvious answer is to involve the members in the team's planning and decision-making. Don't you always prefer to have a say in how decisions will be made and implemented at your place of work?

Employees in a retail establishment, for example, may react one way after being told that they will be responsible for increasing their sales, but will likely react a very different way if they are part of a team that develops the goals, plans objectives to meet the goals, and makes decisions about how and when they will measure the achievement of the goals. This is true for most goal setting, but also for virtually any decision-making done by an organization.

As wonderful as it may sound to work in an environment where everyone can share input for all decisions, not all decisions and planning can be done by all team members for a variety of reasons. Some decisions are passed down, some are time sensitive, some require knowledge not presently held by the team members, etc. While these are legitimate reasons for not seeking input and involvement from team members, they are not normally the reason that leaders make decisions unilaterally or only with other leaders. Quite often, like most people, leaders seek the easiest path to completing a project. Bringing teams together to do this thinking and planning takes time and a good amount of energy and flexibility on the leader's part. For some leaders, it may also conflict with the role they believe leaders should play in goal achievement. They may believe it is up to the leader to assign the work and up to the employees to make it happen according to the prescribed plan.

An analogy for these opposing leadership paths relates to learning time management. A response to the question, "Are you going to the seminar on time management today?" is often, "No, I don't have time for that." On one hand, the person with no time to attend can choose the fastest way to get their work done—by not attending the seminar and instead plowing into their work. However, by taking time to attend the seminar, the person presumably will learn time management techniques that will help them accomplish more in a shorter period. So why would anyone choose the first option of not attending? Most likely, if the person knew that attending the seminar would give them skills to be more productive with their time, they would select it. Often, we just *don't know what we don't know*, which blinds us to opportunities for success.

When we looked at driving styles earlier, you'll recall that the third category was the "Same-Ole, Same-Ole" drivers who continue to drive in the way they have always done it. It worked that way for years, so why should they change? There are many leaders with the same mindset. They have approached their work in one way, and it seems to have worked for them, so why change it now? Like everyone else on the planet, they have a perceived shortage of time, (while in fact, we all have the same number of hours in a day and days in a week) and may see changing to a method of team involvement as time-consuming, risky, and scary.

Effective leaders involve team members in the planning of goals and decision-making because they trust that there may be another way—even a better way. They resist the temptation to grab the challenge and handle it themselves. Over time, they have learned that involving others can create win-win opportunities. Their teams feel more connected to their organization and each other, and the decisions have been much stronger than any one person could have developed. Effective leaders eventually come to embrace the reality of "not knowing what they don't know" and have confidence that involving others makes them look stronger rather than weaker. Additionally, involving others is certainly better than excluding them and later asking them to do work that's now required because the intended goal was not achieved.

In fact, as effective leaders know, involving team members in planning and decision-making ultimately *saves* time, because it leads to better decisions (more heads are better than one) that do not need to be recalculated down the road. As a cherry on top, it also leads to having a set of ambassadors for the project or goal, because anyone who has a hand in developing something will usually defend that effort when it becomes necessary. This tenet of effective leadership is especially important when working in an organization in which trust is not strong and/or there is a history of discord between leadership and employees.

The Traits and Skills Needed by Effective Leaders of Today and Tomorrow

Despite the improbability of being able to determine a single set of skills and traits that are most important for leaders in all situations, the following list represents 44 traits and skills that are critical to most leadership positions, particularly as we envision the challenges in leadership today and tomorrow:

Accountability	Humility
Analysis	Humor
Attention to Detail	Influence/Inspiration
Budget Development and Management	Learner/Learning Agility
Change Management	Loyalty
Commitment/Passion	Open-Minded
Communication/Active Listening	Patience
Confidence	Perseverance
Conflict Resolution/Mediation	Planning
Courage	Positivity
Creativity/Innovation	Problem-Solving
Critical Thinking	Public Speaking

Decision Making	Reliability
Delegation/Empowerment	Resilience
Dependability	Respect for others
Empathy	Stress Management
Emotional Intelligence/Self-Awareness/ Maturity	Teaching/Training/ Mentoring
Feedback (positive and constructive)	Team Building
Flexibility	Technical Competency
Gratitude	Time Management
Group Dynamics	Vision/Direction Setting
Honesty/Integrity/Ethics	Work Ethic

Lists of suggested leadership skills and traits are easy to find online. Some websites list their top five, seven, or ten, and others offer more exhaustive lists of 25, 50, or 100. Many of the categories are generalized, which makes it virtually impossible to offer *THE* perfect list that so many people ask for. In some ways, it may be easier to determine that the absence of certain leadership skills can negatively impact a leader more than others. Also, as was mentioned earlier in this chapter, having the desirable skills and traits without a leadership philosophy will also make a leader sound like someone who is just going through the motions, and has not yet earned the leadership credibility.

This list of traits and skills has been intentionally combined to avoid getting caught in the intellectual argument of whether each one is a trait or skill, and as such, whether it can be developed or is simply a deep-rooted value that many believe exists from birth in some people. For example, when we look at words such as loyalty, it is often hard to determine whether it is a trait or skill. Some would argue that if it were a trait, one could not strengthen it to be more conducive to a leadership role. Most would agree, however, that loyalty is important to effective leadership because it is closely connected to trust, which makes possible the willingness of employees to be creative and take risks, which is closely connected to perseverance, which is closely connected to problem-solving, and so on. Bottom line is that it matters less how these traits and skills are characterized than whether a leader possesses them or can strengthen them to help their team become more effective.

In an ideal world, all leaders would be effective and would possess all the traits and skills mentioned on the preceding page. Not one is unimportant and each of them is routinely utilized by effective leaders, though some more than others, depending on the industry, and the needs of the employees, volunteers, and organization.

On the list of traits and skills, four are underlined. These represent the four skills and traits that I believe effective leaders *most* need to develop, strengthen, and prioritize for today and tomorrow in most professions. These are traits and skills that will be integral to combatting many of the reasons so many leaders today are ineffective and will be crucial in changing the leadership paradigm from *the leaders we have* to the *leadership we need*. For this reason, I call them "super-skills."

Super-skill #1: Effective Communication

Communication is far more grandiose than the word first implies. Yes, it means to dialogue with another person as one does when words are exchanged, but if it were that simple, it would not rank at the very top of the list when employees are asked what needs to improve in their organization. Virtually all studies and surveys show that most employees are either unhappy or very unhappy with communication in their organizations, their departments, and often between themselves and their supervisors.[76]

Communication includes verbal and nonverbal communication and is often associated with active listening and attending skills. It also refers to the timing, frequency, and style that is used by leaders to keep employees up to date, announce important news, and to prepare people for changes that are likely to impact their work and lives.

Timely Communication

Many people are planners and know that having knowledge is a key to planning. How often have we heard people in our workplace say that they are "usually the last ones to know"? Not knowing important information is frustrating, but when you do receive it, information can be very empowering. In fact, there is an applicable expression from Sir Francis Bacon, "Knowledge is power."[77] Simply, the more information one has, the easier it is for them to solve problems and prevent them. Yet, we routinely hear of leaders withholding information from employees. In fairness, sometimes leaders are asked to withhold the information due to issues of confidentiality, and other times, they are asked to hold off sharing information so they will have a business advantage (for example, an interest in purchasing a property). Many times, however, leaders do not intentionally choose to withhold information – they simply do not think to share it. Effective leaders understand that employees feel respected when they receive information, and as stated, they can do better planning and have less duplication of efforts. These leaders continually think outside their own needs and keep those in the organization informed.

Verbal Clarity

Communication, in terms of *verbally sharing information with clarity*, is a life skill that helps a person receiving the information to easily understand the message intended by the leader. In all facets of life, being an effective communicator means being able to be succinct and distinct with words. Effective leaders can share information in such a way that allows the listener to hear the information without losing interest in the topic or becoming tired from listening for too long.

Many of us have been in a conversation in which we said or wanted to say to someone, "Please get to the point!" Time is precious to all of us, and we do not want to spend our limited time hearing information that could have been communicated in a much shorter time period. Plus, listening carefully is tiring, isn't it? An effective communicator is succinct (brief and to the point) and can enunciate their words so the listener will more clearly understand what the speaker intends to say.

So, we know that being succinct is important in one-on-one conversations. However, leaders are also often asked to share information with groups of people, sometimes small and sometimes large. A specific skill set pertaining to verbally sharing information in this way is called public speaking.

Public Speaking

According to several studies on the topic of fear, the number one fear many people have in life is not death, but public speaking.[78] That is a very powerful statement. (The number two fear, by the way, is losing a loved one.) A number of people have this phobia, which is a type of anxiety disorder. The thought of speaking to a group in public creates such anxiety for them that it disrupts their ability to perform one or more daily functions, such as eating or sleeping. For many others, it is scary, but a bit less all-consuming – it may be anxiety producing, very uncomfortable, and something they avoid if possible. If you are in one of these categories, it may be helpful for you to know that you are not alone.

The good news is that many people have overcome their fear of public speaking and have become comfortable in those types of settings. Some people even enjoy public speaking and find it to be a skill they are proud to have.

Most leadership positions involve speaking with individuals, small groups, medium-sized groups, and some involve speaking to large groups, so in terms of communication skills, public speaking is an important skill to develop. Even if you never come to love public speaking, being able to articulate goals, lead group discussions, and effectively share information in different venues can greatly impact how you are perceived in terms of confidence, knowledge, and professionalism.

There are many excellent resources that can assist with this effort to become a confident and comfortable public speaker. Workshops offered by organizations such as Toastmasters International,[79] Ginger,[80] TED Talks,[81] and The Public Speaking Project[82] are available online for viewing. Just a few of the many books that have proven to be helpful and effective are *Presentation Zen* by Garr Reynolds, *The Quick and Easy Way to Effective Speaking* by Dale Carnegie, *In the spotlight: Overcome Your Fear of Public Speaking and Performing* by Janet Esposito, and *10 Days to More Confident Public Speaking – Say Goodbye to Stage Fright Forever!* by Lenny Laskowski. Some of these training materials assume you have a deathly fear of public speaking, and others assume you just need a boost to get more comfortable, but all offer a variety of tips that can be incredibly useful.

Public speaking is one of the most life-changing skills an individual can develop. Leaders are often amazed at how quickly they notice the improvement in their public speaking and how this skill positively impacts so much of their lives in general.

To help you get started on this journey, here are five quick tips from me to you pertaining to public speaking:

1. *Read and re-read your presentation content so much that you feel like you own it.* This will alleviate the need for you to read to the audience from a notepad with your head down and will make the audience want to hear your content.

2. *Talk past the person farthest away from you.* If speaking in a large room, make your words bounce off the back wall. This will prevent you from mumbling and needing to stop to repeat what someone from the audience could not hear. It will also keep the attention of your audience because it signals that you are confident.

3. *Speak much more slowly than you feel you should.* Many people speak quickly to be done with their speech as soon as possible. However, the audience wants to hear ALL your words and needs to hear them slowly

enough to process them. Also, as you know, it is tiring to try to keep listening to and understanding a person speaking at a rapid pace.

4. *Use visual aids when possible.* In the era of multimedia and short attention spans, diversifying the attention of the audience can keep them at maximum alertness.

5. *Use humor if appropriate.* Not all speaking topics are conducive to humor, but where possible, humorous comments that are self-deprecating are generally a safe route to take. The goal of most speeches and presentations, like TED Talks, is to keep things serious but light. Alert listeners are more likely to hear and recall what you say. Likewise, the world is too serious sometimes and people want to smile, and they want to laugh. Humor is often memorable in and of itself, but it also helps to keep the audience alert.

Active listening

Another component of being an effective communicator is being an *active listener.* Active listeners can focus their attention on the speaker, so they are not distracted by other things, such as the time, a car passing by, or the brightly colored tie worn by the person speaking. An effective listener practices this skill by paraphrasing what they hear from the speaker. Paraphrasing is a technique used to feed back to the speaker what you heard them say, so they can tell you if you heard accurately or if you need them to restate something. This demonstrates respect for the speaker since you show that you care about hearing them accurately because their words have value. It also helps you (as the leader) to stay on topic so you can come to a solution more quickly.

As an example, the speaker (i.e., the employee) may tell the listener (i.e., the leader) that they are having trouble meeting the timeline for a project because they had to stay home due to their child being ill. An effective communicator paraphrases back to the speaker something to the effect of, "I'm sorry your child is ill. It sounds like you lost some of the time you had allotted for the project due to needing to be home. Let's see if we can establish a revised completion date."

Nonverbal Communication

As you know, there is an important fourth component of communication skills in addition to timely sharing, verbal clarity, and active listening. The fourth component is *nonverbal communication*. Professor Albert Mehrabian and colleagues from University of California, Los Angeles (UCLA) conducted human research in the 1960s demonstrating that only 7 percent of communication between two people is verbal.[83] That means that 93 percent of those communications are nonverbal (55 percent body language and 38 percent tone of voice). It is important to note that the professor's research has been challenged, since verbal communication such as a speech is obviously more than 7 percent verbal. Unscientifically, however, most psychologists and communication educators today argue that somewhere around 15 to 20 percent of communication is verbal, and 80 to 85 percent is nonverbal. That said, the main point here is not to argue the exact percentages, but to understand that most of communication is nonverbal. The most important takeaway is understanding that an effective leader should be well-versed in all forms of communication.

Nonverbal communication consists of the variety of ways we communicate our feelings, our intentions, and our values through:

- Facial expressions
- Body movements and gestures
- Posture – leaning towards or away from the speaker
- Eye contact – too much or too little
- Space and distance – physically, how close to the speaker one stands or sits
- Tone of voice

- Appearance – clothing, grooming, etc.

- Artifacts in the office – pictures, symbols, etc.

Leaders who bark orders with their heads down are unlikely to pick up on any of the nonverbal cues that their employees share. They are unlikely to know how the individual is feeling, if they understand the assignment, if they trust the leader, and if they can distinguish a serious comment from a sarcastic one.

As an exercise in observation, take a few moments when your television is on to mute the sound and just pay attention to the communication you see from the nonverbals. It can be amazing how much more we understand about the person who is talking as well as the person who is listening when we focus exclusively on nonverbal communication.

Next, keep watching the same show and turn the sound back on. Try to pay attention to the nonverbals while you are hearing the words. Some people can do both simultaneously and others find it tiring to maintain a focus on the nonverbals while the person is talking. Why is this?

In our fast-paced lives and world, it is likely that you have many things going on in your head throughout the day. You have errands to run after work, you need to remember to call your mom or dad, you have a project that is due tomorrow, your car is making a grinding sound when you tap the brake, etc. When someone is talking to you, it is easy to have your mind drift off to think about one or more of the to-do items in your mind. It is also common for a listener to take a quick look at the clock to see if they need to cut the conversation short to get somewhere else. Further, if the conversation pushes one of your hot topic buttons, you may feel the need to interrupt the speaker to tell them your thoughts or opinions, or if the topic makes you uncomfortable, you may be thinking of ways to cut it short or avoid it altogether. In short, each of these scenarios focus on *your* own needs and takes your attention away from what the person is telling you, both verbally and nonverbally.

If it's not bad enough that your mind wanders because you're thinking about any of the to-do items on your list or your discomfort with the topic, the person who's talking likely noticed that you were distracted. This probably made them feel less important, possibly disrespected, and likely less willing to continue the conversation with you. Suddenly, they may tell you that they can try to handle the problem on their own, or simply thank you for your time and slink away. That was not very effective, was it?

As effective leaders, we strive to help our team members be in the best position to be successful. If this team member slinked away, there is not much chance that they feel good about their relationship with you, their leader. They may also read into your actions as being proof that you do not think much of them and their skills. People can have vivid imaginations, as you know.

So how can we avoid these actions that prevent effective communication?

You can physically model effective active listening skills. Gerard Egan developed a model he labeled with the acronym "SOLER" in 1986,[84] and it has been widely used since that time in counselor trainings and student, peer-led trainings. In brief, SOLER establishes a physical presence for a leader that puts most speakers at ease.

The S in the acronym encourages the listener to sit *straight* and face the speaker. Leaning backwards or facing to the side sometimes gives the impression of not caring.

The O indicates that the listener has an *open* posture (not crossing their arms). Crossed arms often appear to be a defensive or unwelcomed stance.

The L indicates that the listener *leans* slightly forward (towards the speaker). It gives the appearance that the listener is reaching towards the speaker's words as opposed to fending them off.

The E pertains to *eye* contact. This one can be particularly challenging since some cultures find looking at someone for too long to be disrespectful. How does one know the right amount of eye contact to display? Too much can feel like a laser beam and probably freak out the speaker. Too little may be interpreted as the listener being disinterested. The desired amount is generally considered to "mirror" the amount shown by the speaker.

Finally, the R in the acronym encourages the listener to *relax* and be comfortable, so they do not come across as robotic.

Cumulatively, these actions are intended to effectively help the person speaking feel that the listener (you, the leader) cares about their relationship and what they have to say, helps the listener to not be accidentally distracted, establishes an appropriate amount of eye contact, and seems more natural. It is important to note that these actions are not foolproof. Much depends on the previous relationship between the individuals. For example, if the two people communicating are roommates who normally talk while reclining on chairs, seeing the listener suddenly sitting upright, leaning towards the speaker, and unfolding their arms may seem creepy. The SOLER model works in most situations, though, because it stops the listener from doing many of the habits and gestures that often make a speaker feel unimportant. When a leader uses the SOLER model, it nonverbally tells a team member or supervisee that they are not burdening the leader, and that they are important to them. All of this happens even when a minimal number of words are spoken.

Electronic Communication

In this day of social media, a large amount of communication occurs via email, Facebook, LinkedIn, Twitter, Instagram, Messenger, texting, etc. Since these applications largely use written words and may not involve nonverbal communication (except for Facetiming or using the occasional emoji), it is quite easy to have these forms of communication be misinterpreted.

When email was first introduced back in the late 20th century,[85] novices sometimes made the mistake of sending electronic messages in all capital letters. The reader most often saw this as the sender yelling at them, which was usually not the intention at all. As email became the primary communication used in many organizations across the world, it was unclear whether emails were replacing letters or memos, or brief thoughts, and as a result, it created the need to consider how the different permutations would be interpreted by the person receiving the email.

At the start of the 21st century, text messages became widely used as a primary means of communicating. An article by Paul Goodman in *TurboFuture* listed 12 disadvantages of text messaging:[86]

1. Misunderstanding

2. Impersonal

3. Expectation to Quickly Read and Respond

4. General Distraction

5. Texting and Driving

6. Socially Disruptive

7. Group Texts

8. Obsessive/Addictive

9. Limitations

10. Sleep Problems

11. Erodes Language Skills

12. Cost

Many of these disadvantages paralleled the early disadvantages associated with email. One significant difference was that the sender needed the receiver's telephone number to send a text message. To send an email, on the other hand, only required knowledge of the intended receiver's email address, which organizations usually provided to employees to facilitate internal communications. For the historians in the room, at the start of the email era, most senior leaders' email addresses were only shared with a select few, to prevent employees from sending emails to the executive leaders instead of their immediate supervisors. As society became more interested in leaders being more transparent and accessible, employees were given email addresses for all employees, including the executive leaders. The ELs, however, often dealt with this by using two separate email addresses – one for the "important people" and one for everyone else. That annoyed a lot of people, but I digress…

For many years, no one took the reins to help email users understand the dos and don'ts of emailing to promote effective communication. In the past decade, however, a few such publications have emerged. In 2016, *Business Insider* published, "15 Email Etiquette Rules Every Professional Should Follow."[87]

1. Include a clear, direct subject line.

2. Use a professional email address.

3. Think twice before hitting "reply to all."

4. Include a signature block.

5. Use professional salutations.

6. Use exclamation points sparingly.

7. Be cautious with humor.

8. Know that people from different cultures speak and write differently.

9. Reply to your emails – even if the email was not intended for you.

10. Proofread every message.

11. Add the email address last.

12. Double-check that you have selected the correct recipient.

13. Keep the fonts classic.

14. Keep tabs on your tone.

15. Nothing is confidential – so write accordingly.

Due to its recency or perhaps the tremendous speed with which new communication applications are developed, many of Goodman's disadvantages are still in existence today regarding the use of both text messages and email. In this era of technology, more and more people communicate electronically rather than speaking by phone or in person. In addition to losing some of the warmth that stems from phone calls and in-person visits, the workplace has been challenged to develop effective electronic communication, or more succinctly stated, to avoid communication snafus. The advent of Zoom, however, seems to have brought the old world and new world of communications together to some degree.

Returning to our automobile driving analogy, we often see angry drivers on the highway making gestures towards other drivers who have presumably offended them in some way. There is a perceived safety for these drivers to communicate (like making a one-fingered gesture) in a way they would be unlikely to do if they were face-to-face with the offending driver. In a similar way, electronic communications have empowered employees to communicate things to other employees and to leaders that in person, they might never do. For this reason, one of the most important practices leaders need to utilize and teach is to never send electronic communications when they are angry. Doing so almost never ends well. However, when the sender takes a few hours to reconsider what they wish to communicate, they often alter the original message considerably. Anyone on the receiving end of one of these angry messages knows this issue well.

Like in-person, nonverbal communication, unintended slights can occur when the sender of a text message or email is unaware of electronic communication etiquette. On a college campus, a faculty and professional staff member shared the following two experiences and brought awareness to numerous others in this vein.

- Student sends an email to the professor of his Chemistry class:
  Student: "hey, when is the final?"
  Professor: "Dear __, I determined your name from seeing the email address on your note. It is inappropriate to send a message of this kind to a professor. In the future, please include a professional address such as 'Dear Professor __' or 'Hello, Professor __.' Write questions as full sentences. Conclude your message with an appropriate salutation such as 'thank you,' and your name. I am happy that you are comfortable writing to me, but please remember that I am your professor, and you are one of the 54 students in my class. Sincerely, Professor __
  P. S. As listed in your class syllabus, the final will be held on May 6."

- Student sends an email to an administrator in the Student Affairs office:
  Student: "Dear __, I need your assistance. I am a student in Professor __'s Sociology 200 class, and he accused me of plagiarism on a paper I submitted last week and told me he may fail me for the class. I did not cheat and can prove it. I informed my parents, and we hope you can help us obtain justice. Thank you for reading this note. __"
  Administrator: "Dear __, I received your email dated October 7, pertaining to your being accused of plagiarism by your professor. I am happy to assist you but want to first ask that you communicate exclusively with me about this matter. As I began to investigate the matter with your professor, I learned that you sent the same email to more than 10 other administrators as well. This makes the process take longer since it involves so many people, all trying to help. Please call my office at __ so we can meet to

discuss your concerns. Thank you, Dr. __."

Student: "Dear Dr. __, I am sorry for sending my note to so many people, but I wanted to be sure someone would help me. I will contact your office today. Thank you for getting back to me. __"

These examples are not unique to higher education in that they simply represent a couple of the communication challenges associated with electronic communications. In the first example, it may never be known if the student was being disrespectful to the faculty member or just ignorant of the rules of electronic communications. Many organizations, service departments in particular, see a lot of communications like this, which make it appear that the sender is being flippant, even though that may not be accurate.

In the second example, the student caused many people to be confused by making each administrator think they were the only recipient of the email. It is not clear if the student intended to create this havoc to insure someone would respond, which could have led an administrator to begin their investigation with a negative view of the student. A similar type of incident could easily occur in other settings as well.

In response to the perceived hidden meanings of emails, emojis were invented in Japan in the 1990s[88] and have become a staple in everyday use over the past few decades. Including emojis can help add emotions to communications, which helps senders counteract the problem of receivers believing that the sender's notes were curt, angry, or sometimes condescending. By simply adding an emoji, the sender can bring more warmth (or humor) to their message.

For example, after an employee received an email from their supervisor reminding them that a report was due at the end of the day, the employee responded with, "I never forget a thing" complemented with a smiley face emoji. Without the emoji included, the supervisor may have found the response disrespectful or argumentative, but the emoji likely added a warmer tone to the sender's words. That said, although the use of emojis may be helpful in social communications, many organizations and executive leaders do not find the inclusion of emojis to be professionally appropriate. The moral of this story— always know your audience.

In summary, communication is one of the skills most in need of attention from leaders today. Problems stem from leaders' hesitancy to include employees in the information loop. Poor leader's verbal skills and listening skills are often the causes of employees feeling disrespected and feeling that the leader does not value them or their concerns. Nonverbal communication is one of the most misunderstood components of effective communication and is often an unrecognized cause of tension between leaders, employees, and constituents. Lastly, electronic communications have increased the ease and speed of communications, but often add to the challenges when used by people to gain speed, sometimes to the exclusion of understanding and in some cases, tact.

Effective leaders must be aware of and learn, refine, practice, and teach ways that employees can effectively communicate to be more productive and to avoid social faux pas (mistakes). With a desire to motivate and satisfy employee needs for involvement, leaders can turn negative exclusion to positive inclusion. Modeling active listening skills and being tuned into nonverbal communication can be the difference between having an employee who feels unimportant and unmotivated and having one who feels respected and like a valued team member motivated to help their leaders and organizations succeed.

Super-skill #2: Conflict Resolution

Conflict resolution skills are needed in today's workplaces and in society more than at any time in recent memory. Everywhere you look, it appears that conflicts permeate the day. Currently, due to the coronavirus pandemic, a polarizing election, high unemployment, an uncertain economy, and decisions to reopen schools and sporting events, etc., tensions and stress are abnormally high, and resilience seems to be in short supply.

Today's examples of stress are certainly unique to the day, but others have preceded these and certainly others will follow.

Political conflicts usually peak during election years, and the last five or six years have been a constant reminder that conflict can place wedges between people that are difficult to dislodge. An adage cautioned that one should not discuss religion or politics at the family dinner table. Today, religious discussions may not be front and center, but political discord seems to grow exponentially, discussion by discussion, and online post by post.

In this era of social media, instead of conflicts occurring primarily at dinner tables, it now occurs on each social application. On Twitter, for example, political tweets can be just plain nasty! Facebook was once a place to read about new births, new jobs, important events, meaningful sayings, and a reminder of friend's birthdays. In recent years, anti-Trump and pro-Trump posts dominated the Twitter and Facebook scene and even with the election long over, still more hatred is being spewed. Amid the coronavirus pandemic, which by March 2021 had already caused 30 million to be infected and 550,000 to die in the United States alone,[89] the political discourse remained front and center. The previous White House leadership had stopped talking about the pandemic in their final month of office, despite millions remaining out of work and millions more desperate for food and/or anxious about the possibility of being evicted from their homes. New presidential leadership has renewed significant focus on the plight of the most vulnerable in the country and has brought a new leadership style which thus far, seems to prioritize action, communication, and empathy. These conflict resolution skills have already done much to slow the intensity of the national anxiety.

Emotions and conflicts like these that occur outside the workplace very often permeate the climate of work organizations as well. Despite the variety of online communications available to the public, the reduced dependence on personal interactions often limits people's skills and ability to negotiate and compromise. Together, these realities make for a danger-ous storm of emotions that are continually stoked and rarely calmed.

When people are stressed and emotions run high, their ability to call on de-escalation skills is challenged, even when these skills have been learned and experienced. In the absence of these skills, attempts to resolve conflicts becomes more of a blame-game and an "I win - you lose" effort. It seems that each person in conflict wants to end the argument by winning it, at the expense of the other person, and often, by any means necessary. This is dangerous thinking and what often leads to informal and formal wars.

The solution to this reality, from a conflict resolution philosophy, is not to go out and acquire additional weapons and allies to end the conflict, but to step back and think about the world in which we all want to live. Do we want a Darwinian culture in which "the survival of the fittest"[90] prevails, or can people become leaders who effectively help to defuse the ticking time bombs and minimize the explosions among people in conflict? With apologies to those who prefer Darwinism, conflict resolution is the better and more long-lasting way toward a war-free world.

In most conflict situations, there are generally four possible outcomes:

- Lose - Lose
- I win - You lose
- You win - I lose
- Win - Win

In the "Lose - Lose" outcome, neither person in the conflict wins. As an example, Darius and his sister fight over a game and their parents intervene by taking the game away and sending both to take a "time-out." Darius is unhappy because he felt he was right and did not get acknowl-edgement that he was right, nor that his sister was wrong. He is pretty sure his sister felt the same way, although reversed. Darius did not think either of them felt the need for revenge after their parents' decision was handed down, but he certainly had no desire to play with his sister afterward.

In the "I win - You lose" outcome, Darius wins, and his sister loses. As a result, he may feel great for a few moments, as one feels after winning a sporting event or any such contest. In a conflict situation, however, Darius' victory may feel like a short-term victory, as his sister is likely to seek revenge or at least seek a way to alter the outcome. Adding to that, he may need to watch his back after the outcome is shared, knowing that his sister remains unhappy, and they will still need to see each other in the future.

In the "You win - I lose" outcome, Darius' sister wins and he loses. He probably does not like the decision, and may be motivated to prove it wrong, especially if he feels strongly that the decision was biased or just plain wrong. Darius is likely not very happy with his sister and probably would not want to play with, much less speak with her soon.

In the "Win - Win" outcome, Darius wins, and his sister also feels like she wins. This is not the same as a tie, because in that case, no one really wins. In a win-win, both sides win at least one thing that is important to them. Since both sides feel like winners, neither side leaves unhappy nor looking for revenge. Most likely, both sides will move on without lingering negative emotions that need to be dealt with.

In a workplace setting, in practice, when the awareness of a conflict exists, there are several techniques used to resolve the conflict. The four primary types of conflict resolution are:

- Informal – *Communication*
- Formal/Informal – *Arbitration*
- Formal/Informal – *Mediation*
- Formal – *Legal System*

Informal Communication

The first option, informal communication, is how most conflicts are settled. You may wonder why this happens, given that so many people want to win at any cost. One large reason that so many conflicts are resolved informally is that time and distance have healing powers. We all have moments in which we are angered by a word, a tone of voice, or a reminder of things the other party may have done that upset us in the past. Any one of these things can be the trigger for us becoming upset and saying or doing something we later may regret. However, having time away from a conflict can allow us to think rationally about our actions and those of the other party.

When a serious conflict arises, one of the least helpful behaviors we use is to go into attack mode and assume that "might makes right," whether the fight be in the form of argumentative words, snide comments, or in the absolute worst scenario, the use of physical force. As many of us learn while we progress through our childhood years, there are often repercussions when we use "might makes right" choices.

Alternatively, there are generally two ways a conflict can be resolved with the informal communication option. First, one or both of the parties in conflict may initiate the idea of getting together at a later time to discuss the conflict. If the relationship is one that has been reasonably positive in the past or if the party requesting the follow-up conversation sounds genuine and sincere, the chance of such a request for further discussion happening is much greater. In this scenario, both parties need to be willing to listen and acknowledge their role in the conflict. When this occurs, and the parties can resolve their conflict, it represents the absolute best likelihood that not only will the issue be resolved, but the relationship between the two parties will be strengthened. In an environment in which the parties will work together on an ongoing basis, this can prevent future conflicts and help to establish an environment of civility, reason, and camaraderie.

Second, the informal communication option can also be utilized when the parties in conflict do not immediately see the value in talking together, but when one or both parties share their version of the conflict with a third party, such as Human Resources or a supervisor/leader. This is yet another time in which the response of an effective leader and an ineffective leader can significantly differ.

A leader who hears about the conflict may plan to arbitrate (be judge and jury) to resolve the conflict, or the leader may see value in speaking with each of the two parties and encouraging them to talk together. A leader who hears of the conflict and quickly moves into the arbitration mode has missed an important opportunity. People in conflict are quite often emotional and may greatly benefit from speaking with a leader who demonstrates a supportive ear. An effective leader is supportive and does not take sides, so the act of talking about the conflict, the issue, and the employee's feelings can be a catalyst for helping to resolve the conflict for the following reasons:

- A leader who simply listens can help the employee to hear themselves as they explain their role in the conflict, thus gaining some clarity on what happened and possibly why.

- The process of reliving the conflict can be educational. An effective leader is now in a situation in which they can ask neutral questions about how either party may have felt, what they may have meant, and other possible ways that things can be phrased. In an ineffective leader's less-helpful response, the employee only hears that the problem needs to be fixed. In the effective leader's response, the employee likely hears that they are important, that the leader cares about the conflict they experienced, and that something good can often come out of responding to conflicts when the parties have good intentions.

After engaging with the employees, an effective leader may ask the two parties in conflict to talk together to see if they can come to an agreement. One way of accomplishing that could be to arrange a follow-up meeting or even better, to plan to have coffee or lunch together, since being in a less threatening environment can be helpful. They can be offered the opportunity to do this directly or to have a third person join them. To be helpful, the third person would need to be seen as a neutral party by both people in conflict. The neutral party's role would be to help engage the two parties in conversation and then let them work out a solution for themselves. People tend to "own" solutions that they help develop, as opposed to having a third party do so.

If there is a need for someone to facilitate the two-person informal meeting, for reasons already discussed, that is preferable to the other option, in which a third party arbitrates and imposes a decision. Often, whether it is stated or not, at least one of the parties is likely to be more comfortable talking with the other party directly, and not under the supervision of a third person. There is also something about sitting down for coffee or a meal that encourages both parties to be less defensive (or offensive) with each other. It is unlikely that either party will leave the shared coffee or meal in anger, unless of course, one party is still too angry to rationally discuss the issue in an informal manner.

Arbitration

The second option, arbitration, is much less desirable than informal communication because it negates many of the benefits of the informal communication option. Nevertheless, arbitration is the second-most widely used method of resolving conflicts in the workplace. Arbitration is quite different from mediation, although many people confuse their usage. Arbitration is a discussion between two parties in conflict that includes a third party, who is formally charged with making the final decision. Although the earlier discussion about the informal communication process sometimes involves a third party, the person in that situation simply facilitates the discussion and tries to get the two people in conflict to communicate and resolve the issue. Arbitration, on the other hand, is extremely different in that while an arbitrator can ask the parties to help resolve the conflict, the arbitrator is deemed responsible for determining the outcome. This method of conflict resolution is often associated with union grievances and is sometimes utilized by the court system because it can be faster than awaiting a trial.

In the workplace, leaders often informally arbitrate conflicts. That is not necessarily a bad thing, as often a simple, quick decision is needed regarding departments and employees under the leader's supervision. Since the leader has overall responsibility for the area, all parties normally agree that a supervisory decision can sometimes be the best response to a conflict. However, can you imagine if every disagreement needed to be resolved via an arbitrator/leader? In most organizations, the leader would spend most of their time solely arbitrating conflicts. For this reason, it benefits leaders to teach their employees how to effectively resolve conflicts on their own. When individuals can successfully resolve their own conflicts, rather than having them arbitrated, they feel more control, increased ownership in their organization, and a stronger commitment to one another.

Mediation

The third conflict resolution option is mediation. In mediation, a third party (who needs to be someone who can be seen as neutral and ideally is not known by either of the conflicting parties) assists the conflicting parties but personally does not make decisions. Instead, the third party seeks to help the parties come to an agreement through their own, self-determined solutions. In this way, mediation is akin to the informal communication process, but with a few significant differences.

Formal mediation has been around since the early 1980s.[91] The first bodies to utilize this method of conflict resolution were courts of law.

Mediation was developed due to court case backlogs, which meant delayed justice and delayed resolve. The courts developed groups of mediators by identifying volunteer community members and training them in mediation techniques. Standard training for formal mediators normally consisted of 30 hours of theoretical and practical training in the psychology of conflict, active listening, problem-solving, stress reduction, positive reinforcement, the use of case studies, and the use of mock cases (role playing). Mediation strives to help people see conflict as a series of "positions and interests" as opposed to winning and losing. The phrase "going to the balcony" comes from the study of mediation techniques. This refers to the concept of envisioning oneself looking down at the conflict from a balcony, where all facets of the issue can be seen more easily.

The early mediation models assigned two mediators to work together to serve as the "third party." This was done to increase the possibility that both conflicting parties would feel a connection to at least one of the mediators. In cases involving a conflict between a male and female over child custody, for example, the mediation team consisted of one male and one female mediator. In a case involving a conflict between an older landlord and a younger tenant, the mediation team would include one older mediator and one younger mediator. Today, some mediation efforts consist of a single mediator, and some consist of two – often depending on how complicated the conflict appears to be.

As stated, both arbitration and mediation intentionally and formally utilize a third party to help resolve the conflict that could not be resolved informally by the two parties. However, there are huge differences. In the mediation model, the mediator (or mediation team) is an unbiased and neutral party whose efforts intend to help the two parties come to agreement. The mediator does not decide anything but assists the two parties to come up with possible solutions. The mediator makes sure all possible solutions are mutually agreed upon. For these reasons, it would not make sense for a mediator to be a supervisor, or even a member of that division or work unit. Any third party having a perceived bias towards one of the parties in conflict would not be viewed as an impartial mediator, and as such, would be unlikely to effectively help the parties reach a mutually satisfying agreement.

Research from the Department of Justice (DOJ) shows that from 2015-2017, 71 to 75 percent of voluntary mediated cases were successfully resolved.[92] The greatest advantage in using a mediation process instead of an arbitration process is that both parties are much more likely to achieve long-term satisfaction with the resolution because the third party helped the parties reach their own agreement.

Mediation normally takes considerably more time than arbitration, which is why many leaders are quick to use the arbitrator approach. An effective leader, however, looks at all the variables, the personalities, the seriousness of the conflict, and the likelihood of more conflicts arising between the two parties, as they decide between these two conflict resolution options. Simply put, one choice solves the conflict and strengthens the relationship between the two parties (mediation) and the other solves the conflict more quickly (arbitration). Ideally, all conflicts that need a third party would be mediated, but this would require a great deal of time. Just as we cannot expect a leader to informally arbitrate every conflict, we cannot expect a leader to refer every conflict to mediation.

Legal System

The fourth means of resolving conflicts is external to the organization – the legal system, which involves police and/or court action. When a conflict involves an alleged violation of law, bringing a lawsuit against the person or reporting the complaint to police or an attorney can initiate a legal intervention. Some people prefer this type of resolve as it does not involve their workplace as the final determiner of action, especially when the person does not believe the issue is likely to be handled fairly by the organization. Like arbitration, a court normally makes a final decision in which one person wins and the other loses, so for this reason, most organizations strongly prefer those conflicts be brought to their Human Resources Office or an organization supervisor, so that there is the possibility of resolution using informal communication, arbitration, or mediation.

All of this is to say that effective leaders would be well-served to develop the skills needed to successfully resolve conflicts and to also help their employees develop these skills. Some employees may have developed conflict resolution skills in high school as peer helpers, or in college as resident advisors or other types of student leaders. Some may have developed these skills in the military, as student athletes, summer camp counselors, or even as parents. Most people, however (as one quick look at Facebook or Twitter posts can demonstrate), have minimal experience successfully resolving conflicts.

When personally involved in a conflict, people generally choose one of the five responses below that researchers Kenneth Thomas and Ralph Kilmann label as:[93]

- Avoiding
- Defeating
- Compromising
- Accommodating
- Collaborating

Avoiding the conflict falls into the "You lose - I lose" category. While you may have hoped time would heal that wound, the conflict is not resolved and likely becomes larger due to inaction. *Defeating* the conflict is a way of expressing the "I win - You lose" strategy. You defeat your opponent, so you get the result you want. As explained earlier, this often leaves the other person with the desire to retaliate. Compromising is a conflict response that most of us were taught is the "right thing to do." If you give a little, they will give a little, right? Often the compromise is not felt to be equal, so the compromise can later feel uneven and unfair. *Accommodating* the other person with whom you are in conflict may seem altruistic and you may feel that you are being the bigger person, but accommodating never feels fair, especially as time passes. This is closely associated with the "You win - I lose" category. The *Collaborating* approach is much like mediation. This occurs when both parties seek to understand the other's point of view and then work together to find ways to resolve the conflict in a fair, reasonable, and long-lasting way.

For those of you looking to develop your conflict resolution skills, two seminal books on the topic were written: *Getting to Yes: Negotiating Agreement Without Giving in,* a national best-seller by William Ury and Roger Fisher[94] and *Getting Past No: Negotiating with Difficult People,* by William Ury.[95] Roger Fisher was the director of the Harvard Negotiation Project and William Ury co-founded Harvard's Program on Negotiation, helped to start the International Negotiation Network at the Carter Center of Emory University with former President Jimmy Carter, and currently serves as a Distinguished Fellow at the Harvard Negotiation Project.[96] Their efforts have taught millions of readers that conflict can be viewed from a perspective of individual needs and interests, which can move from the "I win - you lose" perspective to one of mutual understanding and collaboration.

Super-skill #3: Honesty/Integrity/Ethics

Honesty, integrity, and ethics are deemed critically important traits/values for effective leaders to possess, as evidenced by their inclusion in numerous chapters of this book. Far too often, however, they have shown to be in short supply with the leaders of today.

In an *Inc.* study, 300,000 leaders were asked to rank their four most impactful competencies from a list of 16. These were their cumulative top 10:[97]

- Displays high integrity and honesty

- Inspires and motivates others

- Solves problems and analyzes issues

- Drives for results

- Communicates powerfully and prolifically

- Builds relationships

- Displays technical or professional expertise

- Displays a strategic perspective

- Develops others

- Innovates

Other leadership studies have shown similar findings, with the addition of attributes such as humility, passion, courage, decisiveness, clarity, vision, confidence, positive attitude, adaptability, and resilience.

The 2014 Pew Research Center survey mentioned in Chapter II showed that 84 percent of one 1,835 respondents considered honesty to be the most essential trait for any leader.[98]

Why is honesty so important in leadership?

For many people, it is easier to argue why a leader who is dishonest, lacks integrity, and acts without ethical considerations cannot be effective. When we as team members work with team leaders, we see their leadership as a reflection of ourselves. While we may not have taken part in selecting the leader, by choosing to work where that leader works, we tend to feel some ownership for that leader's actions. That's one reason we may get upset when our leader acts without integrity. We may feel embarrassed because it reflects poorly on us. Who wants to be associated with a person who intentionally misleads people and acts in a self-serving way? Further, when a leader knowingly misrepresents the truth, we often feel that a part of us misrepresented the truth as well.

Outside of how we personally feel when our leader lacks honesty or integrity, our professional lives become more difficult when our leaders misrepresent the truth. We count on receiving the truth in our workplaces.

We make decisions based on what we know to be true and accurate. We are sometimes willing to take calculated risks based on what we believe to be true. When a leader misrepresents the truth, not only are we upset that our actions are now tainted by an incorrect foundation of knowledge, but we can also never again be certain that information coming from that leader is factual and honest.

Since so many people have their identity closely connected to their job, we need to be able to trust our leaders in a similar way that a spouse goes into a marriage trusting their life partner. In marriages, far too often the partnership ends in divorce due to infidelity—a violation of trust the other spouse had in their intended life partner. Similar emotions arise when a leader knowingly misrepresents the truth in a business setting. Good employees tend to leave their leader and their organization when they believe their leader to be dishonest. Has that been true for you? It has been for me – and on more than one occasion.

Unfortunately, dishonest leaders often have no idea how their mis-representation of the truth impacts their employees. They think about their own needs and may make decisions to act dishonestly when they seek more recognition or the limelight, are upstaged by a colleague, are cognizant of their own lack of ability, or simply want something at any cost. Hoping they will not be caught in the lie, they may include details, a strong tone of voice, and assertive nonverbal communication to bluff their way to what they perceive as a victory. And then, when they are caught in the lie, many of these leaders double down on the lie by repeating it or adding more details that make the lie appear more palatable.

Finally, and perhaps worst of all, some leaders are simply unwilling to admit when they are wrong. They somehow believe that admitting the incorrect information they shared makes them appear weak, unintelligent, or perhaps incompetent. Often, being unwilling to admit when we are wrong is based on an insecurity we have as a leader, which is one reason that self-awareness (part of emotional intelligence) is so important as a foundation from which to develop other leadership skills. When leaders violate the trust of their employees or act in a way deemed unethical, such as embezzling money from the organization, they destroy the trust that previously existed. In some cases, that leader will be held accountable by being fired or via legal action. Some are offered an easy way out – they are allowed to resign rather than being fired. However, no matter how the organization responds, many employees who worked with the leader and became aware of these matters will seek to move to a different department or in some cases, seek employment elsewhere. Why? Because they do not want to look guilty by association.

What happens to the employees when they become aware of unethical activity that occurs at their workplace and becomes public? Their personal reputation feels challenged and they will likely feel demotivated for a period of time. No one wants to work with a cheater or a thief, and certainly not someone who would be involved in sexual harassment or violence.

In speaking with candidates for employment, there seems to be a strong link between honesty/integrity and another trait that most employees say they want to see in their leaders – humility. Humility is the opposite of arrogance. An effective leader who demonstrates a sense of humility can laugh at themselves, admit their shortcomings and mistakes, and does not need constant reminders of how important they are. A person with humility does not need to count their wins and losses. They are confident in their skills and experience, and they know that when they take educated risks, sometimes they will lose. In those cases, that person does not seek to blame someone else, but owns the errors and continues to move forward rather than wallowing. Dishonest leaders and those lacking integrity often lack a sense of humility. It seems to almost always be a package deal.

Anyone can be fooled these days by leaders who misrepresent the truth, act without integrity and act unethically for personal gain rather than acting for the good of society, the organization, and their colleagues. Our political world has certainly demonstrated this to be true. Leaders who act in these ways very often are seen as "me-first" leaders. Me-first leaders may accomplish things in the short term, like the narcissistic leaders (of which they are often a subset), but it behooves every organization to have their antennae up for me-first leaders and me-first applicants for leadership positions.

As discussed in Chapter II, "ethical leadership" has become an oxymoron in the minds of many. Leaders are routinely faced with ethical dilemmas, both personally and as leaders representing organizations. Ethics involves the uses and abuses of power, as previously stated, but it also involves much more.

The following represents two examples of ethical dilemmas studied by a group of college students pursuing degrees in leadership and business management, and a group of high school students interested in leadership:[99]

A college student was elected to serve as Treasurer of the Outdoor Adventure Club. In that role, he collected money for trips and was responsible for helping the club's president spend the group's allocated money wisely and responsibly. The group held a fundraiser dance on a Thursday night to help pay for an upcoming ski trip. The admission fee to the dance was to be collected at the door, tallied, and submitted to the college's Bursar's Office on Friday morning for safekeeping.

The day before the dance, the treasurer found himself in a difficult position. He needed to purchase a textbook for a science class that would meet on Friday. He knew the book would be expensive, but when he went to the bookstore, he learned the book would cost $275, which was $35 more than he had anticipated. He would need to find the additional $35 somewhere. After searching everywhere for the $35, he had an idea. The money being collected for the dance Thursday night was expected to be about $900.

The treasurer toyed with the idea of "borrowing" the $35 from the Thursday night receipts and since Friday was a payday for his campus library work-study position, he could simply pay back the $35 from his check. No one would need to know the money had been borrowed and no one would miss it since he was treasurer and would be able to return the money the next day.

If you asked a group of college students to decide if this represents acceptable ethical behavior, what do you think they would say?

This scenario was given to a college leadership class of 20 students who were sophomores, juniors, seniors, and graduate students. Students who thought this "borrowing" of money would be acceptable behavior were asked to stand under a sign that said "Yes." Students who thought this was not acceptable were asked to stand under a sign that said "No." Finally, students who were undecided were asked to stand under the sign that said "Unsure."

The responses varied. A few students stood under the "Yes" sign and said that taking the money and not paying it back would have been unethical, but they thought the behavior of "borrowing" the money on a very short-term basis was acceptable because the student needed the book for an important class and he would immediately pay back the money, so it would not negatively affect anyone. A medium-sized group stood under the "Unsure" sign and said there were too many unknowns for them to be able to answer. It mattered to this group if the treasurer had tried other reasonable avenues to get the money. It also mattered if the treasurer had already asked whether a copy of the book could be borrowed from the college library or from the faculty member. A couple of students in this group said if he told the club president about his plans and the president agreed, then it would probably be acceptable. The largest group stood under the "No" sign and said the behavior was not ethical. They said it was "not like stealing bread to feed your hungry child" and that the money was not his to borrow.

One student from the "No" group said, "It's not only about whether he needed the money or returned it the next day or asked the president. It is about being the treasurer and being trusted by the group to deal with their money ethically." The only way the group would ever be able to trust him was if he asked the whole group if it was okay with them, since it was their money. Otherwise, "someone would find out – someone always does, and then his trust would be shot. He'd have to resign."

An interesting thing happened following the last comments. Some of the students standing under the "Unsure" sign started to physically lean towards the "No" group, as if they were wanting to change their decision. Also, a couple of students in the "Yes" group now had their heads down. They were not asked why, but it was a noteworthy observation, nevertheless.

In another example, a group of 25 high school seniors[100] were asked to engage in a similar exercise, using "Yes, No, and Unsure" signs. Their scenario was different, and this is what they were told:

> You are the town manager in the town where you currently live (an affluent suburb community). The role of town manager is somewhat like a mayor. Although you were not elected, you were hired to oversee all departments within the management of your town. Numerous departments (such as the school department, facilities department, town collector of taxes, town police, town recreation, etc.) all report to you.
>
> This has always been a happy, family-friendly town, with beautiful parks, low unemployment, low incidents of violence, and it has been a place where people felt comfortable walking at night and leaving doors unlocked. For the last few years, however, your town has had financial challenges. Recent storms and an aging infrastructure have meant being forced

to replace many aging pipes, roadways, and bridges. These have left the town with deficit budgets for three straight years. Fortunately, during the good financial years, you were able to save money and maintain a rainy-day fund, so you would have extra money available in case of emergencies. Using this fund has accommodated the deficit-year budgets, but the rainy-day fund is now almost empty.

At an annual Town Meeting, you shared the budget history with town members and asked for ideas of how to save money and/or bring in new money. Town members mentioned a lot of the usual ideas, such as turning down the streetlights earlier and increasing the fees for trash removal, and one member mentioned the idea of bringing a casino to town. She cited the amount of additional money that casinos in other towns around the state have brought in and recommended that the town make this their number one priority. Several town members were excited about this recommendation and before long, it seemed that the whole room liked the idea. You agree to do research and call a special Town Meeting when you are ready to share what you have learned.

After a month of researching the pros and cons related to building a casino in your town, speaking with town officers in towns that had casinos, and bringing a group of town members to visit several of these casinos, you are ready to share what you have learned with your town members, so as promised, the special Town Meeting was called to discuss this single topic. Anyone with information or opinions on the issue was encouraged to attend.

At the Town Meeting, you shared that based on your research, bringing a casino to operate in town could bring in several million dollars each year, with potential for tens of millions. The towns with casinos had recently built new schools, fire stations and police stations, and were able to improve their roads as well as develop new rainy-day funds. The town members who traveled with you to see the casinos brought pictures showing the beautiful new casinos, restaurants, and event facilities they added, and discussed the number of jobs that were added for town residents and residents from surrounding towns.

Next, some of the town residents who joined your tours spoke. They stated that while all the great financial aspects were accurate, they also saw many disturbing things that the research indicated often accompanied the development of a casino in town. Most of the towns with new casinos saw an increase in vandalism to the town properties, homeowner property theft that had increased by double-digit percentages, and an exponential increase in estimated numbers of homeless individuals. The socioeconomic breakdown of the towns had become more polarized as the percentages of both upper-class residents and lower-class residents increased. Simply stated, the casinos reduced the percentage of middle-class residents as the high and low ends increased.

Perhaps of most concern to the visiting team was the information obtained from the towns' quality-of-life surveys. With only a few exceptions, most towns that added a casino showed that crime increased, and overall town pride dropped by an average of 20 percent.

The high school students were asked, "If you were town manager, would you take the action to bring the casino to town?" Like the earlier example, the students' responses varied. About a third of the students stood under the "Yes" sign, meaning they wanted to bring the casino to town. They said that the town needed the money, and this was a great way to create many new jobs for the town's residents as well as people living in nearby towns. They also said that this new source of money could reduce the town taxes that residents complained were already too high, it could be used to knock down the old schools and build new ones and be used to build new facilities for the town's residents, such as a new ice arena, more restaurants, and perhaps a recreational sports complex.

Another third of the students stood under the "Unsure" sign and said they thought the idea was great, but that they felt bad about the possibility of "making the poor residents poorer." They liked the idea of having additional town facilities for all to enjoy, but they were unclear why the residents felt that town pride had dropped after the casinos were brought in.

The final third of the students stood under the "No" sign and interestingly, many crossed their arms, seemingly in defiance of their fellow students under the other signs. Students here said they could not imagine why anyone would value having "new shiny things" over having a town community where residents felt safer. They felt that choosing "Yes" or "Not Sure" was akin to perpetuating racist behavior since they knew that it would adversely affect people with less money, who in their town were likely to be people of color.

At being called out for racist behavior, a couple of the "Yes" group members defended their choice by saying that it was the job of the town manager to bring resources to the town and everyone in town would have equal opportunity to benefit from the wealth that adding a casino would bring. They said the town manager should already be working with other town leaders to find ways to support the needs of the town residents who were most likely to be negatively impacted.

At that point, a member from the "Not Sure" group said that this was not the only way to bring money to the town, and if they already knew that a casino would likely cause hardships for the town's residents, they should table the idea while they considered other possible revenue-creating ideas.

From a leadership perspective, the last student to speak was able to remove herself from "in the box" thinking, which created an either/or situation. By looking at an out-of-the-box model, she sought to keep in mind the needs of all the town residents, not just the vocal ones or the people with wealth that often have influence over such decisions. There was an immediate shift in the aura surrounding the students when she was done sharing her thoughts. Prior to her comments, it seemed that the groups were destined to engage in a positional debate, but after hearing another way to view the issue, the groups all seemed to shift into wanting to generate alternative new and creative ideas that could increase funding for their town.

As the facilitator of both the college and high school groups, it was not surprising that the two different forms of ethical dilemmas resulted in a wide range of thoughts – clearly, neither dilemma had a clear-cut, "right" answer for them. Ethical issues are often like that. If the answers were easy, they would not be considered dilemmas, right?

That said, it was clear that having the ability to hear how peers viewed a situation was instructive to the two groups of students. In real life, it is questionable if they would have listened to each other in the way they felt obliged to do in front of a facilitator and in an academic environment. However, it did not take long for the groups to stop focusing exclusively on the polarized choices of right and wrong and move to consider their values and seek a way to try to meet all members' needs.

One takeaway was that more opportunities are needed to discuss hypothetical ethical dilemmas prior to leaders facing them in their real-life jobs. That is unlikely to alter the choices made by people for whom "power corrupts," such as Idi Amin and Adolph Hitler, but who knows how Tim Cook or Martin Shkreli may have responded had they previously had opportunities to consider the impact of their actions in advance of facing their ethical situations?

When hiring or electing leaders, shouldn't we expect that they already have well-developed ethical values?

Experience tells us that would be a mistaken expectation. What about a high school election or a summer camp team captain decision? Even these examples carry a tone of privilege. Are families with very little income likely to send a child to summer camp? When does that individual have the opportunity to talk about ethics? So, if we cannot expect that most people have the opportunity to think about ethical situations prior to becoming leaders, organizations would be wise to build ethical scenarios into their new employee orientation programs, as would most degree programs at colleges and universities. Ethical considerations are a significant part of critical thinking, which gets to the heart of what an educated individual should have the opportunity to develop throughout their educational career.

Ethical situations can be an effective component in interviews as well. What if you ask a question about an ethical situation and a candidate's response makes you raise an eyebrow or two? Wouldn't that be important information to have? This can potentially allow you to see a candidate's honesty, integrity, and the fit between the candidate and your organization.

You will recall from an earlier chapter that Amazon currently sells more than 70,000 books on the topic of leadership. Another query showed that Amazon currently sells more than 10,000 books on the topic of "leadership ethics." There is good news and bad news in these numbers. On the negative end, for every seven books on leadership, there is only one available on "leadership ethics." Despite the tremendous need to teach young leaders about ethics, it does not yet have the appeal of a more holistic book on leadership. On the positive side, a year ago, the number of leadership ethics books sold on Amazon was about 1,500, so seeing 10,000 now indicates that help may be on the way – or at least it is more available to us. Of course, this access to leadership ethics books doesn't matter unless the books are read and discussed.

In terms of hiring people with well-developed ethical values, it is important to consider that while people are capable of change, it is commonly believed that most people do not change the core of who they are.[101] As a result, when hiring for positions in which ethical dilemmas frequently occur, if a candidate's interview response concerns you, it is not recommended that you hire them and expect them to change.

Super-skill #4: Emotional Intelligence

According to Stephanie Neal, director of DDI's Center for Analytics and Behavioral Research (CABER), "Research makes a clear case that we should stop using the term "soft skills" to describe what are really critical leadership skills. How leaders manage their emotions and how they make other people feel are the strongest drivers of talent retention."[102]

Emotional Intelligence (EI) is a recognized set of skills that some theorists argue are more important to effective leadership than all other variables.[103] EI was developed by researchers Peter Salavoy and John Mayer in 1990 and made popular by Daniel Goleman, an American psychologist, in his books, *Emotional Intelligence: Why it can matter more than I.Q.* and *Working with Emotional Intelligence.*[104]

In his early books, Goleman characterized EI by five components: Self-Awareness, Self-Regulation, Motivation, Empathy, and Social Skills. More recently, he has altered the components slightly, down to four:

- Self-Awareness
- Self-Management
- Social Awareness
- Relationship Management

Pacific Prime Insurance sees six distinct benefits of the impact emotional intelligence can have in an office setting.[105]

1. *Better Teamwork* - Employees with higher EI communicate and work well as a team. They listen, share ideas, and allow space for others to shine.

2. *Better Work Environment* - A work environment consisting of employees with high EI has high morale. Employees enjoy their work and see the value in their colleagues.

3. *Easier Adjustments* - A company of employees with high EI focuses on improving and is less resistant to change.

4. *Greater Self-Awareness* - Employees with high EI know their strengths and weaknesses, accept feedback, and use it to improve their skills.

5. *Greater Self-Control* - Employees with high EI know how to handle challenging situations, remain calm under pressure, and practice restraint to avoid emotional outbursts.

6. *Being One Step Ahead* - Teams with EI gain a productivity advantage by demonstrating positivity and regard for their work and each other, thus attracting new members who value EI.

According to David Walton, author of *Emotional Intelligence*,[106] EI includes skills that help you successfully manage yourself and the demands of working with others. Understanding your strengths and limitations in this regard allows you to know yourself reasonably well, control/manage your emotions, show empathy regarding the feelings of other people, and effectively use social skills to manage your relationships. To do so, according to Walton, one needs to practice "mindfulness," which means being aware of what is happening to you and those around you, being in control of one's own thoughts and emotions, being positive in the face of setbacks and stressful situations, demonstrating empathy (ability to place yourself in another person's shoes), communicating effectively, and seeking to choose emotions that better allow for desired results.

Many components of emotional intelligence will sound familiar because they are closely connected to many of the same skills that we have already noted as desirable traits and skills for leaders, such as empathy, self-assessment, stress management, resilience, positivity, flexibility, feedback, and team building, as well as the three other super-skills discussed at length in this chapter – communication, conflict resolution, and honesty/integrity/ethics.

Since many people often want to know how they fare with respect to possessing various skills, emotional intelligence quizzes can easily be found online to help leaders determine the parts of EI that are already well-developed in them and other parts that need further development to achieve the highest level of success. A homemade emotional intelligence sample question follows:

A member of your team approaches you as the team leader and says he will be unable to participate in the interview of a candidate tomorrow because he has a sick child at home and none of his regular babysitters can be available at that time. What do you do? (Select one)

A. Remind the employee that he had lots of notice about the interview, and you expect him to be there.

B. Let the employee know that you understand his dilemma, you hope his child is feeling better soon, and that you will find a way to manage without him.

C. Let the employee know you are willing to connect him to the interview from his home by Zoom or conference call if he can find a way to be available for the 45-minute interview.

D. Ask the employee if he can get a relative or neighbor to watch his child for a few hours.

Choice A is assertive but demonstrates very little emotional intelligence. This choice reminds him of what he already knows (when the interview takes place) and does not demonstrate any concern for the reasonable predicament the employee is in, nor the effort he has already made.

Choice B demonstrates empathy for the employee's predicament, but simply makes his problem your problem. While responding with anger would not demonstrate emotional intelligence, neither does extreme passivity when his involvement has been deemed important. If you chose choice B, you get a partial credit for demonstrating empathy.

Choice D might be a good attempt at collaborative problem-solving with the employee, had he not already told you he tried to get a babysitter and could not find one. The response, as is, does not constitute emotional intelligence because his response to your inquiry is likely to be, "I tried that already and was unsuccessful."

Choice C is the best demonstration of emotional intelligence of the four responses. You recognized he has a dilemma and acknowledged his effort to find a babysitter by not asking about it again, as was done in Choice D. Your offer to accommodate him in another way demonstrates social skills by seeking to solve the problem with flexibility and common ground. You receive full credit if you selected Choice C.

An ideal EI response would include empathy for his situation, a non-accusatory view of his predicament, recognition that he tried to find a solution, and as was included, a problem-solving effort that demonstrates his value and your desire to help him to meet his (and your) objective in having him participate in the interview.

Self-Awareness

The concept of self-awareness has already been mentioned a few times throughout this book due to its importance. Many therapists believe that before someone can understand and help others, they must first understand themselves. Some people have attempted to measure their degree of self-awareness by taking personality tests, such as the Myers-Briggs Type Indicator (MBTI),[107] and others do not miss an opportunity to take the latest magazine or online quiz. Students studying psychology generally take a plethora of self-awareness assessments along their degree journey, to better understand themselves and the reasons they behave in certain ways under certain conditions.

Emotional Intelligence theory argues that a self-aware person understands how their actions and emotions can affect others and be affected by others. In an interview setting, asking the candidate to tell you their strengths and areas for growth is likely to give you at least some insight into their level of self-awareness. As a word of caution, candidates who indicate they do not have any areas for growth likely have not spent much time seeking self-improvement, which may be a red flag.

In October 2017, emotional intelligence coach Jacqueline Hinds stated that "self-awareness means being aware of what you are feeling; being conscious of the emotions within yourself."[108]

Self-Management

Leaders with high levels of EI can more effectively regulate their behaviors. When people are anxious or upset, a common reaction is for them to respond immediately to a message of disapproval or disagreement they receive. Having a high level of self-management skills, however, means being able to maintain your composure and control under stress and during challenging conditions. A person with high EI understands that responding immediately to a negative situation rarely leads to a desired outcome. To the contrary, it often serves to further escalate a tense situation.

A common practice that a person with high EI may use, for example, is to refrain from responding immediately to an accusatory email. An immediate response from a person with lower self-management skills might include the use of angry or offensive words. While this response may feel good at the time, the person with high EI knows it is highly unlikely that angry words will resolve anything in the long term.

One effective response to receiving an angry or offensive email would be to take a breath and wait a while before responding. Another would be to draft a response but hold off on sending the response for several hours or until the next day. That delay of time will allow you the opportunity to reflect on the effectiveness of the response and the behavior it is most likely to elicit.

This "wait before sending" strategy may be one of the most important pieces of advice you will receive during your career. Even very experienced leaders admit that having responded immediately to such requests in their careers caused situations that became quite problematic. While the other person may have deserved a harsh response, providing it virtually never satisfies you or the situation. With time to calm down and reread a drafted response in the light of day, we often find better and less offensive wording for the response that will best serve our purpose and achieve our goal.

Self-management also pertains to values. When a person faces a moral dilemma or challenge, are they apt to make a quick judgement, or are they able to slow down and fully consider the situation before deciding where they stand? For example, if a medical professional is counseling someone who wishes to explore options related to being pregnant, the professional with high EI is less likely to rush to judgement based on their own values and is more likely to help the person weigh each of the options available to them. In particularly sensitive cases, the medical professional may decide that referring the patient to another person would best assist the person.

Self-management is closely attached to values such as honesty, integrity, and ethics; three separate but highly connected characteristics that are deemed especially important for leaders. As discussed in Chapter II and Chapter V, an area in which some people struggle involves consistently maintaining a high level of integrity in the performance of their duties. Leaders who fall short on this, which potentially results in their taking bribes, sidestepping the law, misrepresenting the truth, etc., would be deemed to have low EI regarding self-management.

Should you be concerned if a candidate you are hiring or electing has low self-management skills?

As an example from one of my favorite television shows, *Friends,* Rachel shared one of her mother's pieces of relationship advice after her boyfriend, Ross, had an affair while they were "on a break," according to him. Her mother's wisdom was, "Once a cheater, always a cheater."[109]

Self-management involves openness to new ideas and a willingness to accept change. Like Rachel's mother believing that men who cheat once will always cheat again, many leaders become stuck in their ways and beliefs about what methods can help them get from here to there. In an upcoming chapter, the lack of openness for change is discussed as one way to know that it may be time for a leader to stop being a leader and move on. Change is part of leadership, and a strong level of self-management helps a leader to creatively attack problems and replace old systems that no longer produce the desired results.

Social Awareness

In a micro sense, having well-developed social awareness skills implies that you understand social situations around you and can respond appropriately to achieve your desired results. In a macro sense, social awareness refers to the larger world in terms of how norms and values impact people and your ability to both understand and effectively respond to them.

Understanding how people are *motivated* refers to self-motivation and others' self-motivation. As you'll see when we later explore the best ways to hire the leaders we seek, one important area to assess in candidates is what motivates them in their work. A candidate with high EI is more likely to talk about how the job they're applying to taps into their motivation. They might share portions of the job that appeal to them and excite them most. This indicates that the job functions related to their interests tap into their already-developed motivations. In other words, these candidates can share what they like to do professionally because they have devoted time to thinking about what motivates them.

Beyond the awareness of their self-motivation, a leader who can learn what motivates their staff members can apply effort toward tapping into these motivations. In a self-assessment document that helps leaders understand their leadership preferences and tendencies, called *Personal Pattern Effectiveness*,[110] there is a sentence that seems to shock most people who take the assessment. It says, "You cannot motivate anyone." It continues by sharing an example of people attending a motivational speaker event. They ask why some of the attendees leave the session feeling motivated to take some sort of action, such as losing weight, selling real estate, or identifying their passion in life, while others leave the session without feeling the motivation. Both groups heard the same speaker, so why weren't both groups equally motivated? The answer is that motivation is not done *externally* to someone. It does not cause someone to do something they did not already want to do. It is an *internal* process, and in the case of this example, the motivational speaker tries to tap into the attendees' already-established motivations and remove obstacles they are facing such as fear, lack of knowledge, lack of alternatives, etc.

Leaders need to know what motivates their staff members to be able to use those motivations to move projects forward. One person may be motivated by getting a paycheck, while another may be motivated by prestige and time in the spotlight. Yet another person may enjoy problem-solving, and another may seek opportunities for public speaking. If a staff member's motivation cannot be uncovered, their performance may suffer in terms of meeting organizational goals.

A person with a high level of intrinsic motivation is not easily swayed from their goals and sees obstacles as challenges to overcome. They may strive for excellence and goal achievement as opposed to extrinsic rewards such as salary and prestige. To have success in this area, the individual is likely to have developed effective time and stress management skills, which are easily measured in a candidate interview.

Social awareness also includes empathy. People with a strong sense of empathy can understand and relate to how others perceive the world. Leaders with low empathy generally come across as robotic and impersonal. They tend to have more interest in the results and the product than how their team members are feeling.

An earlier reference to Sheldon Cooper, one of the main characters on the television show, *Big Bang Theory*, applies here as well. Sheldon struggles to understand how the people around him feel and cannot figure out why his honest words are often so unacceptable to them.[111] Effective leaders with high levels of empathy can "walk a mile in someone's shoes" to better understand how they see a situation and how they may respond to challenges.

Like many components of emotional intelligence, a leader with a high level of empathy can easily focus on the needs and wants of the people around them, as opposed to seeing challenges and achievements from just their own perspective.

There is an academic debate about whether empathy is a skill that can be learned or a trait that you are born with.[112] Researchers have found that by spending time with people who have less advantages and privileges than us, we can learn to understand how others perceive situations. For some people, such as social workers and medical professionals, their everyday mode of thinking is to focus attention on other people. For others, they may primarily see the world as it affects themselves. Leaders who possess or develop a high level of empathy can, for example, more easily "read the audience" in a room full of people and be able to predict how information is likely to impact those individuals.

In our multicultural and diverse world, gaining empathy for people from different backgrounds can be dramatically improved through travel to places where cultural norms are different from one's own. Additionally, reading about the experiences of people can also help a leader to better understand the range of responses that can occur following a crisis, challenge, or success. As mentioned earlier, many leadership books focus on people's responses to crises, which can help to broaden one's sense of empathy.

Relationship Management

Being able to lead change is extremely challenging in any organization because most people do not like change and will work to resist it. They get accustomed to doing things in a certain way, like the "Same-Ole, Same-Ole" drivers from Chapter I. These people often believe "if something is not broken, there is no need to fix it." Convincing them to make changes requires a high level of proficiency in social skills, which includes understanding and managing relationships, finding common ground, knowing how to effectively persuade through words and actions, and developing a high level of trust and rapport with those on your teams.

Many of the skills listed as leadership traits and skills fall under the EI term "social skills." In addition to the skills just mentioned, several other skills are vital to helping a leader make connections with team members, develop the necessary conditions for establishing trust and loyalty, and increase the likelihood that team members will be successful. Some of the more obvious relationship management skills from earlier in the book include patience, perseverance, positivity, reliability, confidence, resilience, respect for others, training, mentoring, team building, dependability, feedback, flexibility, gratitude, humility, humor, and open-mindedness.

From this list, one might infer that the relationship management component of EI is not notably different from what has long been thought of as general leadership skills. The proponents of EI do not make the argument that these are newly invented skills, but that many from the large list of 44 skills and traits can be categorized as significant strengths, as they relate to the four components of EI: self-awareness, self-management, social awareness, and relationship management.

In summary, each of these four components of emotional intelligence can be assessed, practiced, and improved upon. The first and most important way to improve virtually anything in life is to recognize its existence and its value. To be an effective leader, as argued throughout this book, there needs to be a dual focus – one on the desired outcomes and one on the people involved in delivering the outcomes. EI skills are often so obvious in an effective leader that we may easily take them for granted. When we work with a leader who does not possess high levels of EI skills, however, the value of having well-developed social skills, empathy, internal motivation, self-regulation, and self-awareness becomes abundantly apparent.

CHAPTER V

How Can We Hire the Leaders We Need?

At this point in the book, I hope you are convinced if you were not already, that having the "right kind of leader" is too important to leave to fate. Like many things in life, it is much easier to make calculated, intentional efforts to do something right the first time (in this case, hiring the right people) than to try to rectify the problem after you become aware of it. Unfortunately, hiring processes in general have become skewed:

- Our litigious society seems to have caused many hiring-related offices to focus more carefully on not getting sued by a candidate who is not offered the job, than ensuring they are hiring the right person for the job.

- Many people who agree to serve as candidate references are hesitant to say anything negative about the candidate for fear of the candidate not being hired and suing them.

- College seniors are told that networking is the most important thing they can do to land a job, but too many people seem to be hired by *who* they know as opposed to *what* they know. Networking is very important, but it should never replace the need for candidates to demonstrate that they have the necessary skills and traits pertaining to a position.

- Some search committees are not allowed to see the candidates' cover letters and, in a few organizations, even their resumes. The role of the interviewer is challenging enough without removing these informational and often instructive pieces. This can easily change, and in many organizations has changed, with the advent of candidates' online applications.

- Increasingly, organizations strive to make hiring committees more balanced and representative of the general population. This is an important initiative and sends a message to the workplace community that all voices are valued, and to applicants from underrepresented groups that this is a place that "gets it." Unfortunately, in organizations with few members of underrepresented groups, such as people of color, this has placed excessive pressure on these members to serve on numerous search committees, often making it a challenge for them to successfully do the jobs they were originally hired to do. Further, balancing committees should not erase the responsibility of all committee members to be able to evaluate candidates regarding their understanding of and appreciation for the unique challenges faced by underrepresented populations.

Organizations should strive to educate all employees in understanding discrimination, microaggressions, empathic communication, and ways to make an environment more supportive for employees who have not been equitably represented in the past. As you'll see in an online search, there are several companies and institutions that do this well and several books can serve as a basis for group discussions on the topic. These books include: *The Leader's Guide to Unconscious Bias: How to Reframe Bias, Cultivate Connection, and Create High Performing Teams*, by Pamela Fuller, Mark Murphy, and Anne Chow,[113] *Blind Spot*, by Mahzarin R. Banaji and Anthony G. Greenwald,[114] *Allies and Advocates: Creating an Inclusive and*

Equitable Culture, by Amber Cabral,[115] and *The Memo: What Women of Color Need to Know to Secure a Seat at the Table*, by Minda Harts.[116]

There are many causes within the hiring process itself that lead organizations to hire leaders who prove to be less than effective. Fortunately, improvements can help the process result in selecting the best leadership candidates for the job. This chapter will identify 12 areas that are ripe with the need for improvement and some recommendations to help get there:

1. The Internal vs. External Hiring Debate

2. Promotion Decisions Often Happen for the Wrong Reasons

3. Political Hires are a Red Flag

4. Headhunters/Executive Search Firms Do Not Replace the Eyes and Ears of the Organization

5. Let Us Begin the Search

6. Cover Letters and Resumes

7. Structuring Candidate Interviews

8. Assessing a Candidate's Leadership Skills

9. First Impressions and Nonverbal Communication

10. Reference Check Verifications

11. Increasing the Candidate Pool - Preparing Future Leaders

12. The Process for Hiring Executive Leaders

1. The Internal vs. External Hiring Debate

The hiring processes at most organizations are developed by the Human Resources Office, or what in some organizations today is called the Talent Development Office. In many organizations, before *external* candidates (those who do not presently work at the organization) can apply for a vacant position, is it the organization's policy that *internal* candidates (those already working at the organization) are afforded the first opportunity to apply for and land the jobs. This means that the position is announced internally first, and only current employees may apply.

There are many good reasons for having this practice. Giving current employees the first chance at a position tells them that the executive leadership of the organization values them and cares more about their satisfaction than that of a person they have not yet met. This type of policy often leads to good morale, an environment in which employees feel respected, and a feeling that their organization is loyal to them. Internal candidates bring knowledge of the organization's history which can be extremely helpful when there is a large amount of staff turnover. Further, a good employee is less likely to leave an organization if they know they have a good chance of obtaining the next promotional position that becomes available. Of course, if giving current employees the first chance at open positions had no downsides, everyone would implement this strategy exclusively.

The argument against this practice is that bringing in candidates from outside the organization offers an opportunity for "new blood," which can bring new ideas and ways of handling challenges. External candidates can create a block against "circular toxicity." It is one important way that fresh eyes can see the strengths and weaknesses of an organization or department, which is especially important when employees may have become blinded to dysfunctions that are occurring. Additionally, in some cases, applicants from outside the organization may bring more advanced skills or offer a wider range of skills than internal employees.

When an organization's employees are unionized, it is often a contractual practice (meaning it is agreed upon in writing) that all vacant positions are first made available to internal candidates before allowing external candidates to apply. Ultimately, organizations that utilize the internal-first practice potentially limit the skill capacity of their employees, especially those organizations that have smaller numbers of employees. If an internal hiring practice is done exclusively and continuously over time, the leadership skills of its employees could be negatively impacted, since they would not have experienced the unique ways of operating and the training programs offered at other organizations (which external candidates have experienced).

The decision to hire leaders internally versus externally should focus less on the benefits of each, since each carries a package of pros and cons, and instead focus more on the greatest organizational needs, when possible. So much of life involves balance, and this is yet another example. For an organization that has had many of its leaders promoted, the opportunity to bring in outside perspectives can be critical and can provide balance. Conversely, when many recent hires have come from outside the organization, striving to add internal hires and promotions can be an opportunity to emphasize loyalty to employees and demonstrate the value brought by a candidate with a historical perspective.

2. Promotion Decisions Often Happen for the Wrong Reasons

Promotions can be a wonderful opportunity for the right employees. The following real-life example demonstrates, however, that promotions should never be awarded without carefully considering all the leadership components of a new position.

> Don was an assistant director of a department at his organization. He was quite skilled in his area of responsibility, as were his three colleagues, who also served as assistant directors. Each assistant director had unique responsibilities for different components of the department. When the current director was hired by another organization, the decision was made to appoint one of the four assistant directors to the vacant position of director, rather than conduct an external search for a new one. As previously mentioned, internal appointments can be very helpful in building a sense of loyalty among the staff. Additionally, in this case, it would result in cost savings, as the

person taking on the director role would also maintain their assistant director responsibilities.

Of the four assistant directors, Don had been at the organization the longest and had more years of experience in his field, so he was appointed to be the director. Before long, it became apparent that although Don had great skills in his previous role, he had never led a team. He had some of the skills needed for leadership such as budgeting, administration, long-range planning, and assessment, but he lacked many of the "soft skills" of leadership, such as active listening, empathy, communication, and team building. Unfortunately, no one thought these soft skills important enough to include them for consideration when each of the assistant directors were considered for this position.

Don's promotion led to strained relationships in what previously had been a unified and productive team. Don became distant from his previous colleagues and one of the other assistant directors soon left the organization in search of a "more suitable workplace."

Was the fact that Don had been an excellent assistant director reason enough to assume he would be ready to take on the director role? Should interviews have been arranged to assess the soft skills portion of the candidates' skill sets?

In this case, interviews were not conducted and the hiring authority placed little value on the soft skills, so they did not factor that into the decision to promote Don.

Different jobs require different skill sets. No one should ever assume that success in one job will automatically lead to success in another. It may very well be the outcome, but all job-related skills (soft skills and technical skills) should be assessed before any promotion takes place that involves leadership, especially leadership that requires the supervision of employees.

Don's supervisor assumed he needed little training and would be considered "low maintenance" in terms of needing supervisory support. This was not a reasonable assumption. As a rule, newly hired internal leaders with supervisory responsibilities should initially be offered the same amount of support and direction that would normally be given to externally hired leaders.

We can learn a great deal about promotions and leadership from the sports world. In professional sports, there is a myth that the captains are chosen because they are the players with the best skills. In both sports and organizational leadership positions, however, it is not exclusively the technical skill set that makes someone a leader, but their soft skills as well. Two examples from professional sports were Derek Jeter of the New York Yankees and Zdeno Chara of the Boston Bruins. While both men were all-stars in their respective sports, they were seen as leaders by their teammates and coaches because they had strong technical skills as well as strong human-relations skills, like self-awareness, determination, a focus on teamwork, willingness to help younger players, calmness under pressure, and a sense of humility. Strong leaders in professional sports, as in organizations, always seem to make their teammates better. This is the essence of effective leadership.

3. Political Hires are a Red Flag

There is a popular belief that in state and federal organizations, individuals often get jobs because of *who* they know, not *what* they know. While certainly not true in all public organizations, as with most popular beliefs, there are many examples that support this thinking. In the federal government, for example, it is quite common for a person to be appointed to a role in a department or function for which they have never had direct experience. In the Trump administration, we saw these types of appointments for the Secretary of Education, Secretary of Health and Urban Development, Secretary of Energy, and the Head of the Environmental Protection Agency, to name just a few. While appointing underqualified individuals to leadership positions may work in some types of positions, in others it may result in failure, confusion, and derailed progress.

The federal government is certainly not the only industry where political hiring and appointments occur. Another real-life example follows:

> At a public university in the Midwest, employees became highly concerned when two ex-mayors and two ex-city councilors were appointed by the president of a university to fill three vacancies and one newly created position. One of the appointments had legitimacy in the eyes of the campus community, due to the individual being placed in a business development role, an area in which he had strong skills and experience. The other appointees, however, were not interviewed by anyone and did not have experiences that seemed to qualify them to assume their appointed positions. As a result, their legitimacy was tarnished in the eyes of the organization's community. Their colleagues and constituents questioned the appointees' abilities to lead their assigned teams and their staff felt undervalued. These appointments served to increase the existing feelings of mistrust, questionable ethics, and diminished pride on the campus.

In leadership, position *legitimacy* is a critical foundation for developing organizational trust and ethics. In any industry, when a new employee is appointed without a legitimate hiring process and is placed in a functional area in which they have no direct or indirect experience, the appointment will likely have a negative impact on the organization's employees and there is a risk that the quality of the organization's product will suffer. As a result, the productive employees at the organization are likely to lose faith in the integrity of the executive leader and be more inclined to seek employment elsewhere.

4. Headhunters/Executive Search Firms Do Not Replace the Eyes and Ears of the Organization

A "headhunter," according to *Investopedia*, "is an organization or individual that provides employment recruiting services."[117] The term headhunter is often referred to as an "executive recruiter" and the function is often called an "executive search." Although originally developed after World War II to assist with the large number of military service personnel returning to the workforce, these executive search firms (ESFs) took their current shape in the 1970s and 1980s and are often used today to hire senior organization leaders, such as CEOs, presidents, vice presidents, senior managers, and positions that require specialized efforts (due to unique challenges finding suitable candidates). In a business setting, this may include positions such as directors of information technology, development/fundraising, human resources, and business affairs, and in universities, this may include presidents, vice presidents, academic deans, and specialized positions like deans of students, and directors of counseling services, health services, and athletics. Some organizations also utilize these firms when the salary of the desired position meets or exceeds a certain threshold. The search firm may handle much of the hiring process for these positions for a one-time fee, often 25 percent of the position's salary.

For some searches the ESF may handle the entire process from start to finish, which can include everything from recruiting candidates and conducting initial interviews, to verifying credentials and speaking with candidates' references. Other times, the ESF role may be limited to the initial recruiting of a candidate pool. Perhaps most unique to the role of the ESF is their ability to recruit current executive leaders and staff members from other organizations without crossing ethical boundaries.

ESFs strive to meet the needs of those who hire them. However, like most businesses, their bottom-line objective is to stay in business by making money. As a result, the best ESFs normally have numerous searches occurring simultaneously. The ESF normally receives the final portion of their payment after the search has concluded, which has the potential to move the process along more quickly than an organization would if it were conducting the search on its own. Whether searches for senior or specialized leadership positions are conducted primarily by ESFs or by the organization itself, it is essential that appropriate time be allocated for hiring. At times, the hiring authority (the person making the final decision) is anxious to have the senior leader in place and will push the ESF to accelerate the process. When this happens, the risk of missing important input and feedback can be the difference between finding candidates who seem to be great fits for the organization (with skills that match the needs of the organization) and finding candidates who are not as well-matched. Unfortunately, some organizations settle for lesser-skilled candidates, take shortcuts with reference verifications, and shortchange the process from getting enough eyes, ears, and analyses on the finalists, such that the search process results in hiring a candidate who seems to have great potential, but turns out to be a bust.

Candidates applying for high-level leadership positions are generally able to give the interviewers the responses they seek, (e.g., the "right" answers), and sell themselves as strong candidates so their weaknesses are not obvious until much later. As mentioned, when the selected candidate proves to be less than what they advertised, the entire organization can be at risk. For this reason, when utilizing an ESF, hiring authorities need to be cognizant that the ESF has expertise and asking them to rush the process is ill-advised and can jeopardize the quality of the search.

Normally, the ESF will have a senior partner attend all candidate interviews. This allows the firm to assess each candidate in comparison with the myriad of candidates they have seen in similar positions across the industry. As a result, their feedback to the hiring authority normally includes critical information that best informs the organization how a candidate is likely to perform on the job. Organizations need to trust that the ESF wants everyone to be happy when their work has concluded.

In addition to receiving payment when the job is complete, the reputation of the ESF is always at stake, and in most industries, reputation is everything, as it leads to future business. The ESF is not willing to hurt their reputation to accommodate what may be an unrealistic request from the hiring authority of an organization and similarly, they are not likely to recommend a candidate to the organization who they do not believe is a good fit.

While it is important to allow the ESF to do what they do best, it is also vital that the organization not blindly accept the findings of the ESF. The information they provide must coincide with the information learned by the organization. No one knows an organization as well as the organization's employees. At the end of a search process, if everything the ESF learned matches well with everything the organization learned about the employee, a great fit has been found and verified. If not, regardless of the calendar or the anxious president or board, and regardless of what your gut tells you, more work must be done to determine which version of the candidate is most accurate. Often, this means returning to references and others who have worked with the candidate. The importance of finding "the right" candidate has been emphasized over and over here, because hiring ineffective leaders can severely hurt an organization immediately, deeply, and for years to come.

5. Let Us Begin the Search

At this point, I would like you to imagine that you are on a search committee and will be interviewing candidates for a leadership position that involves supervising employees. No executive search firm will be used—it will all be up to you and your colleagues.

Your goal is to use every opportunity to determine whether each candidate is a strong candidate, (e.g., qualified, ready to take this on, and positioned to do a great job). When all is said and done, you and your search committee colleagues will be asked to send the "hiring authority" (the person who will supervise this leader) two to four candidates you believe are each qualified to assume the available leadership position.

In their current state, most hiring practices feel like little more than a crapshoot. It seems that people often cross their fingers and hope that they get good candidates for open positions. After they hire a person, they then hope that person will turn out to be the person they believe they saw during the interviews. In other words, they hope that the candidate is as good in real life as they were in selling themselves to the search committee.

Certainly, some organizations have more success with hiring good employees than others. Why is this? Either their reputation attracts better candidates, their hiring processes are more conducive to identifying quality candidates, or both. We need to improve your chances of getting this part right. Too many people spend a lot of time ensuring that the laws are followed, all "T's are crossed, and all I's are dotted," but spend far too little time establishing a process by which the best candidates are recruited, selected, hired, and then developed. Therein lies one of the biggest reasons that so many of our leaders are ineffective.

As interviewers, far too often we spend time seeking to disqualify candidates or find their weaknesses. The assumption and default position going into the interview is that the individual is presumed to be a reasonable candidate for the leadership position we are searching to fill. Human Resources (HR) received their applications and did whatever they are supposed to do and now you have a pile of resumes. In a leap of faith that HR would only send you these candidates if they were good candidates, you assume that they are good, and your job is to now prove otherwise. Since HR or someone else vetted the candidates before they came to you on the search committee, perhaps you assume that everyone with the proper experience and academic credentials will be a good candidate. However, if only 37 percent of the leaders who were rated in my Facebook/LinkedIn poll were considered effective, our assumption *should* be that everyone with the "proper experience and academic credentials" got to this point, but that much more information needs to be learned by you and your colleagues. How the candidates respond to your interview questions is as important as the credentials and experience they have achieved prior to this point.

When we think of the employees who will be supervised by the candidate you're helping to hire, the colleagues that will work with this leader, and the organization, you need to know if a candidate has *both* the technical skills and the human-relations skills to be successful. You also need to know if the candidate demonstrates any areas of concern which will make you question their readiness to assume the leadership position. Therefore, what you should probably be doing is allowing each candidate to start with a blank slate. Try not to be biased by the resume you have (hopefully) seen. You only know what candidates show or tell you. If you already knew a candidate from a previous experience, you should inform the leader of the search committee so they can determine if you can continue in that role. Often you may be allowed to continue serving on the committee but will need to be clear that your assessments are based on what you see and hear, just like the other candidates.

To begin, you will want to know if the candidate meets the requirements of the position. To effectively do so, an unstructured interview will not work. You will need to develop questions that measure each job requirement and (if the candidate successfully meets a requirement) check the boxes when the interview is over. By doing so, you will begin to know if the candidates are "leadership material." You will also have treated all candidates equally, so later you will be able to compare the strengths and weaknesses of the entire group of candidates. Sounds easy, right? Let's discuss what precedes the actual interview and bring some of the candidates to your interview committee.

6. Cover Letters and Resumes

Human Resources or Talent Development Offices commonly read the applicants' cover letters and resumes to ensure they are applying for the right position and have submitted all materials that the job posting required. If you have interviewed candidates in the past, did you read their resumes and cover letters? If so, how carefully did you read them before interviewing a candidate? Believe it or not, from personal experience, some organizations have historically not shared the applicants' cover letters with the interviewers. A few have not even shared the resumes. They may have reasons for not sharing these important documents that others are not privy to, other than wanting to reduce piles of paper, but since these documents can now be shared electronically, it is unclear why some HR offices would continue to make these private, even to interviewers.

Privacy and confidentiality concerns are certainly important and should be respected. However, if the hiring authority expects you to do a thorough job of vetting candidates who are "leadership material," you need all the information they have about the candidates, as allowed by law and best practices, to make an informed decision. For most types of businesses, the "best practice" is to give all interviewers access to at least the candidates' resumes and, in most cases, their cover letters or cover emails as well.

Carefully reading the cover letter and resume can give you a lot to think about. These are the first impressions the candidate wants you to see, so if it is well-written and sufficiently tells you what you need to know, such as why they are interested, what they have done professionally, that they clearly understand the position, and why the grass looks greener in your organization than the one in which they currently work, you probably feel quite positive about the candidate at this point.

If a candidate's first impressions raise concerns about their candidacy, what do you do with that? What could that mean about the candidate? What if the candidate misspells the name of your organization or has typos in their cover letter? What interview questions could you ask to find out if the errors were indicative of their working style?

Cover letters and resumes are not rhetorical pieces; they are important first impressions that have more meaning than just the words on the paper. Starting with the resume and cover letter, and throughout the entire hiring process, you will want to ask yourself a series of questions, such as, "Is this person leadership material?", "Does this person possess the necessary skills to make them effective in getting things done, helping others to get things done, and helping others to become the best they can be?", "Would I want this person as a leader of my department?", and "Does this person understand what people will expect of them as a leader here?" Most importantly, as mentioned earlier, ask yourself, "Why does this person *want* to be a leader?"

People take on leadership positions for many reasons: more money, prestige, a next step in their career path, encouragement from others, because no one else would do it, they have the confidence they can do it, they are seeking a new experience, to help the organization, and to help group members grow, etc. Why a person wants to take on a leadership role matters a great deal. So, how can you learn this about the candidate and answer the above questions?

7. Structuring Candidate Interviews

Candidate interviews can be tense or enjoyable, boring or interesting, and either a waste of time or instructive. The ways that you and other interviewers establish your questions and the ways you interact with candidates will determine whether you create an environment that is conducive to helping you assess each candidate's true strengths and weaknesses.

Just a few decades ago, the interview norm was to fire questions at the candidate and make them toss back responses. It was a "sink or swim" approach and assumed that a good candidate either knew the correct responses or did not. It was a "Can you handle the pressure?" type of scenario. This approach seemed to parallel the approach for teaching a child to swim at that time. The swim instructor would toss the child in the water and expect that the child would magically begin to swim. Since that time, there are many good reasons that this approach for learning to swim has been abandoned and similarly, that this approach to interviewing is not widely considered useful either.

Today, skilled interview teams learn "interview basics," such as which questions cannot legally be asked, but they also need to learn how to help the candidates feel comfortable during the interview process. Few organizations talk about interview basics, which may be one reason that candidates often show a different persona in interviews. Remember, if they do not show you their best, you may end up disqualifying an excellent candidate simply because your organization has a hostile interview process.

How do we set up the interview environment so we can get a realistic view of each candidate?

The goal for the interview team is, of course, to develop and ask questions that will elicit responses which indicate to the interview team whether the candidate is ready or not to take on the position. The goal for the candidate is to give their best, honest responses. In the pressure-style interview, few candidates leave those interviews feeling that they gave their best answers. However, when interview teams are trained well, they can make candidates feel comfortable and thus able to give their best and most genuine responses. Unless someone is applying to be a 911 operator, it serves little purpose to put undue pressure on candidates.

How can this "comfortable interview environment" be established?

There are several ways. The interview committee should be physically set up in such a way that all participants are on an equal level, (i.e., no one is behind a desk, and it's not set up with all committee members' chairs pointed at the candidate, like a lecturer in front of a classroom). The committee members should introduce themselves and explain the process they will use. For example, they might say, "We have about 45 minutes to spend with you, and we have 10 questions. There is some water for you next to your chair. If we use terminology you are not familiar with, please let us know and we will be happy to try to clarify the question. At the end of the interview, we will try to leave you a few minutes in case you wish to add something to your responses or to ask the committee questions."

A skilled interview committee uses supportive nonverbal cues (smiles and open body language, for example) and helps the candidate get warmed up by asking a couple of the easier questions at the start of the interview. Imagine if you were being interviewed and the first question asked was, "What would you do if you learned that one of your employees had a drinking problem?" Instead, interview teams should be encouraged to ask questions such as, "Can you tell us about your experiences that relate to this position?" or "Can you share why you are interested in this position and how it fits into your career goals?" The goal is to allow the candidate to give you their best effort, as opposed to being blown up by the first question and wondering for the rest of the interview how badly they screwed up that response.

Some organizations ask interviewers not to take notes while the candidates are speaking. The explanation for this is threefold. First, note-taking may be distracting to the candidate. Second, it is hard to make eye contact with the candidate if your head is constantly down while you write notes, and third, if you write something during the response to the first question and then write nothing during the response to the second question, the candidate will likely wonder which question they messed up – since you only wrote during one of them. Ultimately, writing during the interview may distract the candidate from giving you their best responses and ones that are most representative of their style.

The set of questions that your interview team develops, as mentioned earlier, should intentionally measure each of the skills the organization seeks to analyze. If the skill is important for you to evaluate, there should be a question that will elicit a response from the candidate to demonstrate an effective use of that skill (or lack thereof). You should not leave this to chance. If you want to know about the candidate's leadership style, asking a question about a challenging person they once supervised may not elicit more than what you specifically ask. If you want to know about their leadership style, it is best to simply ask the question directly.

Most effective interview teams divide their questions among all members, so each member asks at least one question. They also try to use different approaches when asking the questions. For example, one common approach is to ask, "Can you tell us of a time when you gave someone feedback and how it was received?" A different approach could be to use a scenario such as, "Let's assume you are the department head and during a staff meeting you notice one of your employees falling asleep. How might you respond?"

A third type of question or approach can be used to assess specific skills, such as work prioritization, time management and stress awareness. To measure these skills directly, the interviewer might say, "It is Friday afternoon at 3:00 p.m. and you have an appointment across town that you need to leave for at 4:00 p.m. You have two tasks due before you leave, and each will take about 45 minutes. One task is to complete your weekly payroll and the other is to finish a proposal that your supervisor is expecting from you by the end of the day. As you contemplate these, your administrative assistant knocks on your door to ask if you can speak with one of your employees who seems to be in distress. How might you respond to this situation?"

A fourth type of question or approach involves role-playing. Fewer organizations use this style during an interview because it can make a candidate feel uncomfortable, thus not likely to respond with their best or most realistic answer. In certain industries and for certain types of positions, however, role playing can be very effective. For a role-playing question, the interviewer shares a scenario and asks the candidate to act out their response with them. The situation may be as follows: "You are my supervisor and are scheduled to meet with me today to do my annual performance review. You plan to share several positive performance areas as strengths and need to also tell me that you are concerned that I may be showing favoritism towards one of my staff members. Let me know when you are ready, and we can begin."

After considering the skills listed in the job description and the different interview question approaches, the interview team needs to develop a series of questions. Using these guidelines, you can get clarity about the strengths and areas in need of growth for each candidate. You and the organization should be able to get a good sense of whether this candidate is "leadership material." Additionally, the way your team supports the candidates and asks a clear and challenging set of questions will give the candidates a good sense of your workplace. Showing that you care enough to make a candidate comfortable may prove to be the difference in their decision to choose your job offer rather than one from another organization. Finding a talented person to fill a leadership role is absolutely a two-way street. You want to feel good about what the candidate offers, and they want to feel good about the way they are treated.

8. Assessing a Candidate's Leadership Skills

What skills does a candidate need to be an effective leader/supervisor?

Many job postings and descriptions for leadership positions include a phrase such as, "experience supervising professional staff is required." However, *experience is not a skill*. A skill can be intellectually learned (such as in a book or classroom) and an experience offers the opportunity to practice a skill.

Many candidates face a *"chicken and egg" conundrum* regarding supervisory experience. The candidate wants to gain supervisory experience but cannot do so when the job requirement says, "must have experience supervising professional staff."

If all the supervisory positions expect supervisory experience, how can candidates gain this experience?

The fact that some candidates already have previous experience with supervision does not mean that they are good at it, right? If we want to have more effective leaders, it stands to reason that we want to open this window of opportunity to as many candidates as possible. Listing previous supervisory experience as "required" limits the candidate pool.

Some upper-level leadership positions involve supervising mid-level leadership employees. Certainly, it makes sense in most cases that someone applying for an upper-level leadership position should be required to have "demonstrated successful supervisory experience." Some leadership positions involve supervising multiple employees – often more than the best practice recommended number of six to eight. Having "demonstrated successful supervisory experience" makes sense here as well. For leadership positions that involve supervising one to three employees, however, do all candidates need previous supervisory experience or could it be considered as a "preferred" experience instead of a "required" one? Preference can still be given to an experienced supervisor, but why not allow the committee to also consider a candidate who may have great skills and appears ready to take on the supervision of others?

What needs to happen if we want the search committee to be able to consider candidates with no supervisory experience?

If you want the committee to have this discretion, the hiring authority needs to be sure to clearly state it on the job description *before* the position gets advertised. The "supervision experience" section of the job description would need to be listed as "preferred," not "required." If it is listed as "required" and a candidate has never supervised anyone, most organizations will not allow you to interview that candidate, regardless of how wonderful they seem, because they don't want to open themselves up to lawsuits based on "discriminatory practice."

With that hurdle cleared, how can you determine from the interview if a candidate is ready to supervise others?

The interview team can ask questions that allow the candidate's human-relations skills to become clear. For example, this can be accomplished by asking a situational question in which the candidate is given a scenario such as, "An employee with a history of no disciplinary problems and very good productivity has missed a few meetings and was late with a few assignments over the past month. As the employee's supervisor, how might you approach the situation?" A person not ready to assume a supervisory role may simply inform the employee that their behavior is unacceptable and needs to change if they wish to keep their position. Conversely, a candidate more ready to assume supervisory responsibility may respond that they would speak with the employee in private to try to understand what may be going on. They may also share how they would try to support the employee, so that together they may be able to address the problem and find a mutually acceptable resolution. Which of these responses demonstrates a concern for the individual as well as the behavioral expectations of the employee? The latter, of course.

Too often, the committee agrees on the questions they wish to ask but spends no time at all discussing the responses they will find acceptable. This is one of the greatest problems in many interview processes. A less-experienced interviewer needs support in learning how to evaluate a response – it is certainly not something people "naturally" know how to do and leaving it unsupported may cause the interview results to look skewed since the hiring authority reading the evaluation notes will be comparing "apples and peaches" as opposed to "apples and apples." Interviewers need to know what a successful candidate's response sounds like.

Whether a candidate has experience supervising others or not, what specific skills are associated with the experience of supervising another person?

Some examples of supervisory skills and traits include:

- Knowledge of human development
- Active listening skills
- Coaching skills
- Conflict negotiation skills
- Teaching skills
- Feedback skills
- Evaluation and assessment skills
- Approachability
- Patience
- Role model skills
- Positive attitude

This is by no means an exhaustive list of the skills and traits associated with effective supervision, but in thinking about these examples, could measuring some of these skills demonstrate that a candidate is likely to be effective in a leadership/supervisory role?

As discussed earlier, there are many ways to ask candidates a question in an interview. Some ways may feel more appropriate for lower-level leadership positions and some for higher-level leadership positions. Whatever you decide, you need to be consistent in asking all candidates the same questions so you can compare all responses to the desired skill set (apples to apples). As stated, the interview committee also needs to establish a minimal-level response for the skill to be demonstrably met. Of course, a higher-level response would always be preferable.

It is important to note that interviewers should seek to measure candidate responses against the required job description skills objectively, rather than comparing candidates against each other subjectively. This serves to ensure that each candidate is viewed fairly. Once this has been accomplished, you will hopefully have identified at least a small group of candidates who meet all the required (and possibly some preferred) criteria, with some candidates who are stronger in certain areas and some who are stronger in others. This is the type of information that the hiring authority will want to see. A skilled hiring authority wants to see how the candidates' skills measured up against the job description as opposed to candidate comparisons, because in addition to seeing the search committee's evaluations, they are (hopefully) seeing evaluations from multiple interviewers/evaluators across the organization, some of whom may have only been able to interview three or four of the candidates due to their availability. To rank the three or four they interview will not be very helpful, but to see how each of the candidates was evaluated with reference to the job skills will be useful in looking at the overall picture.

The search committee is the one group that normally needs to interview all candidates, so they often feel an obligation to rank all the candidates against one another. Sometimes this can be allowed, even though the committee might not see the evaluations from the other groups in the organization that interview the candidates (which is a different area of concern).

9. First Impressions and Nonverbal Communication

Numerous books have been written about first impressions, which as you know, are critically important and often quite accurate. According to a survey conducted by the Harris Poll, approximately 49 percent of interviewers know within the first five minutes if a candidate is a good or bad fit for a position.[118]

A large part of that first impression is based on nonverbal communication and the rest from the candidates' responses to the initial interview questions. The Harris Poll shared examples of candidates' behaviors during interviews that created strong first impressions of candidates. For example, in one interview, the candidate had his head down for the first five minutes. Whether or not this is a true reflection of the candidate's self-confidence, the behavior greatly influenced the interviewer. Another candidate answered a text message during her interview, and another played with her hair during most of her interview. These first impression candidate behaviors are an important part of the overall evaluation process.

As mentioned in Chapter IV, researcher Albert Mehrabian argued that when communicating in a face-to-face setting, 55 percent of the communication is body language, 38 percent is tone of voice, and words account for only 7 percent of the communication.[119] The body language portion of face-to-face communication includes body positioning, eye contact, facial expressions, head nods, fidgety hands, furled eyebrows, crossed arms, watery eyes, muscle tension, shaking hands, and so on. Many people believe they can determine the sincerity and trustworthiness of an individual they meet within seconds, based on some of these nonverbal forms of communication. When you get a "gut feeling" about a candidate, it is often due to these types of nonverbal communications.

Your brain will likely pick up many cues from candidates throughout their day of interviews and presentations with your organization. It is important to accept these cues and connect them with your other observations of the candidates.

Did a candidate's facial reaction to your question about working with people from cultures different from his own tell you something? What did it mean to you when the applicant folded her arms after you asked about how she handles stress? Would any of these actions give you possible information about the candidate that corroborates other parts of the interview?

On an episode of the television series, *Friends,* Chandler interviewed with his potential boss for a leadership position. Every time the interviewer said that Chandler would have a lot more "duties" in this new position, Chandler smirked. The interviewer did not notice the smirk, and when the interview was over, the interviewer told Chandler he thought he did fine. Chandler told him he "almost lost it" when he mentioned the increase in his "duties." The interviewer appeared confused by what Chandler said, so Chandler added, "You know, duties... doodies." After seeing the look on the interviewer's face and realizing that he now probably thought he was immature, Chandler quickly tried to convince him that nothing said after the interview should count. But of course, it did count.[120]

First impressions are very important but are not always foolproof in their accuracy. When first impressions are positive, we often expect they will be followed by more positive impressions and indicators that the candidate would be a good fit for the position. When a first impression is not positive, it often makes a lightbulb go off in our heads. Did we just witness a candidate's weakness? While important to remember that this first impression may be perceived negatively, it is important to store that information away, but not to let it taint the next communications you receive from the candidate. Each of these circumstances are simply first impressions, but nothing more than that—yet. At the end of the day, it is important to ask yourself the question, "Do other responses from the candidate reinforce these positive or negative first impressions?"

10. Reference Verifications

The industry standard and best practice before hiring an employee at any organizational level is to conduct a series of reference verifications. You simply want to know if the people who the candidate previously worked for/with agree with your assessments from the on-site interviews. This is too important to leave to chance, so you need to triangulate information wherever possible, (i.e., seek to view the information from a variety of perspectives). Some organizations and hiring authorities prefer to do reference checks before bringing final candidates in for interviews, and some prefer that be a final step in the decision-making process. Both have pros and cons, but the more comprehensive and detailed the reference check process, the more likely the organization is to gain an accurate view of the candidate.

Despite its huge importance, many hiring authorities view the reference verification process as a nuisance that is either required by organization policy or in some cases, by law. As a result, hiring authorities may assign or delegate this task to a staff member who is lower on the organizational chart. Often, that staff member has more time, but likely also has less-developed skills in analyzing information from a reference call (and less experience doing so). These delegates may ask fewer questions to verify the quality of the candidate's work experience and may not gain detailed knowledge of the candidate's work style or interpersonal skills.

Further, the reference check process is often underutilized. This may occur because a hiring authority has already put candidates through a lengthy interview process and received dozens of feedback evaluations from those who met with the candidate, and now does not want anything to change the collective opinion. Sometimes the hiring authority takes the interview feedback, compares it to the input received from references, and discovers there are discrepancies.

Should the reference checker assume that the candidate's previous supervisor was the problem, so of course they would say negative things? If the hiring authority trusts their interview teams, should their feedback supersede anything the previous employer or colleague has to say?

As this is so important, they need to (at least initially) trust all sources of information. Reference checks can be viewed as the most revealing information about a candidate. Those offering a reference know the actual work style of the candidate. They do not have to read between the lines of what the candidate has told them – they have seen it, and often over a long period of time. That said, the fact that the candidate has requested that their references write or speak on their behalf is a pretty good sign that these people will say positive things.

Some people will answer your reference question, "In what areas can the candidate improve?" by saying, "Nothing I can think of." This is usually a red flag. Any valuable reference should be able to give you positive information but also a sense of the areas where the candidate can improve. Press them on this if need be. Conversely, some references will surprise you by seeming very noncommittal about the candidate. Occasionally, a reference provider will even share reasons that they do not believe the candidate is a good fit for your open position. These instances are rare but can be eye-opening. Skilled reference evaluators need to know how to ask questions that elicit feedback about the areas in need of growth.

Do you need to settle for feedback from only the people whom the candidate has preselected?

This is an enormously important question. Many organizations limit the reference calls to those people, and as a result, may receive reference evaluations that are generic and not very meaningful or useful. Other organizations, however, make it known to the candidate that if they become a finalist for the position and wish to continue in the process, the candidate will need to give the organization permission to contact other individuals from whom the organization wants to hear. This is the potential game-changer.

So, if speaking to people who aren't on the candidate's list is so helpful, why doesn't every organization use this practice?

One reason an organization may shy away from asking a candidate to speak with additional references is the fear that the candidate will refuse to give this permission and drop out of the interview process. If a candidate took this action, however, would you really have wanted them as a candidate, anyway?

What possible reason (other than the obvious) could there be for a candidate not wanting additional people contacted about their work style?

In another episode of the TV show, *Friends*, Rachel has a lunch interview for a job with a representative from Gucci, a competitor of the current company she works for (Ralph Lauren). By a quirk of fate, her current boss is seated right behind her, so she tries to make him believe she is on a date. When her boss finds out she was at an interview, he fires her for not being loyal to the company.[121] Many of us have heard stories about people being fired for interviewing at another organization, but it is a rare occurrence in most professions. On the other hand, an executive leader may not want the public to know they are considering leaving their organization if the organization is owned by shareholders, since the stock values could drop. Most often, however, when a middle-management employee does not want anyone to be contacted as a reference other than the names they already shared, it is likely a cautionary flag that they have something to hide.

The organization invests a great deal of time in the hiring process and intends to invest a great deal of time and resources in their selected candidates, so minimizing such an important part of the process makes little sense. Despite the importance of speaking with references, many organizations and hiring authorities bypass or find shortcuts for this portion of the search process, often to the detriment of the process and the result.

Here are a couple of situations that demonstrate the importance of reference verifications (based on real-life examples):

- Sam's resume indicated that he worked for short periods of time at several organizations over his seven-year career. When asked about this during an interview, Sam responded that his spouse had received several opportunities for promotions over the seven years, and they agreed to prioritize her career. This sounded reasonable and to some, showed Sam to be sensitive to and supportive of women's challenges in the workplace. Upon speaking with supervisors at two previous organizations that had not been included on Sam's original list of references, however, it was learned that at both places, he had been accused of serious infractions and mutually decided that he would leave.

- Valerie's resume indicated that she had five years of experience in a job that was comparable to the one for which she applied. She communicated well and certainly seemed to understand the industry. When asked why she was leaving her current position, Valerie shared that she was originally from the region and wanted to be closer to her family, including her aging parents. This sounded reasonable and the search committee was thrilled with their luck in finding a person with Valerie's skill set who was interested in joining them. Upon speaking with her previous supervisor, who had not been included on her original list of references, however, it was learned that the organization had received numerous complaints from the staff Valerie supervised about her alleged bullying and a variety of ethical concerns. As a result of these concerns, Valerie's contract had not been renewed.

With the increase in litigious actions in society to what some believe to be absurd proportions, certain organizations no longer allow their employees to serve as references for internal candidates and instead, have all such requests come through their Office of Human Resources. While this removes much of the risk of a reference person (and the organization) being sued by an applicant for sharing negative information, it also removes one of the most important components of the hiring process and makes it significantly easier for a poor candidate to pass through the hiring process. As an alternative, some organizations advise employees serving as references to only share positive or neutral information. It is unfortunate that the fear of lawsuits has forced some organizations to create ethical dilemmas for these employees. This will undoubtedly result in many people being hired who would likely not have been otherwise, but for these unnecessary blind spots. Of course, this may result in a poor leader simply moving to a new organization to continue ineffective leadership. Many of you are likely familiar with someone who fits this profile.

Despite these concerns, it is still most common today for references to offer their assessment of a candidate when asked. For less-than-stellar candidates, it is also common for them to give a neutral evaluation and assume that the person asking the questions understands that this is an indication of a concern. One possible solution could be for organizations to offer (or require) professional development workshops on the practice of giving effective feedback. In addition to supporting new leaders doing performance reviews for the first time, this education could help those writing or giving references to successfully offer feedback when asked about previous employees and reduce the likelihood that fear of a lawsuit will alter the flow of honest reference information.

11. Increasing the Candidate Pool - Preparing Future Leaders

Much of this chapter has focused on resumes, first impressions, developing questions that match specific leadership skills defined by the job description, ways to structure candidate interviews, and maximizing the use of reference verifications. An earlier chapter touched on the need to increase the size of applicant pools. That information focused primarily on external candidates (those who do not currently work at the organization).

But how can the size of the leadership candidate pool be increased by focusing on possible candidates who already work at the organization?

In 1539, Richard Taverner authored the proverb, "Better the devil you know than the devil you don't know."[122] In this circumstance, it means that hiring a person you already know may be a better choice than hiring one you do not know, because the new person may be worse. Negativity aside, this is simply because knowing a candidate maximizes the likelihood that you know how they will handle the new position. This is sometimes called the "no surprises" framework. Internal candidates are a known commodity, so you know their strengths as well as their weaknesses. With an external candidate, we always wonder if they will handle their job in the same way we see them in the interview. Were they giving us the responses they thought we wanted to hear or were they being genuine and honest? With the internal candidate, you may not know if they are ready to make the jump to a new level of responsibility, but at least you already know their work ethic and their heart.

Before we jump to judgement that internal candidates are always preferable because we already know them, though, we should remember a competing adage, "The grass is always greener on the other side." This implies that the strengths we do not yet know from external candidates may surpass the strengths of the person we already know. They may not have the weaknesses we know the internal candidate to have. Additionally, with an external candidate, there is the potential benefit of them bringing new ideas and different ways of handling situations from their previous organization. This can bring new energy and freshness to an organization or department.

Obviously, both beliefs can be proven correct, and both can have exceptions. What is important, however, is that you never "settle" for a safe candidate or assume that someone you already work with cannot do the higher-level job they apply for. Quite often, people rise to the level of expectations. This means that a person may not demonstrate a skill set until assuming a position which requires that skill set. It happens in professional sports, and it happens in the workplace. Assistant coaches often become head coaches and assistant directors often become directors. Sometimes just being given the opportunity to demonstrate a skill set is all someone needs to take on the higher-level responsibility. Of course, this is not a given, as some very good assistant coaches and assistant directors become lousy head coaches and directors.

Why is that?

Again, because they are different positions with different skill sets.

As previously mentioned, some organizations have a policy of hiring from within the organization before looking at external candidates. For these organizations, and others who wish to develop a pipeline of future leaders within the organization, it is important that potential leaders be given opportunities for growth *before* leadership positions become available. Opportunities such as coordinating a special organization-wide activity or serving on a task force allow internal employees to get a taste of leadership and at the same time, show themselves to others in their community as they engage in these roles. Often, employees who have never held a leadership position do not see themselves as future leaders and may need someone they respect to offer them encouragement to explore such a move. Not too many people will push away a supervisor or mentor who says, "I see leadership potential in you."

The practice of encouraging future leaders is important for all employees, but even more so for the underrepresented populations in your organization, because they are less likely to see people who look like themselves already in leadership positions. In many organizations, this means giving thought to how you can encourage women, for example, to be willing to step into a previously male leadership arena. For anyone thinking it is not fair to give more encouragement to women (or another underrepresented population), there are two important points to consider. First, the increased recruitment of underrepresented groups does not exclude the need to continue encouraging populations that currently serve in leadership roles in greater numbers. The organization needs as large a pool of potential leaders as possible if it plans to intentionally beat the statistic of having only 37 percent of its leaders considered effective. Second, as mentioned earlier, some people have never thought of themselves as leaders for a variety of reasons. Perhaps they have not had family members or friends in leadership positions or perhaps they were actively discouraged from seeking such a role in the past, so as to not bring attention to themselves.

If there is a much lower number of leaders who are female or people of color in your organization, is that indication of a problem?

That depends on many factors, such as the mission of your organization and its geographical location. As already mentioned, increasing any underrepresented population increases the applicant pool, which increases the odds of hiring effective leaders. Additionally, if an organization wants the demographics of its leaders to reflect its employee memberships and/or constituents, someone will need to do the math to determine an optimal demographic representation or balance. For most business organizations, there currently exists a less-than-desirable number of leaders who are female and people of color. In Fortune 500 companies, for example, there are currently only 41 female CEOs[123] (which represents an all-time high). Does anyone really think that women are less qualified for CEO positions than men?

Another reason an organization may have fewer than desirable numbers of females and/or people of color in leadership roles is the existence of an unconscious/unintentional bias against these populations.

What is an unconscious or unintentional bias and what would one look like?

An unconscious/unintentional bias could be something going on within an organization that limits or unfairly disadvantages a person or group without people being aware of it and without it being intentional. For example, it may be as simple as a group of men golfing with their male boss and discussing the vacant leadership position at the clubhouse afterwards. They did not intentionally exclude females, but their golf group is male-only, and the job opening was one of the many topics discussed. As a result, however, the golfers took the opportunity to encourage male staff members to apply but did not have a similar opportunity to do so for any females, since none were there. Look around your organization.

What is the breakdown of gender and race pertaining to your leaders? Were you aware of this before being asked to think about it right now?

If you were not aware before, it may be considered an unconscious result. If, however, everyone knows about situations like the golf example, but no one acts to alter the inequity, then it would be considered a conscious result.

That said, my intention here is not to dictate the demographics of anyone's senior leadership team, but to point out that if there is an inequity, more effort will likely be needed to increase the number of applicants from those populations for leadership positions. As with most societal inequities, one important way to change the status quo is to change *unconscious* actions to *conscious* actions so they can be discussed by an organization's board of directors or leadership team. Very often, if people knew those inequities existed, they would have already acted on them because they do not intentionally favor one population over another. They simply want the best candidates for the leadership positions they are trying to fill, right? If not, a second block to having a representative leadership team may exist.

By understanding where leadership inequities may exist in your organization, that knowledge will often allow you and others to build bridges for underrepresented populations where they did not previously exist. When we open leadership opportunities for all populations, we not only make the playing field fairer, but the results often lead us to get more candidates and more potentially high-quality candidates. To achieve this, we need to ask ourselves the questions, "What stops more members of ___ group from applying now?" and "What can we do to eliminate the road-blocks so that more members of __ group will be comfortable applying for leadership positions?" This may be hard work, but the alternative may be maintaining an unbalanced leadership team, and one that may consist of only 37 percent who are considered good by those they supervise and 63 percent who are considered to be not good, if my Facebook/LinkedIn survey[124] is to be believed - or any of the surveys and reports by Pew, Gallup, Accountemps, BetterUp Labs, BambooHR, Career and Workplace, and DDI. Sorry to be blunt, but the goal is to improve leadership and if it were easy to do, everyone would have already done it, right?

12. The Process for Hiring Executive Leaders

Never are the results of hiring leaders more important than when hiring an executive leader such as a CEO or president. Likewise, nothing is more devastating to an organization than hiring an ineffective one. This point cannot be overstated or overemphasized.

Granted, the hiring or election of an ineffective leader for any group can be destructive to the goals of the organization, but the mushroom effect of hiring a bad executive leader or the election of a bad regional or national official (e.g., governor, mayor, representative in congress, senator, president, etc.) often negatively impacts multiple layers of employees, staff, and/or constituents. Many of you have probably experienced this in your work lives – perhaps in your current work life. If so, you may already have ideas about how this can be fixed. There are certainly safeguards and actions that can be taken to minimize this risk. Others of you may be wondering why this is being addressed because all you have ever known in your work life are effective leaders. Quick reality check – you are very fortunate. Remember the 37 percent statistic from my survey – far less than half of the 1,412 rated leaders were considered "excellent/good."

In the U.S. government, the election of a bad president can be off-set, to a degree, by the checks and balances that were developed when the United States wrote its Constitution. Ideally, the checks and balances counter the notion that a single individual can bring the country to its knees through ineptitude. In most organizations and elections, however, the hiring or election of an ineffective or bad executive leader can negatively impact the entire organization and/or community immediately, and potentially for many years to come.

Given the potential constructive or destructive environment that an executive leader can create and influence, it is critical that we think carefully about the ways that we search for, assess, and decide to select candidates for these senior leadership positions. Unfortunately, when seeking to hire an executive leader, people involved in these hiring processes may *not know what they don't know*. Often, at least a few people associated with the organization have been involved in hiring high-level leaders in the past. If those experiences were positive and the selected candidates were successful, these few people are likely confident in their ability to successfully orchestrate such a search.

Often, executive leader search committee members lack the experience of hiring a high-level employee, and either need to count on the chairperson or on learning the hiring process from the HR office and learning the nuances as they go. They may see a resume or vitae that outlines the candidate's experience, educational achievement, and their activities, such as membership on national or regional boards. However, as you well know, *what* these candidates have done in their work histories is only part of the story of their candidacy. In addition, search team members must also learn *how* they performed these activities. This includes how successful the candidate was in each role, but equally important is the way in which the activities were accomplished. In other words, there are what we call "hard skills," such as budget development, forecasting, strategic planning, and product development, and there are also what we call "soft skills," which are sometimes called human-relation or emotional intelligence skills, as discussed in the previous chapter.

As you recall from Chapter V, Daniel Goleman, author of *Emotional Intelligence*[125] focused on four skills:

- Self-Awareness – the ability to recognize and understand one's moods, motivations, and abilities

- Self-Management – the ability to control one's impulses

- Social Awareness – the ability to understand other people's emotions and reactions and be aware of how societal dynamics impact employee production and satisfaction

- Relationship Management – the ability to develop strong, trusting relationships and find common ground with others

As an example of emotional intelligence, you have likely heard the story of a discussion between two people in a relationship that sounded like this: "Yes, I am upset, but it is not because of *what* you said, but *how* you said it." The response that follows this statement will usually demonstrate the level of "emotional intelligence" the person possesses. The two people in this conflict may exhibit either higher or lower levels of emotional intelligence based on their awareness of how their words connect to their moods, if they can control their impulses, and if they can understand the reaction of the other person before responding.

The importance of EI is greatly enhanced when a person takes on a leadership role, and even more so when it is an executive leadership role, due to the number of people with whom the executive leader will interact. Some theorists believe that people either have the empathy trait (and are born with it) or they do not, while others believe that empathy can become an acquired skill. Either way, most agree that an executive leader needs a healthy dose of EI to be successful, but many interviewers have little idea how to measure it during the search process.

To assess these skills in the 1980s and 1990s, some organizations utilized the technique of visiting the final candidate's current organization to view their community and be able to freely speak with the people who worked closely with the candidate. While perhaps not a perfect way to evaluate a candidate's EI, this visit was a creative effort to understand the candidate "off paper" by seeing their impact in real life. A few organizations still use this approach today, but most have abandoned it due to concerns about disrupting the candidate's current community, discouraging people from applying, and not achieving the goals they envisioned from this activity.

However structured, the search process for executive leaders must be extremely thoughtful, inclusive, and well-run. To ultimately hire an excellent EL, this hiring decision cannot be a political favor or simply a legacy selection. There cannot be trustees or board chairs saying, "Trust me, I know how to find top-notch leaders" and the organization cannot hand the search process to an executive search firm, wash their hands of the process, and expect the results to magically work out. This executive leader search is far too important and will impact the core staff, the core product, and both the short and long-term future of the organization.

A philosophy regarding the hiring process should generally reflect that the higher the stakes, the more time the search process needs to take. When searching to fill an executive leader position, as opposed to a position that falls more in the middle of the organizational chart, more time should be allocated to find qualified candidates, interview them, and validate strengths and challenges with references. There are a few exceptions here and there, but you likely understand the logic for this philosophy. Despite this, some organizations simply *appoint* a new executive leader without the benefit of using a search process.

The executive search process must look far and wide for candidates who have what the organization needs. If this takes a long time, so be it. In the meantime, an interim executive leader can be appointed who will "do no harm" and hopefully encourage and facilitate some growth in preparation of the new executive leader. Over the past couple decades, new agencies have been developed that create lists of retired executive leaders who are willing to take the reins for six months or a year while a search process takes place. This approach is often more desirable than appointing a senior leader, such as a vice president, to do their own job and the executive leader's job simultaneously for a year while the search is conducted.

A vice president from the organization may have a smaller learning curve regarding the organizational norms, but an ex-president with a stellar track record and reputation presumably already knows how to be a successful president. Such a person can also help the organization by allowing the vice president to remain in their regular position. To use another expression, saving a dollar (by asking the vice president to do both jobs in the interim) may sound "penny wise," but it often appears to be "pound foolish," as the vice president can easily get overwhelmed and fail to do either job well. Whether choosing to use a vice president or an ex-president, appointing a placeholder may not be something an organization wants to admit having to do, but it is without question far less detrimental than rushing to hire someone and later learning they are a latent narcissist or one who proves to be toxic to the organization.

Peter Northouse's book, *Leadership: Theory and Practice*,[126] shares several theories that explain the success or failure of leadership. As mentioned earlier, one of these theories is called the *Contingency Theory*. This theory argues that leadership is most likely to be successful when the candidate's skills and style closely match what the environment needs and wants. For this to occur in an executive search, it is in the best interest of the final decision-makers to hear feedback from *all* types of constituents of the organization – the senior-level leaders, middle-level leaders, entry-level employees, as well as customers and other constituents.

Generally, no single person or group can realistically understand the perspectives of all workplace members. Including many voices in a search process serves to invest all these members in the success of the selected candidate. Sure, it is easier not to do so, but including a variety of voices makes it more likely that the candidate's hidden weaknesses and areas of concern will surface. Gaining this level of input about candidates may be the only way to gain insights into how the candidate will interact with the entirety of the organization. This only works if the hiring authority (in the case of hiring an EL, that would be the board, owner, etc.) is honestly willing to hear and value diverse opinions, as opposed to exclusively their own.

Another reason an organization needs to take special care when hiring an executive leader is because of what occurs immediately after the new executive assumes their position. Often, a new executive leader will immediately ask the current vice presidents to submit their letters of resignation, so that the new leader can select their own leadership team. The new executive leader generally waits a period of time, and then accepts the resignation letters from those vice presidents they wish to replace and rejects the letters from those they wish to retain. Although logical, this can cause a great deal of disruption to the organization. Some vice presidents may choose to leave before the new executive leader begins, because they have seen enough of their new boss from interviews and reputation to know that this person is not someone they want to work with. During this period, some department heads may report to different people on a temporary basis and long-range planning efforts may need to be put on hold until the new executive leadership team can get an adequate feel for the needs of the team and the organization.

As a result of these organizational realities and challenges, it makes sense to take the time to do the EL search thoughtfully, so it does not need to be repeated soon. As stated earlier, selecting a leader who is not a good fit for the executive leader position will most certainly exacerbate the primary reason that good employees leave organizations.

After a new executive leader is hired, another significant but less-discussed challenge may occur. Since the search committee and the hiring authority put a lot of work into the hiring effort, they likely feel assured that their selected candidate will be a great fit. There is now reputational pressure for them to not have to admit they were fooled by the candidate they selected. Sometimes, after the dust settles and the new executive leader is on the job, cracks in their foundation appear and the new "golden child" shows significant areas for concern.

When a new executive leader is seen as making significant errors or demonstrating a style that differs from the one they demonstrated during interviews, the hiring authority will need to take time to determine if the new EL is just having growing pains or if they are not well-suited for the position. While this consideration takes place, the executive leader may still need to hire their senior team and move forward on organizational initiatives.

To remove a new executive leader from their position within their first year risks placing the organization into chaos – again. Conversely, leaving an executive leader in place who cannot move the organization forward risks the reputation of the organization and possibly its future. If these possibilities do not terrify boards, owners, and everyone involved enough to take every precaution to hire ELs "right" the first time, nothing will.

While few board members believe they will be negatively surprised by a new executive leader, it should also be noted that when they *are* surprised, there are ways to respond to these challenges gracefully and productively. Doing nothing and hoping for the best, however, is virtually never the appropriate way of responding.

When new concerns arise about the executive leader, many boards or owners may place band-aids on their organizations while investigating the issues that led to the dissatisfaction. Earlier, we looked at the pros and cons of appointing an interim or past executive leader from within the organization. A different but possible strategy would be to call a retired or ex-leader of that organization (or a similar organization) to coach and support the executive leader through this challenging time. That person may be asked to function as an invisible coach. However, this is a situation that works best when the EL recognizes their predicament. In cases in which the EL does not see or admit to the existing problems, and chooses to place the blame on previous leadership, the current staff, or the board, the alternatives in the situation may be limited to saying goodbye and helping the EL leave gracefully. This scenario is more likely to occur when a new EL is product-smart but simply lacks emotional intelligence skills such as self-awareness and interpersonal skills. Unfortunately, this trend seems to be on the rise.[127]

While these scenarios and challenges can still occur after an exceptional search process, they are more likely to occur when a search process is not well-designed or well-run. Given the 37 percent leader satisfaction rate previously discussed, this scenario often catches people by surprise, and is usually not resolved until a great deal of damage has been done to the organization.

CHAPTER VI

When Is It Time for A Leader to Leave?

Many authors share suggestions for how an individual can successfully begin a leadership journey, but very few discuss when it is time to stop leading. This is different from asking when someone should be a good follower as opposed to a leader. This chapter addresses a challenge for today's leaders—deciding how and when to move on to another role or retire and pass the baton to a new leader.

Many of us have worked with leaders who held onto their leadership positions past their effectiveness date because they liked their title, salary, and/or the recognition and influence that came with it. Some of us have also worked with leaders who stayed in their leadership roles despite hating their jobs so much that they found reasons to not come to work on a regular basis. These folks attended numerous conferences, often worked from home, joined too many external boards, and used every minute of vacation, personal, and sick time available to them. Still others of us have worked with leaders who withheld information from colleagues to make themselves appear nonexpendable. In this way, they believed their supervisor would not relieve them of their duties. A few of us have even worked with leaders who were widely disliked by their supervisor, colleagues, and constituents, but remained in their leadership roles for years because of the political influence they held. Perhaps you have additional examples as well.

Why do people stay in a leadership position when deep inside, they know it is long past time to leave, either to seek alternative employment or retire?

Having leaders stay in leadership roles past their effectiveness is yet another component of circular toxicity that can destroy an organization. It is also another reason that surveys routinely inform us that more leaders are ineffective—they stay past their "best to leave by" date. This is a significant problem from at least two vantage points:

- As stated, organizations need strong leadership to meet the needs of their constituents and to facilitate the development of their employees. Ineffective leaders who remain in their positions prevent this from happening.

- Leaders often begin their leadership journey strong and with very positive results. Many of the leaders mentioned earlier were not always so skeptical, distrustful, lacking confidence, egotistical, or whatever led them to take these actions. Many were, in fact, outstanding.

On a positive note, based on anecdotal evidence, it seems that many leaders do leave at a time that makes good sense for them personally and for their organization. They are likely to be celebrated as innovators, role models, mentors, and people whom others aspire to emulate. Some receive large send-offs and leave in style, often with coronation-like festivities. Another portion of these effective leaders are also greatly appreciated but desire to avoid the limelight, so they leave quietly, and we are unaware of their transition details. Unfortunately, however, when leaders who outlast their prime remain in office, we hear a lot about them (usually in the breakroom), so their negative impact on the organizational culture is high.

Using the highways as an analogy, we tend to pay more attention to the car crashes we pass by and less so to the cars that avoided crashes and just have dents or taped plastic for a window. We wonder what happened and stop to stare at someone's misfortune, which causes traffic slowdowns, and gives inquisitive minds a good amount of time to wonder why nothing seems to be happening. Isn't this what happens in the workplace as well? When an unpopular leader leaves, especially involuntarily, everyone hears about it, talks about it, and stops working while they ponder the reasons for it. Leaders at the workplace are not just another car on the road – they are not just another employee at the workplace. They are in the limelight and people pay attention to them.

Workplace leadership "car crashes" are memorable. Unlike the real car crash, the effect of their demise in the workplace is not an immediate reaction. Because leaders are responsible for the performance of the employees they supervise and determining the direction and priorities of employees' work, we spend a lot of time hearing and talking about them (to the distraction of our work) when they are no longer productive. This is not helpful to anyone.

All of this is to say that leaders who remain when they shouldn't not only cause departmental productivity slow-downs and employee development problems, but also organization-wide problems associated with the car crashes. They can interrupt the functioning of the entire organization. For these leaders who suddenly go from being effective to ineffective, we need to understand why so we can help prevent these occurrences or in some cases, prepare for them.

To gain insight into the metamorphosis that occurred between their early days as "an effective leader," "golden child," "future of the organization," etc. to their later days, when they are sometimes referred to as "budget-busters" or "irrelevant," we need to better understand what occurred. Something happened to change this person who enthusiastically supported employees and strategically accomplished organization goals into a person who became apathetic, lethargic, mean-spirited, or whatever else their ineffectiveness came to look like.

Unfortunately, there is no singular reason that these negative behaviors may become prevalent at the end of some leadership careers. While some may have been foreseeable, others may have been the result of personal challenges that the leader faced in their life. Sometimes, the issue may have been as simple as a leader accomplishing their goals and needing to increase their challenges but being unable to do so at their current organization. Other times, the cause may have been political, pertaining to external constituents with whom they negatively interacted, and who have influence with boards and organization ownership. Both scenarios can lead to feelings of resentment, apathy or other ineffective traits and characteristics.

The key to minimizing these examples of "good leaders gone bad," is for ALL leaders to pay attention to the development and well-being of the people they supervise. Seeing and disrupting a pattern of ineffective leadership can serve to spare the leader and the organization years of headaches.

In management, it is argued that the higher the level of responsibility one has, the less supervision, support, and direction they should need from their supervisor. While this may be true for some leaders, other leaders may want or need this type of developmental connection with their supervisor. If we accept this argument, we need to also be aware that no one is ever free of personal circumstances that can impact their leadership effectiveness.

There are numerous reasons that it is time for a leader to leave. Here are 10 of them:

1. The Goals Have Been Met

2. Leadership Transitions

3. Going Through the Motions

4. Waiting for Retirement

5. What Else Would I Do?

6. Attitude

7. I Can Change – I Just Do Not Want To

8. I Can Not Afford to Leave

9. Spite

10. Real Leaders Know When It Is Time to Leave

1. The Goals Have Been Met

Effective leaders, like everyone else, take on their positions for different reasons. We can assume that effective leaders take positions to help the organization and its employees and constituents accomplish established goals. Beyond that commonality, leaders assume these roles for a wide range of reasons, as discussed in an earlier chapter regarding responses to the question, "Why do you want to become a leader?" Supervisors of these leaders can help by asking the leader about goals they have set for themselves while in their role at the organization. As the leader closes in on achieving these goals, the next step for the supervisor should be to discuss career plans. Is this the time to stay and establish new, challenging goals, or is it the time to leave? If they stay, what will continue to motivate them and spark their interest? If they need to leave, how can the supervisor be helpful in this transition?

Internally, how can an effective leader know when it is time to leave or stay? The concept of emotional intelligence has been discussed throughout this book and applies here as well. This is another reason that having well-developed emotional intelligence before taking on a leadership position is so important. The extent to which a leader knows themself and their values and beliefs will encourage them to periodically self-assess whether the current environment is conducive to meeting their career goals. For some leaders, this may be accomplished in three years. For others, their goals may be the driving force that gets them up each morning for 36 years. The only way to know is to ask the question periodically, honestly, and realistically.

2. Leadership Transitions

A change in leadership can substantially change a work environment. When a leader's supervisor exits the organization, the introduction of a new supervisor may require that the leader reassess their fit in the organization. This is equally true when the leadership transition involves a new CEO/president or when a professional sports franchise hires a new president or general manager. Some new executive leaders wish to hire their own leadership team, so their staff members either need to wait and see if they meet the new leader's needs or update their credentials to prepare for a job search. In these situations, as with all new leadership situations, it behooves a leader to think about what it will be like working with their new supervisor. A new executive leader normally needs to prove their capabilities early and determine which staff members can be considered allies in support of their efforts and style. If the early view of a new supervisor does not seem conducive to the type of environment in which the leader can thrive, it is probably a good time for the leader to look for new employment elsewhere. It is virtually always better to job-hunt when you have a job than to wait until you are unemployed.

3. Going Through the Motions

Despite starting their leadership position with initial joy and excitement, at some point in time, leaders may find themselves "going through the motions." They may not have achieved all their established goals but have been effective for a long period of time. Now, however, they may receive little joy from their work. While they used to say they would do this job for free, they now use all the vacation, personal, and sick time they have available. All employees deserve to follow their passion, but when the passion is gone, leaders owe it to their organization and the staff they supervise to make room for a new supervisor who will bring that missing enthusiasm to the organization.

4. Waiting for Retirement

Some leaders were effective for much of their career and began to tire late in life due to physical ailments or fatigue. Some jobs require a lot of physical energy, some require a lot of mental energy, and some require both. These leaders may now lack the energy needed for the position and feel entitled to ride out the wave until retirement. They may earn a respectable salary due to their length of service. They daydream about what retirement will be like.

The elder leaders at an organization who are no longer effective are often the most difficult to help leave their positions due to the political connections they may have made in the surrounding community, with governmental leaders, and with internal governance structures, etc. Most often, these leaders are allowed to float a bit during their final years as a sign of loyalty to them for their years of leadership and due to their advanced age, which can also trigger a lawsuit if they perceive themselves as being pushed out of their position.

There is certainly a case to be made to keep the wisdom and experience a leader has brought to the organization, but only if the leader is still producing results and sharing the history when useful. "Out with the old and in with the new" may have a ring to it, but when we lose the most experienced leaders, we also lose their history. That said, however, if the leader is simply waiting for retirement, they need to ask themselves if this is fair to their staff, colleagues, and the organization. Unless they are operating at a level that is sufficient in their eyes and the eyes of the executive leader, they need to remember the critical importance of effective leadership in the organization. In this case, the leader needs to step aside, whether that means retiring early, taking on a new position developed by their supervisor with their special skill set in mind, or announcing their retirement and expressing willingness to help onboard a new leader as they transition someone to replace them. What is not acceptable management behavior, however, is knowingly working around a nonfunctioning, ex-leader who is largely uninvolved in important decision-making. That scenario mocks the concept of effective leadership.

5. What Else Would I Do?

Leaders are often highly skilled in their role, but when their drive and productivity contract, they may want to stay in place because they have no idea of what else they can do if they leave the organization or are asked to step into a temporary role while their replacement is hired. A self-aware leader recognizes their own needs, but also strives to respect the organization. That leader can often request a meeting with the executive leader to explore future options. Certainly, there is risk in taking this route, but staying in a position when you know you are just "taking up space" is not how any effective leader wants to be remembered.

6. Attitude

In leadership, as in life, attitude is everything. Effective leaders are often easy to spot due to their positive and upbeat attitudes. They smile, enjoy working with their staff and colleagues, and consider it a privilege to be paid well for giving their all (and then some) to their organization. Leaders must always remember that they are in the spotlight, whether it is obvious to them or not. Employees are motivated by enthusiastic leaders, but that does not mean all leaders need to be traditional cheerleaders that yell and holler their support. A book by Susan Cain titled, *Quiet: The Power of Introverts in a World That Can't Stop Talking*,[128] demonstrates the power of the introvert, and the reality that many quiet leaders are the most effective goal achievers and employee supports around. I am certain that many of you either know of these quiet, effective leaders, or ARE these leaders.

When you stop smiling on Monday mornings as you enter your building and the Sunday night blues become so pronounced that you spend more time planning vacation days than thinking about how to help a staff member or the organization move forward, it may well be time to say goodbye to this experience and begin the search for the next one.

7. I Can Change – I Just Do Not Want To

When leaders are new, they despise hearing that existing staff are resistant to change. After all, that is likely one of the main reasons they were hired – to bring effective change. They spend months listening and offering new perspectives, but they hear that people like the way things are. At some point in their career, these leaders become the "organization elders" and one day they are surprised to hear themselves respond to a new colleague's idea with, "If the system we use works, why do we need to change it?" Some people love change and others would rather visit the dentist for a root canal. If you lean more towards the latter, or hear yourself uttering those words, it may well be time for a change. You are not bad – you simply have done your part to bring in new changes and build on them. Now it is time for someone else to bring in new ideas.

8. I Can Not Afford to Leave

A very common reason that previously effective leaders may remain in a position long past the time they know they are no longer effective pertains to money. Altruism is all well and good, but according to eminent psychologist Abraham Maslow, we cannot move to higher levels of personal development until our lowest-level basic needs have been met.[129] Having enough money to pay the mortgage, buy food, and send your kids to college are considered basic needs to many of us these days. Some leaders who have lost their effectiveness may know the time is right for them to leave the organization but are afraid of not finding another job with the pay and benefits of their current position.

This condition may be the one most frequently experienced by leaders who either have fallen out of love with their position, their organization, or both. Those around them can hear the Wendy Whiner imitations on a more frequent basis. It is unrealistic and probably unfair to ask someone to voluntarily give up their financial security so the organization can replace them with a more effective leader. In a case like this, however, either the organization's Human Resources Office or the executive leader would need to offer to help. In Chapter II, we looked at humane ways to support an employee moving on to a new position with a new employer. Despite the possibility of the organization feeling like a concierge service, it makes much more sense for the organization to help the leader who wants to leave to be able to do so, rather than keep a disgruntled person on staff, and in a leadership position to boot.

9. Spite

A much less common reason for a leader wanting to remain at an organization despite knowing they are no longer effective pertains to spite. In an episode of the television show, *Seinfeld*, Jerry went to a store to return some clothing he had purchased the day prior. When the manager asked him why he wanted to return the clothing, Jerry replied, "Spite!" After the manager told him that spite is not a reason for making a return, Jerry explained that the salesman who sold him the clothes the day prior did something he did not care for and as a result, he wanted to return the clothes so the salesman would not get his commission. Jerry argued that the sign in the store says, "merchandise may be returned for any reason." The manager told Jerry, "Yes, but it cannot be returned for spite."[130]

Some people have a strong expectation of life being "fair." They expect karma to strike when someone acts in a way that is unjust, and they wait for the satisfaction they feel when justice is eventually served. Even effective leaders may have momentary lapses. Ideally, self-aware people make the decision to leave a place that treats them unfairly, but occasionally, spite enters the equation. In these cases, if a leader is treated unfairly by the executive leader, for example, the leader may choose to stay in the organization, hoping to get justice in some way. They may plan to tap colleagues to help gang up on the leader, make the EL look bad in the media, or spread rumors through the organization's clientele. In situations like this, there are often no winners and many losers, so it is considered best to speak directly with the unhappy employee to remind them that "the best revenge is to live a happy life."[131]

10. Real Leaders Know When It Is Time to Leave

Throughout these examples, many of you may be shaking your heads and thinking that this author has no experience in the real world if he thinks management is going to push these folks out or that these leaders will forgo their paychecks and egos to step aside and allow new leaders to take their place. Well, not being overly naïve, and having had experience working with thousands of real-world people and innumerable challenges over a lengthy career, tells me that despite knowing it is the right thing to do, you are probably correct in thinking that many organizations will not assertively push ineffective leaders out the door, but many may be willing to initiate conversations about the leader's future.

It is widely believed that Albert Einstein once said, "The definition of insanity is doing the same thing over and over again but expecting different results."[132] (It was not actually Einstein, but for the sake of argument, let's make believe he said it.) In this case, doing nothing differently maintains the status quo, which is simply unacceptable because the effectiveness of leadership is at stake. Leaders cannot "stand pat" at the expense (perhaps literally) of the trust, integrity, forward thinking, and employee development that are so often lacking. It is reasonable and necessary to ask organizations to recognize the importance of effective leadership and the destructive capabilities of ineffective leaders, and to consider acting in the best interests of the organization and its constituents, despite the legal risks and personal energy it takes to make those things happen.

Most of my optimism in this regard, however, points to the leaders personally. Once we can determine the reasons that individual leaders become ineffective after years of productivity, these leaders must act, and many will do so, with organizational respect and support. Most leaders want to leave a legacy that emphasizes their successes – not overstaying their effectiveness.

Regarding leaving a desired legacy, my personal experience and the experience of many colleagues over the years has demonstrated to me that when leaders become aware or are made aware that it is time to leave, a great many will take the necessary steps to do so. As important as we all may believe ourselves to be, it is nevertheless important that all leaders recognize the ebbs and flows their organizations take and actively decide that they are ready, willing, and able to give 100 percent or to move aside and allow the organization to replace them with someone who is ready, willing, and able to do so.

Leadership is not about *me,* but *we.* As you all travel down the leadership path, you will hopefully consider when the time is right for you to leave – with consideration given to your needs, but also to those of the leadership environment in which you have been privileged to serve.

CHAPTER VII

What We Can Learn from Experienced Leaders

Do we learn more from reading and thinking about leadership or listening to people share their leadership experiences?

Most people will say they prefer to hear from those who have experienced something rather than reading about theory. That is why real-life and hypothetical examples have been included in previous chapters. Storytelling is always more appealing and interesting. Hearing directly from those with experience also has a certain believability factor (or credibility).

Developmental theorists dating back to philosopher John Dewey (1859) and Maria Montessori (1870) argued that the best way to learn about a profession or to develop a skill is through a "theory-to-practice" approach.[133] This means that learning how to do something and then trying it out is one of the most effective ways for many people to learn. If we were in an actual classroom, you would have been asked, upon starting this journey, to either take on a leadership position at work or in your local or regional community, or to focus on a leadership role you already have. In this classroom, as we read each chapter of this book, you would have been asked to think about the chapter topics in relation to your leadership experiences, interactions, and observations. All students would have been asked to write a weekly journal entry to document their thoughts about how their reading and personal experiences matched up. You would be asked to discuss these thoughts and observations with classmates on a weekly basis as well, so others could hear how theory informs practice and practice calls for theory. In this way, each student would have a personal dialog with their instructor and additional opportunities to engage with their peers, as they experienced the trials, tribulations, and joys associated with leadership.

Given that we are not in class together, this chapter aims to offer you information right from the horse's mouth, so to speak. Several very effective leaders, both young and well, less young, have graciously agreed to share information about themselves and their experiences with leadership, and to respond to a series of questions that have been developed by students from my leadership classes over several years.

You will have the benefit of reading the unedited responses from these special leaders and get a good sense of what has helped to make each of them so effective. One of these leaders has more than 50 years of leadership experience to call on, and the other three leaders are in their late twenties/early thirties, having been extraordinary student leaders in college and accomplished leaders in their vocational areas thereafter. All are extraordinary individuals, as you will see.

Each of the four leaders have responded to the interview questions listed below.

Interview Questions for Experienced Leaders

1. Please tell us about yourself and talk about what has drawn you to take on leadership roles throughout your life.

2. Please share some of the leadership roles you have held.

3. What is your leadership philosophy?

4. Please share the qualities or attributes you believe are important to being an effective leader.

5. Have your views about leadership changed over the years? If so, how?

6. What have been the most enjoyable and least enjoyable parts of being in a leadership role?

7. What leaders have inspired you throughout your life?

8. Please describe one or two of your most memorable leadership successes and one or two of your most memorable leadership missteps or mistakes.

9. What advice would you offer to future or current leaders?

10. How would you most like to be remembered as a leader?

Jim Collins

1. Please tell us about yourself and talk about what has drawn you to take on leadership roles throughout your life.

My name is Jim Collins, and I have been privileged to serve in a number of leadership positions, both in paid and volunteer capacities over the last 50 years. I learned quite early in my career that I was drawn to effective leaders and felt that I needed to live up to the role models that I had worked with. I also was challenged to always work on improving organizations for the benefit of achieving their missions and the performance of the people charged with the responsibilities of leadership and management.

2. Please share some of the leadership roles you have held.

My primary leadership role has been as Chief Financial Officer, Treasurer, Executive Vice President, and Chief Investment Officer for Clark University, a 3500-student research and doctoral university in Worcester, Massachusetts. I filled one or more of those roles over the 41-year period from 1979 through 2020. In my professional career, I had previously served as Business Manager for Cornell University Dining Services in Ithaca, New York, and as Budget Manager and Associate Treasurer of Brandeis University in Waltham, Massachusetts.

For the last 18 years (2002-2020) I also served as Trustee and Treasurer of the George I. Alden Trust, a $230 million charitable foundation established to promote education and educationally related activities. We supported primarily independent colleges and universities with less than 5,000 students and located in the six New England States, New York, New Jersey, and Pennsylvania. We also supported YMCAs in Massachusetts, the Worcester Technical High School, and a large number of Worcester community organizations and independent secondary schools in our geographic area. In this role, I had the benefit of observing and working with a wide range of leaders and enjoyed measuring the relative effectiveness of different leadership styles, particularly of college and university presidents.

I also held leadership roles in many Worcester area community organizations, including as Chair of the Board of the United Way of Central Massachusetts, Treasurer and Chair of both the Finance and Investment Committees of the Greater Worcester Community Foundation, the Worcester Art Museum, and the Worcester Business Development Corporation.

Earlier in my career, I had been one of three founders of CBORD, Inc., now a division of Roper Industries, and had also been involved in the early days of SCUUL, Inc, a liability insurance captive created to provide coverage for educational organizations, now doing business domestically as United Educators.

3. What is your leadership philosophy?

I would not say that I have a singular "leadership philosophy." I do have several principles that guide my work and my thinking about organizational effectiveness and the responsibilities of leaders. First and foremost, I do believe that "leadership matters," and is almost always the single most important factor leading to organizational effectiveness, or lack thereof. This may seem obvious, but I am continually exposed to people who do not agree with this basic principle, and instead focus on a wide variety of other factors. I do not discount those other factors, but I have too often seen examples of both strong and weak leadership that result in quite rapid organizational change, whether for better or worse. To me, it is always the first area to consider. Interestingly, I have not found that the mission of an organization changes the primacy of this principle.

A second principle to which I am drawn is simply one of hard work, continual presence, and leadership by visible example. Leaders need to be present to understand the challenges of the organization and its employees, and they need to listen to suggestions from others as to creative solutions. They also need to be "seen" as being attentive and involved – and committed – to the need for organizational success. Some of this is catego-rized as "leadership by walking around," but to me that is only the first step; the real difference is made in fully engaging with the staff members and working to both inspire them and to use the leader's knowledge and exper-tise to help arrive at optimal solutions. To me, this is mostly a function of fully taking responsibility for both the job and the people for whose perfor-mance you are responsible. Having just finished reading an excellent book by Doris Kearns Goodwin, entitled *Leadership in Turbulent Times,* which uses case studies of the lives of Abraham Lincoln, Theodore Roosevelt, Franklin Roosevelt, and Lyndon Johnson. I was struck by the degree to which she ascribed each of their successful leadership careers to having been the hardest working people in every job they took on, especially early in their careers.

Other principles follow logically from these two. Leaders need to be empathetic, and they need to care for people, and to have an ability to remain calm in crises. They need to be habitually honest and be both trust-ing and trustworthy. It does no good, and instead is harmful, if in being present the leader models behaviors that are neither inspiring nor aspira-tional. A leader needs to be optimistic, but not "Pollyannish." Subordinates have strongly developed antennae for bullshit, and a "leader" who forgets that will not be successful in achieving her or his mission. I also believe that effective leaders need to always work to promote fairness in decision making, and to ensure that the leader is perceived as always working to "be fair." I also have seen that effective leaders work very hard to be helpful whenever possible, and to whomever is present and in need of assistance.

4. Please share the qualities or attributes you believe are important to being an effective leader.

My answer above speaks to the qualities that I find needed in an effec-tive leader. Determination to succeed in achieving the mission is probably first. Beyond that, I would add emotional and interpersonal intelligence, self-confidence, optimism, and warmth. Being a strong judge of character and having a genuine concern for others' well-being and need for organizational belonging are also important.

Thoughtfulness is important, but a leaning toward action and experimentation will probably be better appreciated by those who are looking for direction. Not unrelated to the above, an effective leader needs to be able to make decisions, and to act upon them quickly, both for the good of the organization and its employees and customers/clients. There have certainly been leaders who do not demonstrate all of these, but most good ones display most of them.

5. Have your views about leadership changed over the years? If so, how?

My personal views of leadership have not changed markedly over the years, due in no small part to the lessons learned from one of my first mentors in my first professional position (more on this person later). Rather, the lessons learned early have been reinforced and refined by my additional points of observation as my career progressed. Unfortunately, there were times when the observation point was a negative one. That is, I was able to see the negative impact that subsequent people's behavioral traits had on their organizations, and this helped me to understand that my early lessons really were as important and significant as I had believed at my young age and inexperienced background.

6. What have been the most enjoyable and least enjoyable parts of being in a leadership role?

By far the most enjoyable part of being in a leadership role has been when measurable success has been achieved. I grew up being very competitive in a variety of athletic pursuits, and from that I learned to study what led to "winning," and what behaviors were detrimental to that clearly defined objective. I remain competitive, and this leads me to structure my personal goals and objectives toward "winning," even as I work to reach consensus on which set of achievements would fit that definition for all or most stakeholders. I know that I am competitive to a fault, as demonstrated visibly, and unfortunately, at a university staff picnic when I decided to run into the catcher during a close play at home plate. The catcher was my boss, the University President, so this was not my finest moment. Because of this competitive streak, I am drawn to measurable achievements, whether it be in university rankings, winning one-on-one competitions for the best students and faculty, or earning awards for rising to become the best university food service in the country.

The least enjoyable parts of leadership for me, not surprisingly, are when we fail, or fall short of our aspirations. This can occur on an overall level for the entire organization, or it can be the failure of a particular person, including myself, who was unable to meet the challenges needing to be overcome. This might involve the need to separate that person from the team, which no one likes to do, even if that action is ultimately best for all concerned. It is especially demoralizing if a great deal of energy and time were invested in that person's success, and that failure can be difficult to overcome for the entire team, but especially the leader.

7. What leaders have inspired you throughout your life?

My most inspiring leader was Arthur A. Jaeger, the former Director of Dining Services at Cornell University, and the person who hired me as Business Manager (a kind of Assistant Director) for what became a $20 million true enterprise within the university's Division of Campus Life. Cornell Dining had lost hundreds of thousands of dollars annually for many years, and suffered from a horrible reputation among students, faculty, and staff. Art was hired with a simple and clear mandate. "You will have almost unlimited freedom to operate, but if you do not turn this operation into a programmatic and financial asset within three years, we will have no choice but to outsource the entire operation." (Also, there was to be no mandatory board program, so everything had to be achieved through market success.) Given such clear direction, Art went to work with the goal of having Cornell become the best and most innovative university food program in the country and achieved this goal in only three years. We went from having 12 students on a voluntary board program to over 6,000, including many who did not live on campus.

Art was tireless in setting high aspirations, and bringing in managers, supervisors, and employees at all levels who could help us improve rapidly. He/we pioneered such innovations (now common in most universities) as unlimited food options, unlimited changes in meal plans, multiple restaurant concepts, guest chefs from the best and most famous restaurants in the country (the "Cross Country Gourmet" program), grocery stores to accommodate students without time to sit down for meals, computerized menu planning (the above mentioned CBORD system), which was ultimately sold to hundreds of colleges, universities, hospitals, and corporate dining clients, computerized card access (CBORD system still used at Clark University), vending operations, a low calorie board program with its own dietitian focusing on healthy eating habits, and a high-end catering program, which also allowed our board plan participants to dine once per month in the white tablecloth table service high-end restaurant we opened. He also developed a cash bonus program for managers, which was anathema to university administrators at that time. We also introduced weekly financial statements to help guide our work and increase manager accountability.

Art's leadership was based largely on his sense of urgency, determination to succeed, his full acceptance of his responsibility, and his attention to training, marketing, and the highest quality standards. He was relentless, and his creativity was boundless and contagious. He insisted that his management team dine at the best restaurants and come back with ideas that could be implemented for the student board plan. (And my challenging job was convincing the Cornell auditors that such expenditures were valid uses of university resources!) He was fearless in dealing with the university bureaucracy, but very attentive to the student customers, who often railed against him personally, but flocked to his programs and restaurants. Arthur was also an early proponent of "affirmative action," based on merit and providing opportunity for education, training, and advancement. He was able to find some of his best supervisors and managers from within his operating units, and many of these were women and historically underrepresented people in management.

In fact, one of my other most admired leaders is Margaret (Peg) Lacey, a young woman with a 2-year associate degree who was hired as a pantry worker, and was quickly promoted to supervisor, manager, and area manager, before leaving Cornell to be Director of Dining Services at Columbia University, before ultimately returning to Cornell as Art Jaeger's successor as Director of Cornell Dining. She subsequently served as the Midwest Regional Director for Aramark Food Services. Peg was always very staunchly supportive of her employees, and she was known to be highly visible "on the floor" and in the kitchen with her chefs. She, too, was fearless, and always trying new ideas to advance the university dining experience.

Another outstanding leader for whom I had great respect was John Hughes, my three-year Cornell apartment mate, and captain of the undefeated (29-0) NCAA Hockey championship team of 1969-70, the last college hockey team to complete a championship year with no losses. He received not only his BS and MBA degrees with me in an accelerated program, but then decided to attend Cornell Law, and became a very successful attorney in New York City. As with Art Jaeger, John was among the most competitive, goal-driven persons that I ever met, and he led his team to several victories based upon determination alone. He was not the most skilled player on the team, but he was THE leader, and in the ECAC championship game he had scored what appeared to be the winning goal in the last minute, only to have it called back for an offsides ruling. With only a shrug, he proceeded to score again – this time it counted – in the next 20 seconds. He also had become a teaching assistant in the MBA program while only an undergraduate, demonstrating his salesmanship, optimism, and drive for success.

John was an expert at cajoling and inspiring teammates, faculty members, fellow students, and all others with whom he came in contact. (In this latter example, he achieved a small level of "fame" when his two daughters, Sarah and Emily, competed on the U.S. Figure Skating Teams in sequential Olympic Games, with Sarah winning a gold medal in 2002. All of us who knew John attributed a small portion of their great accomplishments to the examples set by John and their mother Amy, throughout their childhood.)

I have also had the good fortune of being the son-in-law of a very effective leader within the Worcester, Massachusetts area. Paul Patrick Foran served for a great many years as Assistant Superintendent of the Worcester State Hospital, the first facility for the mentally ill in the United States. As Assistant Superintendent, Paul was responsible for all hospital functions except for medical care, which was under the direction of a licensed psychiatrist. Paul also found time to serve his country, both in World War II and subsequently as a General in the Massachusetts National Guard, in which he served for 42 years. In this role, Paul commanded the Emmett Guards, which had been created in 1855 as the "Irish Guard."

A Worcester legend and hero to Paul Foran - General Thomas Foley, had served in the same capacity in World War I, and subsequently became Chief of Police in Worcester. Foley Stadium bears his name in honor, and our mutual friend Jack Foley is the General's grandson. Thomas Foley and Paul Foran shared the leadership traits of extreme diligence, careful attention to detail, an almost obsessive devotion to subordinates, all joined with high levels of compassion, kindness, and warmth. Both were admired and loved by their employees and soldiers under their command. It was always a mantra of Paul Foran's that "a general leads from the front."

I would be remiss if I did not include the above-mentioned Jack Foley as another very effective leader with whom I have worked. Jack serves as the Vice President for Government and Community Relations at Clark and has also found the time and the interest to serve six terms on the Worcester School Committee. He is a long time Board member of the Main South Community Development Corporation, which works on improving this area of Worcester. More recently, he has been elevated to be Chairman of the Board of Trustees of the YMCA of Central Massachusetts and serves as a Trustee of the Greater Worcester Community Foundation. He remains very active with Special Olympics and a host of other agencies serving those with mental disabilities. In each of these areas, he is one of the true leaders of the organization, working diligently to find solutions, and communicating frequently and effectively with the wide range of stakeholders involved with these very different organizations. Jack accomplishes this huge amount of work with good humor and a high level of both energy and empathy for the people with whom he interacts. Every organization in Worcester is looking to include Jack Foley as one of their key leaders.

There are more people with whom I have worked that I find admirable, and from whom I have observed leadership skills and characteristics. But this is a pretty good list of five of the most outstanding leaders from my experience. I have learned from them all, and all have helped shape my expectations for leaders of important organizations.

8. Please describe one or two of your most memorable leadership successes and one or two of your most memorable leadership missteps or mistakes.

Two "successes" of my career in leadership roles both involve Clark University. Following my work at Cornell, I spent about four years at Brandeis University, an organization which was in transition during my time there, and badly needed some leaders to help replace the just retired founding President (and then Chancellor). I had in four years been asked to take on roles as interim Director of Dining Services, Budget Management, and Associate Treasurer, working on investment matters, including with the Investment Committee of the Board of Trustees. I was able to learn a whole lot about university management and leadership and was able to receive strong references from all Vice Presidents, the Dean of Faculty, the President, and the Chair of the Investment Committee, when the Chief Financial Officer position at Clark became open. Despite just turning 30 years of age, I was proud to be so recognized by my leadership colleagues at Brandeis and given the opportunity for that leadership role at Clark.

The second success was more important, and more durable. With a lot of help from a great Board of Trustees and several strong administrators, we were able to "turn around" a struggling organization with recent deficits, an endowment of only $11 million, and a physical plant that badly needed some refurbishing and major new investments. Despite a year or two of struggling to make payroll each week, we were able to stabilize the organization, and start it on its way to being a much more attractive option for potential students, faculty, and staff. We have not had any further operating deficits, and our endowment now stands at $430 million. Our student acceptance rate is down from about 85 percent of all applicants to just over 50 percent. These are of course not the only measures of success, but many of our stakeholders have been very pleased with these and others.

I have of course had many failures of leadership over my career. I have made errors of judgment relative to people, and their potential. I have also erred in not obtaining enough opinions on decisions from various stakeholders. If I had the opportunity to start over, I would consult more widely, and I would have more self confidence in my ability to obtain and filter advice. I think that I would try to laugh and smile more often and be more open with subordinates and others with whom I work. I would certainly try to take criticism less personally.

I also was fortunate in the mid-1990s to have hired a particularly talented and ambitious assistant, who had been a young mother, and accordingly had not yet had an opportunity for any post high school education. I promoted her to a Business Manager role (very good decision!)

and supported her desire to work toward her college degree, which she began in the evening program (also a great decision!). But I then allowed her to leave for WPI (a very bad decision!), where she was hired as Associate Treasurer, continuing an exemplary career path that had her serve as Director of Financing Programs for the Massachusetts Health and Educational Facilities Authority, and stints at two universities larger than Clark (Suffolk and Poly Pomona in California) as Chief Financial Officer and Executive Vice President. Along the way she finished both her bachelor's degree and MBA at Clark, and also received an MPA from Harvard's Kennedy School. I was simply late in identifying the opportunity that giving her a second promotion into the investment area would have provided. This mistake had a happy ending recently when we hired Danielle Manning back to Clark as EVP/CFO, and Treasurer. This mistake went from a leadership low point to a high point in my experience.

9. What advice would you offer to future or current leaders?

My advice to future leaders follows from all the above comments and reflections. First, work very hard, and be especially diligent in working to achieve consensus among stakeholders on the objectives you are seeking to achieve, and the path you are taking to reach the organization's goals. Primarily, take responsibility for the role you have been asked to assume. Be willing to take a lot of managed risks, especially with ambitious people who are eager to chart their own path to a leadership role. I would also encourage leaders to be willing to admit mistakes somewhat earlier than I had done, and to move on with people and programs with more potential.

10. How would you most like to be remembered as a leader?

I would like to be remembered as a person who was able to lead effectively, and to have done so with integrity and good intentions. I hope people will remember me as creative and focused on decisions that were aspirational and long term in nature. My hope is that people will say that

I served my organizations VERY well, with no hesitation and no "buts" in their recounting of my time. I would also hope that the many people with whom I have worked over the years would say that I helped them in their careers, and that they had enjoyed a stronger and more rewarding career in part because of my mentorship and leadership.

Paula Cruz

1. Please tell us about yourself and talk about what has drawn you to take on leadership roles throughout your life.

My dream has always been to become a global health nurse. I am now a global health nurse. I always knew that I wanted to work with patients through education and empower them to engage in their care. My vision is to enhance the health and well-being of the children and families in the community. This vision has been my north star for creating and implementing programs and projects. I think about how I can improve the care I provide to patients and families. My motivating force is the opportunities that I am privileged to have. I believe that every child deserves an equal opportunity for health care and a chance at life. My dream would be to eliminate the health disparities dependent on one's race, community, and socioeconomic background.

Being a first-generation immigrant, I have always felt that I needed to work extra hard in order to achieve success. I grew up seeing my parents working two jobs from 7 AM to 11 PM and still having time to keep up with my siblings and my activities. Working two jobs was not only normal to me, but also expected.

I was born in the Philippines, moved to Saudi Arabia at 2 months old, and migrated to America when I was 8 years old. The beginning of my life was full of travel and adventure with my family. I was privileged to see places in the world that others may never have been able to see. At a young age, I was always curious. I always asked why. As much as my parents wanted me to remain within the status quo, I always seemed to deviate from that.

What drew me to leadership roles? My curiosity and belief in the opportunity for better - every day. My caring nature. My ability to relate to different people. My drive to bring people together to achieve a vision.

2. Please share some of the leadership roles you have held.

To start, I am the eldest of three. Although I was the eldest, I do not think I was ever strict or tough on my two siblings. I believe my parents were already strict enough that my role was to be the person my siblings could go to if they ever needed anything or if they were ever in trouble. I learned how to lead, discuss, argue, and succeed with my siblings. This is my longest leadership role, and every day there is something to learn as we are all so different and similar to each other.

In high school, I was the captain of our volleyball team. This is probably one of the first experiences I had working with a team and working together on a daily basis to achieve a goal - to win our games. I also learned the importance of improving individually as an athlete to best serve the team during games.

In college, I was the Endeavor Program leader. The Endeavor Scholars Program was focused on expanding education opportunities for women and underrepresented minorities. The Endeavor Scholarship rewarded academic merit and leadership capability and provided recipients with a full-cost scholarship for eight semesters. "The Endeavor Scholars Program sought to enroll a diverse group of outstanding students who understood that leadership is not innate, but fostered, believe that women and minorities own a place at the table of change, appreciate that hard work and scholarship are required for success, embrace the idea that students can change the world through service, and who are committed to sharing their skills and knowledge with the wider community and world."[134] This role made me realize the importance of perspective. When I reflect on this experience now, something that resonates with me is how happy I would be to see other's success - to be able to be a part of their journey - to be able to support them through the good times and the tough times - to be able to listen when all they needed was to be heard. I knew then that there really was not much I could do except for providing my peers with support and encouragement.

I use a similar approach now with the team that I work within the Colorectal and Pelvic Malformation Center at Boston Children's Hospital. We are a small multidisciplinary team of around 20 people which is composed of nurses, a social worker, a psychologist, a dietitian, administrative staff, and surgeons. Each member of our team has a different role in providing care to patients within our center. Within our team, we all have varying strengths and weaknesses. In my role, I can support and encourage each member of the team to excel within the scope of their practice while addressing the needs of our patients and families. I continue to use what I learned from being an Endeavor Leader to now leading our team.

3. What is your leadership philosophy?

I believe that fostering positivity, an environment of creativity and innovation, and commitment to providing the highest quality of patient care within the Colorectal and Pelvic Malformation Center, is a priority. To do this, it is important for me to make myself approachable and accessible to the team, with a promise to lead at all times.

My thoughts focus on delivering seamless care to patients from their initial outreach to the time they arrive in Boston. I achieve this by providing collaborative care while working closely with every member of the multidisciplinary team. I recognize each individual's strengths and perspectives to promote a healthy environment for patients to receive care. My words are based on mutual respect and honesty. I encourage my team to perform at the top of their scope of practice. To do so, I am direct with my team when there is something I do not know, and I provide honest feedback when appropriate.

I lead by genuinely listening to the patient's individual needs. I lead by appreciating the strengths and weaknesses of every team member. I lead by making decisions using the input of every member of the team. I am open to feedback and consider different perspectives when making decisions in challenging situations. I am approachable so that every team member is comfortable speaking up when they have any questions or have any doubts regarding the patient's care.

4. Please share the qualities or attributes you believe are important to being an effective leader.

- Care and Compassion
- Honesty (Transparency) and Respect
- Trust and Integrity
- Positive Influence

5. Have your views about leadership changed over the years? If so, how?

Yes, I would say at times I was a micromanager. A part of it comes from expecting and wanting perfection. Over time, I have learned that as humans, we make mistakes and the best way to succeed is to know how to get back up when you are knocked down. I have learned that there is no one answer that is right, but many answers that might work. I have learned to trust other's strengths. I have learned to let go of having to be in control of things I cannot control.

Based on Arianna Huffington's book, *Thrive*, I have learned to reinvent myself, personally and professionally, by prioritizing the balance between rest, play, and work.[135] Huffington emphasizes the importance of rest and sleep. Increasing the amount of time that we rest and sleep can help improve the quality of the work we produce on a day-to-day basis.[136] In relation to leadership, this would lead to being a more effective leader by reducing sleep deprivation which "reduces our emotional intelligence, self-regard, assertiveness, sense of independence, empathy towards others, the quality of interpersonal relationships, positive thinking, and impulse control." Huffington highlights the importance of thriving instead of just surviving. By learning how to thrive, I would not be living by the status quo of today's culture. As nurses and leaders, it is important that we take care of our personal well-being, as this leads to optimal outcomes for the patients we care for.

6. What have been the most enjoyable and least enjoyable parts of being in a leadership role?

The most enjoyable part of being in a leadership role is being able to see a team achieve their goals and at the same time, observe teammates' individual growth. I personally also enjoy being creative as the leader of a team and thinking outside of the box to solve problems or promote change. It is enjoyable to consider each individual's perspectives, which leads to making an impact as a team.

The least enjoyable part of being in a leadership role is disappointing the team because the goal achievement was unsuccessful. Another part that can be difficult is getting buy-in about your vision from the whole team.

7. What leaders have inspired you throughout your life?

- Mom, Ofelia Cruz – passion, hard-working, perspective
- Dad, Mamerto Cruz Jr. - belief in following rules, discipline
- Sister, Shereen Cruz - hard-working, discipline, strength
- Dr. Belinda Dickie – trust and belief in each person's success
- Herminia Shermont - empowering and encouraging growth
- Dr. David Milstone - motivating and believing in every individual's potential

8. Please describe one or two of your most memorable leadership successes and one or two of your most memorable leadership missteps or mistakes.

Most memorable leadership successes

Class of 2014 Dream Scholarship at UMass Dartmouth—The scholarship provides support and empowers a student who has courage to share their dream, along with a plan of action to demonstrate how they will realize their dream. It was an honor to co-lead the $25,000 Dream Scholarship Endowment as a gift to UMass Dartmouth with a team of talented individuals. We continue to help with facilitating the selection of the annual $1,000 scholarship recipient.

Global Surgical Missions to Haiti, Ghana, China—Being able to function as an operating room nurse alongside international health care providers has been an honor and something that I will always be grateful for. I have learned so much from every person with whom I have worked. Most of the surgical missions are not only dedicated to helping patients but also collaboratively working with local surgeons and nurses. It has been an eye-opening experience to be able to exchange knowledge and experience in order to improve patient care and patient outcomes.

Most memorable leadership mistakes

Taking on more than what I could realistically manage - leading to getting sick and needing to take a break. I have a really difficult time saying, "No." I look at every challenge as an opportunity for growth. In the beginning of 2020, when I went to Ghana, I got very sick. It was a combination of a bad cold and fatigue. From that experience, I learned how important it was to listen to our body's needs. I learned the importance of slowing down and appreciating what we have around us. I learned that "There is no rush" to life. This became my new mantra—*There... Is... No...Rush...* It sounds silly but it was very hard for me. I needed to teach myself how to take a break, relax, and recharge. I had to learn the value of rest. With rest, our minds are able to process information better, be more creative and think outside of the box.

9. What advice would you offer to future or current leaders?

- Trust in the process.
- Continue to be curious about everything and how you can make things better for yourself and others.
- Try to learn as much as you can.
- Listen to others' needs and perspectives.
- Pursue every opportunity you can get.
- Hone in on your passion.
- Prioritize rest - to recharge your energy.
- Balance Work, Rest and Play—*There... Is... No... Rush.*

10. How would you most like to be remembered as a leader?

I would prefer to be remembered for sustainable projects and changes I have implemented throughout my life. I would like to be remembered for how I made people feel. I would like to be remembered as someone who genuinely cared about people—someone who genuinely cared for the growth of each individual, and someone who listened.

Joshua Encarnacion

1. Please tell us about yourself and talk about what has drawn you to take on leadership roles throughout your life.

Born into project housing with a loving mother who never let outside circumstances determine the attitude with which she carried herself, I learned through her experiences, and later in life through experiences of my own, the power of visualizing and communicating what's possible, and never giving up on realizing those dreams.

Lucky to have started life the way I did, at a young age I learned to live with gratitude for all I had, while aspiring to solve problems for myself and others. Whenever I could, I learned to share solutions with the people around me who found themselves in situations similar to my own. I was born into a "tough reality," but always had the support of a loving community which taught me the importance of working with people to move through challenges.

Through being coached, investing in therapy, and with a lot of self-study and reflection, I've learned my life has been shaped by the roles that communication, collaboration, and community have played in my survival, upbringing, and whatever "success" I can claim, as someone learning to properly manage the various leadership roles I've taken on over the years.

My mother is a strong, first-generation, Dominican-American woman who never failed to communicate the importance of exploring worlds beyond the ones we found ourselves living in during my adolescence. In me, she inspired curiosity, wonder, and an ever-present state of reverie. The grounding and reality of shared poverty and duress that the project housing communities I was born into and experienced forced us to traverse life in highly interdependent ways, and this is where I find the roots of my sensitivity for the word, the term, and what I've come to adopt as a lifestyle, leadership.

A leader, in my opinion, is someone who can communicate the worth and potential of another individual so clearly that the person can see it in themselves, believe it for themselves, and act on it. To do this, the leader must understand and accept their own worth and potential, so they can move from selfish to selfless motives and drivers, which allow them to use their talents to serve the people around them in an altruistic way.

I am drawn to the responsibility of solving problems and sharing solutions with as many people as possible. This requires constant practice and refinement of my communication and collaboration skills. Assuming a leadership role is the #1 way to accelerate the practice and refinement of these skills. Deciding on the right leadership roles to take on is a matter of understanding the needs of the communities we will serve by doing so. I've made it a hard rule for myself to lead teams, people, and communities that can benefit from my values and principles for navigating life, which makes it easier to be myself as I dedicate time to leadership.

2. Please share some of the leadership roles you have held.

The first leadership role I ever held was as an older brother. "Holding down the fort" figuratively, and sometimes literally (depending on the games you played at home with your sisters, brothers, and cousins), is not easy - so I want to give a big shout out to the eldest sibling in families!

In middle school I became captain of my local baseball team in Springfield, Massachusetts. I was responsible for getting everyone into my mom's van on time, so we were never late for practice! This was followed by becoming the captain of my football team in high school. I never asked to be the captain of the team, but my coaches always recognized my desire to keep the team together and communicate in ways that kept spirits high through the ups and downs of a sports season—I was a go-to for support and direction for my teammates. The best part about these experiences was learning how to handle the responsibility of titles like "captain" and "team leader," which meant keeping everyone together and making sure we all stayed focused on our goals.

In college, I served in a number of different leadership roles. These taught me a lot about who I was as a person, and more so, how I could direct my skills in the service of others. Those roles consisted of Resident Assistant, Orientation Leader, Admissions Ambassador, Student Trustee, and Senior Class President. I came upon most of these roles due to the absence of football in my life after being diagnosed with atrial fibrillation. The sense of community afforded by the "student leadership" positions on campus at the University of Massachusetts Dartmouth really spoke to my need for a sense of belonging. To pay the university back for creating such a personally and professionally healthy atmosphere amongst the groups and with the support of Dr. Milstone, I assumed responsibility for improving the quality of education and student life on campus through my involvement in events and a variety of collaborations with campus administrative leaders. Some of these efforts positively (I believe) influenced decisions made by university Trustees as well.

I was proud to have been on leadership teams that have created events such as the "2014 Dream Gala," which raised funds of $25,000, allowing the class of 2014 to endow an annual $1,000 scholarship for future students seeking to fulfill their dreams. I was fortunate to work alongside another group of leaders to create a Torch Relay from New Bedford to Boston, MA in solidarity with the community rallying from the Boston Marathon Bombing incident. I was also grateful for the time I spent alongside university officials who came together to design and deliver a university-wide strategic plan for bettering the student experience and allocating university funds to impact thousands of futures as the University continues to serve as an economic engine for the South Coast and Massachusetts at large.

Since college, I served in a number of leadership roles which have allowed me to see the world with an international range of perspectives. I have supported teammates as the Head of People Development for Outco

Inc., where I built emotional intelligence learning experiences. I have also supported engineering leaders for Uber Inc. as a technical learning and development program manager, where I built technical-skill development systems. I have further supported department heads as a Talent Learning and Development Partner for Simply Business, where we built the recruiting and training arms of a growing business. Most recently, I served as CEO of Outco Inc. where we grew the organization through the pandemic to increase our capacity to help job-seeking software engineers earn jobs in a fluctuating job market.

Other roles I am proud to mention include serving as leadership coach for Braven in support of youth transitioning from college-to-career and serving as a teacher for the Citizens School to facilitate skill-development programs for middle school students after traditional education hours.

3. What is your leadership philosophy?

My leadership philosophy is pretty simple - grow and help others grow. As leaders, I truly believe it's on us to continue doing the hard work to develop self and social awareness and continuing to practice responsibility and self-control as we develop our abilities to positively influence the world around us, and more importantly, the people in it. As long as we remain committed to lifelong learning and sharing those learnings with the people around us, we will continue to be leaders that inspire folks to continue developing themselves as effective communicators, collaborators, and community advocates. My personal leadership philosophy—grow and help others grow.

4. Please share the qualities or attributes you believe are important to being an effective leader.

- Empathy and the ability to understand (with compassion) how to enable collaboration

- A growth mindset and the skills that invite others to think from the same place in a psychologically safe way

- The ability to accept responsibility for peoples' behaviors and for the well-being of those who trust them, while never giving outside circumstances power/control over what they can accomplish

- An action-oriented attitude and the energy to mobilize the people around them

- Integrity of character - building on the reputation of being someone who does what they said they would do

- A focus on balanced living and the long-term sustainability of mental, emotional, physical, spiritual, financial health

5. Have your views about leadership changed over the years? If so, how?

Yes—very much so. I used to believe leadership was a one-person sport, and that way of thinking placed a lot of pressure on me and made me place a lot of pressure on others in the role(s). Internalizing the exemplary heroism displayed by my mother as she single-handedly pulled our family out of dangerous situations made me think leadership is an act put on by a savior. Not until middle and high school sports did I learn the roles of interdependence and team building in effective leadership, and even though I didn't have that language in those years of my life, I felt a shift in how I viewed leadership responsibilities. In college/early career is when I grew into a more collaborative teammate which shaped my views on leadership and how successful leadership brings focus to ensuring the group you are responsible for is well taken care of so we can accomplish the task at hand, ideally deriving from a unified mission and vision.

6. What have been the most enjoyable and least enjoyable parts of being in a leadership role?

- Most enjoyable:

Bringing others joy when we create a vision together and being able to celebrate together when we accomplish a goal.

- Least enjoyable:

Being misunderstood when I must make a decision that benefits the majority even though it may mean not satisfying a part of the group I serve.

When I make a decision in service of people, and they do not realize the benefit in the moment because they are projecting their pain or unrealistic expectations on me.

Having to accept failure in delivering on promises as part of the process of learning and leadership development. When we miss a target for ourselves, it is hard to recover - when we miss a target for and with others, it's ten times harder to recover because everyone involved will also have to process the disappointment.

7. What leaders have inspired you throughout your life?

- **Rosemary Hernandez,** my mom, for the never-ending love and joy she gives to her family and the people she meets throughout her life

- **Jaisha Encarnacion,** my sister, for her patience and deep understanding of the world around her. She is the complete opposite of me energy-wise, and because of this her presence alone has taught me the importance of balance at all times

- **Mario Encarnacion,** my brother, for his ability to re-energize at a moment's notice and his commitment to showing up after every failure and continuing to live through the harsh realities presented to him, and to us, while accepting his mistakes as lessons for growing as a better human, and as of late, a better father, every single day

- **David Milstone** for his patience, compassion, and genuine care for everyone with whom he comes in contact, as he remains committed to his responsibilities as a servant-leader

- **Ryan Leslie** for his ability to take control and responsibility for his life and for creating art, music, technology, opportunities for the people he wants to help succeed, and in the ways he finds effective, while not having to sell-out to the mainstream to be popular

- **Drake** for his ability to empathize with all cultures and backgrounds to make music

- **Stephen Covey** for his manifesto on principle-centered leadership and his ability to communicate those principles in an effective and impactful way

- **Barack & Michelle Obama** for their reminders of staying true to oneself and one's own vision

- **Brene Brown** for her teachings on the power of vulnerability and exercising the courage to understand and express how we feel

- **Angel Kyodo Williams** for her teachings on living with fearlessness and grace in the face of other's unreasonable judgements and our own insecurities

- **Pema Chodron** for her teachings on living with an open heart and a present mind as we experience life through the lens of gratitude and appreciation

- **Big Sean** for using his platform as an entertainer to educate and uplift people

- **Ozuna** for his commitment to keeping his culture alive through music, storytelling, and celebrations

- …and so many more!

8. Please describe one or two of your most memorable leadership successes and one or two of your most memorable leadership missteps or mistakes.

Successes

One of my most memorable leadership successes has come from committing to supporting my community when beginning my technology career. The tech industry has less than ten percent representation from Black/Brown people. Having recognized this fact early in my career made me acutely aware of my potential, as a tech industry processional of Caribbean descent (Black/Hispanic, Dominican), in being able to share knowledge and make connections with employers who will find value in the talented professionals from the Black/Brown communities in which I grew up. Today, I know many tech professionals who grew up in cities/towns or neighboring communities from my upbringing. There is still a lot of work to do in democratizing access to the tech industry, but if we all work on making one connection at a time, we'll make change through habits that reimagine who can benefit from an ecosystem like the tech industry which boasts access to perhaps the most (physical/financial/political, etc.) resources in the world.

Mistakes

Most of my most memorable leadership mistakes have come from not fully expressing myself in moments when I had something to say but feared speaking up and gave into imposter syndrome. It is very easy to discredit our thoughts and emotions in the presence of others because we believe they are more accomplished or have more sense than we do. Thinking this way is not always wrong, as many people are talented in many ways, but at the end of the day, there is always room for more than one opinion and more than one answer. What we want to do is make sure we do not put ourselves down in the process of lifting others up, even when we are impressed by what they have to say or how they say it. This can be easier said than done, and I have made this mistake many times.

I once worked in a leadership role for an employer that was hiring aggressively for a growing team of ten. I remember fearing to speak up against my boss when we rejected someone for a role with no real basis for doing so. The way the potential candidate was described was "too shy and not really interesting." My training in hiring has taught me that we need to ensure we consider specific and measurable criteria pertaining to a person's ability to do the job so we can avoid making biased decisions that default towards bringing on folks who use their charisma to sell us on their likability but leave us underwhelmed when it comes to delivering the work. In that specific moment when I read the feedback, "too shy and not really interesting," I should have pushed back, but I did not. As a result, the team of ten grew to be skewed in one direction which indicated bias towards my then boss' comfort. I still lament over the moment, but I have learned to speak up in moments when decisions are being made that disrespect your principles, training, or understanding of what is fair or true. It may feel like a risk, but the true risk is being complicit in a decision that is not healthy and then having to live with the discomfort and reality that follows.

9. What advice would you offer to future or current leaders?

All current and future leaders should heavily invest in developing emotional intelligence (EQ/EI). At its core, the art and science of EQ is understanding ourselves enough to be in control of ourselves, and understanding others enough to influence them, while recognizing our motives both positive and negative. Ideally, we should use EQ like a tool to help us be more effective in moving ourselves and others toward positive goals.

Additionally, seek out leadership coaching, therapy, and regularly invest in relationships with friends and family.

10. How would you most like to be remembered as a leader?

I would like to be remembered as a leader who was committed to growing and helping others grow as he journeyed through life in the most grateful way possible.

Jacob Miller

1. Please tell us about yourself and talk about what has drawn you to take on leadership roles throughout your life.

Leadership has always been something I was drawn to, but not in the sense that I think I was born to lead or have an ego about it. My view of leadership has always been and continues to be deeply entwined with concepts of fairness and creating visions of improving the conditions for all. My first real memory of putting leadership in action was in 2004 when I was in the fourth grade. I remember being home and watching the devastation caused by the Indian Ocean tsunami. Seeing people's families, livelihoods and communities stripped away in real time on live television left me feeling that something had to be done.

When I returned to school, I created a loose class council and began working on a fundraiser. We sold bracelets with "Wave of Hope" written on them and raised thousands of dollars to send to the disaster relief organizations. This was the first instance in which I saw the importance of standing up and getting others organized. Leadership is relational, cannot happen in a vacuum, and is a creative art. These elements have always drawn me to trying to find ways to build relationships to creatively try to make others' lives better.

2. Please share some of the leadership roles you have held.

I was a Student Trustee at UMass Dartmouth, the founder of the Student Run Business Association, the Senior Policy Advisor and Community Development Director for State Senator Mark Montigny, a union organizer with the Greater Southeastern Massachusetts Labor Council (MA AFL-CIO), and project coordinator for multiple local community development projects.

3. What is your leadership philosophy?

My leadership philosophy centers around being of use, building and maintaining authentic relationships, and creating visions of fairness and equality of condition. Much of my thinking around leadership is centered in compassion and a deep understanding of an old stoic saying, "What can happen to one, can happen to all."[137] None of us are immune to the challenges the world has for others, thus we should treat ourselves and others compassionately.

Too many leaders see themselves as the answer, but I view myself at best as a sorter and messenger. My view of leadership is much more vocational than the way leadership is discussed in most of the reading I have done. There are requisite skills that leaders tend not to learn because society often ascribes leadership to the loudest, most outspoken person in the room who knows how to say the "right" things. I have never found these folks to be able to do much other than posture.

Another element of my philosophy is a deep commitment to learning and self-analysis. I take the self-analysis too far sometimes though and stifle myself by overthinking every move and rehashing ways I could have approached things differently. There is a line from a song that I often remind myself of, "the tighter the fist, the looser the sand." I always find when I try too hard to control things or put too much pressure on myself, the thing I was after always dissipates.

4. Please share the qualities or attributes you believe are important to being an effective leader.

Caring, caring, and caring. I have seen numerous leaders take on positions because they saw it as an opportunity to better themselves or their resume. It is remarkably easy to tell when someone's heart is not in the thing they are doing. The worst thing is to come across a leader who does not intrinsically care about their role or community. We are all human and can waver, but there should be a baseline of care that we expect from our leaders.

Caring breaks down into several sub-elements. When a leader cares, they often know how to listen, view themselves as a steward striving to leave whatever they are doing better than how they found it, engage in critical self-reflection, and improve themselves to improve others.

5. Have your views about leadership changed over the years? If so, how?

I am going to give the worst answer: yes and no. I feel like I have always had a baseline view about leadership and my approach to it. There have been variations though, especially when I began studying leadership more deeply. I found myself trying out different tactics. Like I mentioned, I view leadership as a vocation. I was looking for different approaches. Some of them integrated into my style and others have fallen away.

One leadership and life view that has definitely changed recently is knowing when to react. So much of leadership is about pace and I have learned that quick reactions do not produce the best results. That does not mean complacency is the answer either. There is a fine balance that must be struck. Often when there is a rush to react to things that do not turn out as planned, more problems are caused.

6. What have been the most enjoyable and least enjoyable parts of being in a leadership role?

The most enjoyable part is the ability to help others. I love seeing people being able to get what they need and know that I was able to tear down the bureaucracy for them. On the flip side, human dynamics are extremely difficult. Being in leadership roles often makes people skeptical of your intentions and building trust can be extremely difficult.

7. What leaders have inspired you throughout your life?

My dad. When I was young, he stood up against the sheriff in a union fight that ended up in a long legal battle. The case made it all the way to the Supreme Court. He and his colleagues won. He worked tirelessly to make that case work. Our dining room table was always covered with papers and the phone seemingly never stopped ringing. He always instilled in me the importance of fighting for fairness and standing up against the powers that be no matter how difficult that can be.

8. Please describe one or two of your most memorable leadership successes and one or two of your most memorable leadership missteps or mistakes.

My most memorable leadership success was after I assisted in passing a state law that expanded health insurance coverage to low-income students. I was able to give a talk about the experience and after the talk a single mother approached with her kids. She told me that the healthcare coverage that she was receiving because of this legislation allowed her to go to school and change the course of her family's trajectory. She is someone that I think about a lot. Interactions like that are the best leadership successes that I could ever ask for.

I make leadership missteps every single day. Communication is an art that I am constantly trying to master. Being able to marshal a project from inception to completion takes acts of diplomacy that are nearly impossible to anticipate. All of my leadership missteps have centered around not knowing what others do not know and the miscommunication that ensues.

9. What advice would you offer to future or current leaders?

Be nice and build solidarity with others because it allows for you to make mistakes that do not create catastrophes. People should want to answer your phone call and get back to you. Leadership is not a monolithic act; it is something that is practiced every day. Do not be afraid to admit that you have been doing it wrong. I find myself realizing that I have been doing so many things wrong over the past couple of years. This does not imply you should be mean to yourself, rather give yourself the space and compassion to explore the negative aspects of your style. It is better to invest that time now.

10. How would you most like to be remembered as a leader?

I would like to be remembered as someone who truly cared and left things better than the way I found them. I think back to Voltaire who famously said, "one must cultivate one's own garden."[138] There is something modest about this statement, yet deeply profound. While I do not have a green thumb, I recognize that gardening takes constant work, adjustment, and care. I would like to be remembered as someone who made the world, even if in small ways, a fairer and nicer place to live with dignity.

CHAPTER VIII

How Can We Change the Leaders
We Have to the Leadership We Need?

As you have read in the preceding chapters, the recruitment, selection, supervision, training, and support for leaders can be strengthened by a paradigm shift from a focus on the leader being the singular point of our attention to the leader's ability to positively influence their teams and constituents. Leaders are given an amazing opportunity and awesome influence. As Peter Parker (Spiderman) reminds us, "With great power comes great responsibility."[139]

Effective leaders often seem like normal, everyday people. They do not have a large "L" on their shirts, but in many ways, they are extraordinary. They help others to think about, reach for, and achieve more than they ever thought possible. We need them, but it is extremely challenging to find them, and once found, to keep them. Why? Many people:

- Believe it is all they can do to bring their own best efforts to their jobs

- Wonder why anyone would want to be responsible for what others do – their accomplishments and failures

- Do not want to have to decide that someone loses their job or doesn't get a raise or promotion

- Don't like to be the focus of attention

- Just want to be part of the group

- Have so much going on in their lives that they simply want to go to work, earn their paycheck, pay their bills, and enjoy their weekends

- Do not believe that the extra pay, the title, and the leadership perks are worth the price leaders pay

Effective leaders:

- Generally, do not take on the role for the higher salary, the title, and the leadership perks

- Understand that their efforts will be in the public spotlight

- Understand that they can lose their jobs if they and their staff do not accomplish what is expected of them

- Often wish their title did not distance them from those they supervise

- Understand that some people resent that the leaders receive higher pay and more perks

- Understand that some people dislike them because they are "different now"

- Are motivated to achieve success

- See potential in others

- Seek to find ways to encourage their team members to give their best

- Devote their time to help their team members be successful

- Treat everyone with whom they are in contact respectfully

- See themselves as not having a choice to be a leader or not – they are driven to be effective leaders

Some leaders take on leadership positions to have power and influence they can exert. Some leaders take on the position because they have good technical skills in their vocation and people tell them they "should run the place." Some leaders take on the position so they can afford to send their children to good colleges. Some leaders take on the position because they have been at their organization the longest. Some leaders take on the position because they did not like the way the previous leader acted. Some leaders take on the position to impress mom and dad, grandma and grandpa, and their friends.

By the nature of their new role, many people consider themselves "leaders." However, having the opportunity to become a leader is incredibly different than having the desire to become an *effective* leader. Many people might say they have "always wanted to be a vice president," but few say they have "always wanted to be an effective vice president." Of course, they want to be effective, but too often, people assume the skills they already have will make them effective – as do the people who place them in those leadership roles.

Some leaders feel a passion to positively impact their organization. Some leaders genuinely want to help their team members grow as professionals. Some leaders are willing to take the blame when things go south and share the victory when their team is successful. Some leaders are willing to honestly self-assess their skills and seek to strengthen them to be more effective and helpful to their organization. Some leaders are willing to take calculated chances to improve their organization. Some leaders do not actively seek the spotlight, but they also do not shy away from it and routinely and generously share it with their team members. These are the "effective leaders."

There are a multitude of leadership positions out there. Most organizations cannot function without identifying a certain number of employees as formal leaders, people in charge, supervisors, management, etc. Management theory tells us that it is optimal to have one leader for every six to eight employees. This is necessary to ensure that employees have someone holding them accountable, supporting their efforts, and encouraging them to reach their potential. The odds of these leaders accomplishing these goals, unfortunately, is not high, as we know from the research done by organizations such as the Pew Foundation and Gallup. Why is this? Simply, we have plenty of leaders, but not enough effective leaders.

An example of what we have compared to what we need is highlighted by television cartoon character Homer Simpson, the paternal head of the *Simpsons* family, which includes his spouse, Marge, and their children, Bart, Lisa, and Maggie. As you likely know, Homer works in a power plant as a safety inspector. The power plant is owned by Montgomery Burns, a less-than lovable, wealthy Springfield influencer. In one episode, Homer is promoted to be a supervisor and is given the mandate to make his employees more productive. To do this, Homer asks the employees, "Are you working hard?" They respond "Yes." Homer then asks, "Can you work any harder?" They indicate that yes, they can do that, so Homer tells them to do so. The result, as one might expect, is that the employees use all the energy they have to increase their productivity, and experience short-term success, but soon thereafter, burn out and collapse.[140] This demonstrates leadership, but not effective leadership.

How do we make such a significant change in the culture of the workplace, which has for far too long taken the easy path to finding and hiring leaders, focused on only the leader to the exclusion of the other team members, and assumed that through some sort of magic, leaders would all be competent without internal and external reflection, assessment, and support for continual development?

The preceding chapters have identified numerous ways to improve the various processes to which this challenge refers. The problem is, like the rest of the challenges in society, that "change" does not come easily. People like their "Same-Ole, Same-Ole" driving habits and change is at odds with the comfort zone of many people. Fortunately, we have a remedy called *Change Theory.*

Anytime one seeks to effect change in an organization or in the world in general, it is helpful to consider the basic tenets of "change theory." Due to the complexities involved in creating change in an organization, there are numerous change theory models. Dr. John Paul Kotter, the Konosuke Matushita Professor of Leadership, Emeritus, at Harvard Business School, and author of *Leading Change,* offers the following eight-step model for effective change:[141]

1. Create sense of urgency
2. Form a guiding coalition
3. Develop an inspired vision for change
4. Convey the new vision
5. Empower others to enact the vision
6. Generate short-term wins
7. Sustain acceleration of the vision
8. Institute permanent change

After reading and considering the previous chapters, I hope that the first step, "Create a sense of urgency," pertaining to changing the current ways we find, develop, and support our leaders, has been established. Sharing data and information from this book with others and raising the main points of concern with which you agree should help to create the impetus for others to also seek to understand these issues and determine that action is needed. We need you to be a beacon.

By creating the impetus for change and engaging others to join your efforts, you would be "Forming a guiding coalition" that is needed to think more about these concerns. "What concerns?" you ask? The concerns that are associated with having only 37 percent of supervisors and past leaders being rated as excellent or good. The concerns that are associated with good employees leaving organizations, businesses, companies, and institutions primarily due to poor leadership. The concerns that are associated with having a large population of women and people of color who are ready and capable of effectively assuming leadership positions, but a society that is accepting these changes at a snail's pace.

I humbly offer the following takeaways in a Top 10 format, made famous by the former host of the television show *Late Night* and the Top 10 guru, David Letterman.[142] To change the current leadership paradigm from "the leaders we have" to the "effective leadership we need":

10. Do not take my word for it. Do not take the studies from the Pew Research Center, Gallop Reports, BetterUp Labs, Career and Marketplace, Business Insider, TurboFuture, Inc. etc. as the only data that exists. Prove to yourself that current leadership is not effective. Review the research, talk to employees or group members, think about the past leaders you have personally experienced. Your information will likely confirm that far less than half of today's leaders fit your definition of "effective."

9. Albert Einstein already told us that the definition of insanity is doing the same thing over and over again and expecting a different result. The status quo is not working, so we need to change the leadership paradigm.

8. Ask what and why. What exactly is not working and why is that the case? Leadership is complex, so look at problems associated with leaders today, as was done in Chapter II, but keep exploring. Implement as many solutions as you have read here and agree with but know there are certainly more.

7. Keep and improve what works well. This is an important step. Too often, when making changes, we inadvertently alter something that was working well. As Burt Lance, director of the Office of Management and Budget under President Jimmy Carter said in 1977, "If it ain't broke, don't fix it."[143]

6. Involve populations that are presently underrepresented in leadership as you move to develop a guiding coalition. Let us not make the same mistake in resolving the problems that helped to create them.

5. Agree on the changes you most want to see, including those mentioned in this book, and list them with clarity in terms of identifying specific actions you plan to take.

4. Seek help from those who can help make the changes occur. Share the vision and expected results.

3. Identify some "low-hanging fruit" (easy wins) at the start of your action planning. Coalition members need to see some success to help them fight through the more challenging components of these changes.

2. Build on the successes. Remind the team and the community of the successful changes and the plans for the next successful changes.

1. Work with all partners to institutionalize each of the changes. Once a change is made, the only way to avert accidental fallback is to put the changes in writing in all the right places.

If more inspiration is needed, think about how much less "road rage" will exist once we have removed all the ineffective leaders and replaced them with effective ones. This is probably a daily reminder for most of us as we see the tailgaters, non-yielders, and the drivers who believe blinkers are optional. Road rage is certainly caused, at least in part, by drivers who do not practice the rules of the road. It may well also be caused by employees spending eight hours a day with ineffective supervisors and leaders who take away their control, treat them poorly, negatively affect their livelihood, and create toxic environments in the workplace. We have much to do, but fortunately, we have great people to do it – starting with you!

I'll bet you are now ready to act but may have a few questions first. Hopefully, this last chapter will cover at least some of those questions (and answers).

CHAPTER IX

20 Questions (and Answers) With the Author

No book can possibly answer all the questions pertaining to leadership, but this book has attempted to address several of the most important questions, including:

- What is the current state of leadership?

- Why are so many of today's leaders ineffective?

- How do you know if a candidate would be a good fit for a leadership role?

- What skills and qualities do leaders need to be effective?

- What hiring techniques need to change for us to hire effective leaders more consistently?

- When is it time for a leader to leave?

- What can we learn from experienced leaders?

- How can we affect the change we wish to see?

This chapter shares a variety of questions that have been raised by leaders, supervisors, employees, student leaders, and wannabe future leaders, as well as my responses to each.

Bonus question:

Who or what the heck is BANO?

BANO stands for "Blinkers Are Not Optional" (the title of this book) and serves as a reminder that effective leaders need to do the work to be successful—it is not optional. At the end of the chapter, I will provide you with an opportunity to connect with me if you have questions related to the goals and concepts of this book or about leadership in general.

In no specific order of importance, here are my answers to 20 leadership-related questions:

1. If someone in a leadership role makes an ethical mistake, can they ever get people to trust them again or should they just hang it up?

It likely depends on what the ethical mistake was. If they got two candy bars from a single pull of the vending machine, not too many people are going to stop following them on Twitter. However, if the leader took money or physically hurt someone, for example, their ability to gain or maintain respect from constituents is likely in jeopardy. The best one can do after violating the trust of their constituency is to be honest. Defending the action or finding someone or something else to blame for its occurrence would not go far toward reestablishing trust, which is critical for a leader. If the leader has a reputation that has been free of unethical actions, some people may be willing to give them a second chance. Of course, it is always best to think the situation through prior to committing the unethical behavior.

2. How can people elect a person who will campaign honestly and do what they said they would do when in public office?

If someone develops a potion for this, they will become quite rich. This is exactly the reason that politicians, as a group, are often mistrusted by the public. For some, it is the norm for a person running for office to promise the moon and in practice, to deliver far less. In fairness, sometimes the politician means well but is unrealistic or unlucky about the roadblocks that may be in the way of the progress they seek.

All things equal, however, since trust is such a major component of gaining one's vote, leaders running for office would do well to be honest, genuine, and realistic in the things they promise, and voting members of the community should ask questions that force the candidate to go beyond naming their goals - they need to also discuss exactly how and when they will be accomplished. As the saying goes, "If it seems too good to be true, it probably is." Once in office, reminding the candidate of their verbal commitments may help, and certainly reminding folks come re-election time of what was promised and what was delivered will go a long way toward not allowing the cycle of misrepresentation to continue.

3. Why does it seem that people are hired for positions based more on their personality than on their skills and ability to do the job?

Since perception is reality, it is hard to dispute this argument. Sometimes from our positions looking in, it certainly appears that extroverted people, for example, have an easier time being hired for jobs that involve a lot of schmoozing. Alternatively, this could be a case of you seeing a candidate in one way and others seeing the same person as having skills you have not seen in them.

An important factor in looking at any position is the job description. If the job needs the candidate to earn people's trust, ask them to tell you of a time that they earned people's trust. Make them convince you that they are a good investment. Having an engaging personality is one thing but requiring the candidate to demonstrate overall competence is vitally important.

Anyone who has read the book, *Quiet* by Susan Cain[144] knows that introverts can be the most effective problem-solvers and can earn trust as well as or better than extroverts – but there seems to be a societal bias towards extroverts in the U.S., in particular, for some yet-to-be-understood reason. Best advice for when you are the candidate is to work to your strengths. Be sure to understand what the employer or constituency needs and explain confidently and creatively how you would plan to meet those expectations.

4. Why do so many people seem to change after they get hired to be in charge?

Here is where Lord Acton's statement, "Power tends to corrupt; absolute power corrupts absolutely"[145] from an earlier chapter may be in play. I assume by your question that you do not mean that the person changes for the better, although that circumstance can also be true. Some people rise to the occasion and find the extra confidence, skill, and attitude they need to be successful, despite some thinking they could not.

In other cases, some people may enjoy the authority that some positions grant, and while they may not have taken the position for that reason (or perhaps they did), they may find that emphasizing their authority over people and decisions makes it easier for them to fulfill their position requirements.

In a college setting, for example, both circumstances happen with more frequency than people may realize. For example, student Resident Assistants (RAs) are hired to work in the residence halls. They are tasked with developing community, helping individuals solve problems, responding to crises, planning programs, handling administrative functions, and interpreting and enforcing college policies. Some RAs surprise themselves at how social, caring, and trustworthy they can be, but unfortunately, it seems each year that a few RAs appreciate the authority given to them to enforce policies a little too much and lose sight of the balance that all leaders need between being approachable and being assertive.

With helpful feedback from a supervisor and/or a constituent, many leaders who fall into the power-hungry model can recalibrate their efforts to approach their positions with greater balance. It's important to remember that leaders are human, too.

5. I am in college and have never held a leadership role but would like to try one someday. How should I get ready so people will give me a chance?

One way to prepare for leadership in college is to watch a current student leader. If you are a member of an organization, you could approach the student leader that holds the president title in private, to let them know of your leadership interest and ask if they would be ok with you asking them a few questions about their leadership style from time to time. By observing them and hearing how they think about leadership, you will be able to see some of the issues you should be prepared to face.

Another way to get ready could be to find a book (or five) on leadership that current leaders recommend. There are thousands of books on Amazon that focus on leadership. Most are written for all types, levels, and ages of leaders. Some books focus on the types of challenges leaders face and others focus on specific skills leaders should develop. Some books read like beach novels and others are more textbook-like, but as the reviews will show, most are well-regarded and can be very helpful.

As most leaders will tell you, though, nothing can prepare you for leadership like doing the job. Expect to make mistakes, own up to them, and learn from them. People will give you a break if they feel your reasons for taking on the leadership role are pure.

6. Why does my community organization only seem to attract so-so candidates for our open positions?

The section in Chapter I on "circular toxicity" describes how an organization can fall into a situation in which good employees leave and only so-so candidates apply to join a group, thus leaving the organization with only mediocre staff and a fairly unproductive environment. Now that you have read the other chapters and have this question, it may help to reread that chapter. Please feel free to reach out if you still have questions in this regard.

Additionally, each of the hiring practices discussed in Chapter V plays a role in changing the strength of the candidates you hire, as well as increasing the odds that the person you hire will demonstrate, in practice, those skills you saw in them during the interviews.

7. I am a college student who was elected to be the president of a student group. I cannot understand why my organization only seems to attract younger students who have never been student leaders. We need some older, experienced students, too.

It could be instructive to have a conversation with the staff members who advise and train student groups at your college. Perhaps they can share some history about your group. Has it always been like this or is this year different for some reason? They may be able to help you connect with last year's president to ask about that group as well. In some groups, it is normal for the newest members to be younger and the older members to be the elected officers. Having the more experienced members teaching the less experienced members is often a model that works well in leadership. As the group leader, however, you should feel free to seek to alter the status quo – that is what a leader does when they identify an area of concern.

8. I know people say that leaders are "made not born," but I know several people that have been leaders since they were playing tee-ball (youth baseball.) How do you explain that?

The current leadership theory that leaders are "made" as opposed to "born" does not intend to say that all people grow into becoming leaders in the same way, and at the same time in their lives. It really argues that effective leaders are generally made up of *traits* that are helpful to their leadership – such as intelligence, energy, curiosity, appreciation of team-work, etc., and learn the *skills* to enhance the strength of their leadership – such as communication skills, conflict resolution, coaching, time management, etc.

Each leadership position calls for different skills. A team captain, which sounds like the people you knew as "tee-ball leaders," may know how to make other people feel included and valued and help them strengthen their confidence. These are young people who likely have had strong role models who demonstrated these skills to them, and they learned to incorporate them with their other skills and traits. Some people are astute observers of what goes on around them. Other people learn by reading or hearing about a skill and putting it into practice when possible.

The change in thinking that leaders are "born" with certain abilities to thinking that leaders are "made" has come about over the years due to seeing that effective leadership is not exclusively connected to traits one is born with, but also a series of skills (like those discussed in Chapter IV) that can be learned and developed.

9. I just took on a leadership/supervisory position at work and was advised to look at my staff's personnel files. Wouldn't that just bias me against my staff? If they thought someone should have been fired, shouldn't they have done that before I arrived?

It would be helpful for you to know if the person recommending that you read the personnel files did so as a message about one or more specific people, or as a recommended practice in general. In most organizations, you can certainly read personnel files without the world needing to know you are doing so. As a supervisor, it is normally within your prerogative to read the personnel files so you can offer feedback as well as know about any type of accommodations or discipline the employee may have received in the past.

Some supervisors prefer to start with a clean slate so those employees who may have been less productive in the past can gain some energy in having a new supervisor to work with. In many cases, even if an employee had trouble in the past, having a new supervisor who is rooting for them to succeed is enough to motivate the employee to perform well. Like the athlete who moves to a new team and suddenly finds their mojo, having a new supervisor can be the same sort of inspiration. That said, however, it is generally a good idea to know what happened in the past. As the section *Lazy Leaders Ignore History at Their Own Peril* argues in Chapter II, there are very few good reasons to ignore history and many good reasons to pay attention to it.

10. When you are hiring for a leadership position, can you say "no" to all the candidates, even if some had the qualifications for the job? I was told that is illegal.

First things first—I recommend that you speak directly with your Human Resources Office, as they hold responsibility for hiring practices and decisions at your organization. In general, however, the answer is "yes."

In fact, it is generally considered much wiser to not just seek to hire the best of the applicant group you see, but to only hire the best *fit* from the applicants whom you believe meet the required skills and experiences pertaining to the job. Hiring the most skilled candidate without paying attention to their possible fit in the organization could well result in their becoming one of the 63 percent of the ineffective leaders discussed in Chapter I. [146]

Effective hiring needs to be both objective and subjective. If you have two candidates that meet the requirement of the job description, great! Now you can be subjective and select the best fit of the two. If none objectively meet the requirements or appear to be good fits for the position, find a temporary solution and open the search for more candidates.

Sometimes you will feel pressured to hire someone quickly and hope you can give them enough support and training to make them effective. That is noble, but unwise. If the person is not "ready" to assume the leadership position now, move on. Maybe they will be ready next time, but for now, you need someone who is deemed ready, knowing that the support and training they will be given will make them even stronger and more effective.

11. My boss always seems to focus on what I do wrong as opposed to what I do well. My annual evaluations make it appear that I am a lousy employee. Should I contact Human Resources?

One way to respond to this challenge is to ask yourself, "How would I want an unhappy staff member to respond if I was their leader?" Most of us would want to have an opportunity to hear a concern about us before the person tells a third party. That said, it is often not easy to share this kind of feedback with your supervisor. As awkward as it may be, however, the person will normally appreciate you bringing the concern directly to them.

Think about how you might best hear this information. A "you-statement" such as, "You only gave me negative feedback" would likely elicit a defensive and negative response from the supervisor. Using an "I-statement" can be more effective. To do this, according to Thomas Gordon, who in the 1960s developed the I-statement technique, you share three things:[147]

1. A brief, non-blaming description of the behavior you find unacceptable

2. Your feelings

3. The tangible and concrete effect of the behavior on you

With these in mind, you could ask to speak in private with your supervisor about the evaluation. An example of the I-statement could be, "Mary, when you only share negative feedback with me, I feel confused and resentful because it makes me think you do not see the positive things I do in my work."

Hopefully, this interaction will produce positive results. It is important to know that if the supervisor's response does not satisfy your concern, the option to consult with Human Resources remains a useful possibility.

12. One of my staff got drunk during their lunch break and had to be escorted out of work last week. He is still not back to work yet. Human Resources has been in contact with the employee and his family. A few of his colleagues have inquired about the health of the employee. Am I allowed to tell them?

This is an issue of confidentiality. As a supervisor, you can certainly contact Human Resources to ask how the organization handles these types of communications. Almost certainly, they will advise that you let your staff know that the organization is involved as is the employee's family. Regarding specifics, unless the employee states that detailed information may be shared with others at the organization, all parties involved need to maintain the confidentiality that the employee deserves, and the law provides.

Often, this will not totally satisfy the colleagues, who are likely concerned for their friend's safety. The organization should not be deciding who gets informed about what, though—that is the right of the employee to decide. Most people will understand.

13. I chair a committee and it seems like pulling teeth to get anyone to talk. I do not want our decisions to come just from me. How do I get people to get comfortable engaging in discussions?

You may be experiencing a piece of what some people call the "Teacher Syndrome." A study was done by Mary Budd Rowe in the 1970s to determine how long a teacher waited after asking a question before they would move on. The average wait time was one and a half seconds![148] This happened, in part, because external thinkers are comfortable responding immediately, but internal thinkers often need time to process the question and contemplate their possible response. In groups of any kind, encouraging members to pause before responding can help the external thinkers be more reflective and give the internal thinkers more time to process their response. In her study, Rowe learned that by simply pausing for three or more seconds, there was a noticeably positive impact on student responses. Adults can also be thought of as external/internal or extroverted/introverted thinkers, so this is one technique to consider trying.

Additionally, by setting up some committee ground rules, expectations of the members can be established that help encourage involvement. For example, one expectation can be to allow each member to have some talking time by not allowing anyone to dominate the airtime. In Robert's Rules of Order,[149] a process that generally guides the functioning of student governance and city/state/federal committees, this requires that all members have the opportunity to speak once before any member is allowed to speak a second time. This tells the members that you want to hear from everyone if possible. Another ground rule can be that members come to each meeting prepared (i.e., having done any reading or advance thinking requested by the chairperson).

To further increase committee member involvement when time allows, you can ask a question, give members time to write their thoughts on paper and share them in groups of three, and then share them with the larger group. This allows everyone to begin to talk in very small groups in case anyone is not a fan of public speaking. When people are asked about their greatest fears in life, guess what is always at the top? No, not death, but public speaking. Even some professionals may be uncomfortable speaking in large groups, so breaking the ice is often helpful in encouraging further sharing.

Another way to get folks talking is to use the process called "brainstorming." In brainstorming, the topic is explained and the members each verbally share their thoughts while the leader writes the shared thoughts and ideas on a whiteboard or something similar. One important rule when brainstorming: tell the group that there are no dumb ideas. As an example, if the topic is to decide on a staff development program to offer, brainstormed ideas may include bowling, an ice cream social, book club, a skill-based series focused on career development, etc. If someone says, "family carnival" while brainstorming, no one should evaluate the idea, even if there is no money available – all ideas are accepted, and no one feels foolish. Later, the group can look at the list of ideas and pick a few to further discuss or vote on, etc. These are effective tools, and there are others, but having an optimistic and supportive leader can also do wonders.

14. At my work, I am what most people call "a newbie." I have heard that a lot of people look for mentors. Should I have one and if so, how do I find one?

Having a mentor can be incredibly helpful, especially when you are in a position that involves many complicated situations and challenges. Some industries are more invested in assigning mentors to employees while others do not do anything in this regard. For those who organically find mentors, they generally find that establishing a mentor-mentee relationship is a combination of luck and privilege. For these people, a mentorship comes naturally – it evolves from a single professional interaction to a situation in which the experienced leader either says or demonstrates a willingness to help the person on an ongoing basis. Like any relationship, a mentor relationship can vary in time spent together. Some mentors, as in the book *Monday Morning Leadership by David Cottrell*,[150] spend structured and consistent time together while others get together to talk when one of them wishes to do so.

If you believe that having an experienced professional (who is not your direct supervisor) would be helpful to your growth and development, ask around. Do any of your close colleagues have this type of relationship with someone? Is there someone at your current place of work or at a previous place that you have great respect for? If so, you might start by posing a general professional question to them and see if they seem interested and willing to share their thoughts with you. It is often obvious by their initial response if they are comfortable with you. If so, continue to ask for their thoughts as you desire – but be careful not to overtax them. Obviously, you want to let them know that you are extremely appreciative of their time and thoughts.

Like any relationship, if you do not have someone in mind but want to develop a mentor relationship, keep your antennas up—there are many great people in the world who have received help in their careers and want to "pay it forward." When you find a great one, you will indeed feel privileged and very fortunate.

15. I received a call from a customer who said one of my male employees was very rude to her. She also told me that another employee was in the area and likely heard the whole interaction. I asked the employee who was in the area about the incident, but he said, "I am not a rat, so I stay out of people's business." I hate to put that employee in a bad situation, but I need to know what happened.

When it is possible to resolve a problem directly at its source, rather than bringing other people into the mix, it is normally best to take that route. By speaking to the employee who was allegedly rude to the customer, you can gain their perspective, and you already have the perspective from the customer. It is important to let your employee know why you are following up on the interaction and what you hope can be an outcome from this conversation. This is where "conflict resolution" skills can be very effective – for you, in trying to resolve a complaint and for your employee, who may have been perceived as rude when they attempted to resolve a customer's problem or concern.

"Rudeness" is one of those things that can be in the eye of the beholder. What is considered rude to one person may be considered "direct communication" to another. At the same time, we know that the customer's *perception* of the communication is their *reality*. Regardless of what was intended, that customer perceived the employee's behavior as something less than acceptable.

If this is not the first time you or someone else has received a report of this employee being rude, you need to determine if the employee is demonstrating a pattern of unacceptable behavior. Does he understand what is expected of him in terms of customer communication? Is there a certain comment or type of customer that causes him to become defensive?

If so, perhaps you can offer tips or another perspective on how employees can maintain what a customer considers acceptable behavior while striving to resolve the customer's problem.

At some point, and independent of your follow-up about the complaint, it would probably be helpful to speak with the employee who witnessed the interaction between the employee and the customer, to address his response about not wanting to be "a rat" and "wanting to stay out of people's business." It would be appropriate to let him know that in a business setting like yours, your goal is to help people be more effective in meeting customers' needs. When a supervisor is asking for information, the expectation is that employees will be honest, and see themselves as an important part of the organizational culture. For the goal of achieving excellent customer service, all people need to bring their strengths and help others to further develop their skills into strengths. In this sense, following up with this employee is like planting a seed for their future communications.

16. I am a supervisor at my organization and several employees asked me if our CEO understands how driving her Porsche to work every day makes people feel when more than half of the employees and all the families that use our center live just above the poverty level?

Sometimes even the best-intentioned leaders have blind spots—we are all human. Whether it involves using words that are considered offensive to some people, or being, as the television show *Seinfeld* identified, a "close-talker," a "low-talker," or a "high-talker" (one who stands too close when talking, speaks too quietly for anyone to hear, or speaks in such a high pitch that a male high-talker is often mistaken for a female on the phone, respectively),[151] many of us do something that drives someone else bonkers. On one hand, when someone raises our consciousness about how we interact or show ourselves, there is a natural inclination to become defensive. Even if it is possible to use an I-statement, as explained in question #11, there is risk involved, so it is recommended that you give much thought in deciding how important it is that you make the CEO aware of this. There is another expression that may apply here. "Is this the hill you are willing to die on?"

If you deem it worthy of your effort, do you know how the CEO handles feedback? If not, is there someone that can answer that question for you, such as a Human Resources director or a Staff Development Coordinator, etc.? If the answer is that the CEO welcomes feedback and is very self-aware, then almost any thoughtful approach can work, and she will likely appreciate the feedback and concern. If the CEO does not respond particularly well to feedback, is there an organization suggestion box or a support office where the concern can be confidentially shared?

While the concern could certainly be well-founded and be something others believe as well, it is important to think about the issue from the other person's point of view. What if the CEO has one car and enjoys having the Porsche because she travels a lot and at this stage of life, she wants to ride in comfort? Will it be worth the effort if the CEO cannot really do much to resolve the issue? Here is where a combination of critical thinking skills and emotional intelligence comes in most handy for leaders.

17. Are there books or videos that can help me become a better leader?

Yes, there are many excellent materials that have been produced to help leaders learn about responding to different situations and developing additional leadership skills. If you do a Google search for books on the topic of leadership, you will see more than 70,000 different leadership books that are sold there at this moment. Each has a description and reader reviews, so you can easily find some that will be suited to your interests.

Additionally, there are professional organizations for most types of jobs that offer materials especially related to the work you do, and many times, they offer seminars on a variety of professional development interests, such as leadership. Your Human Resources Office or your supervisor are likely aware of these and can often recommend some that would best fit what you are looking for.

Depending on how much time and interest you have, there are classes taught at local colleges on leadership, whether they are in business management programs or education, public policy, etc. Again, your Human Resources Office may be able to help with these and in some cases, your organization may even pay for such classes as part of their commitment to your professional development.

18. I really want to try to take on a leadership role, but I absolutely hate public speaking and do not want to freeze up every time I have to address the group. Do all leaders need to be good public speakers?

Good leaders come in all shapes and sizes and leadership positions are as varied as the leaders. Some leadership positions involve extensive public speaking and others involve much less, but it is safe to assume that all leadership positions will involve some amount of public speaking. Even if the first leadership position you take on does not involve much public speaking, it is likely that the next one will. As a result, it is a good idea to see public speaking as an important skill to develop.

As mentioned in Chapter IV, the greatest fear many people have in life is not death, but public speaking. It certainly can be challenging to put yourself out there in front of a group where people can judge you. Most people who have engaged in public speaking will tell you that the more you practice speaking in public, the easier it gets. If no other resources were available, most leaders could learn how to be more effective with public speaking by trying things and noting the audience's reactions, making alterations, and trying them again. We can also learn a lot about effective public speaking by watching other people do this. As you know, there are numerous resources to help you become more skilled (thus more comfortable) with this.

We go to the dentist even though we may not love the sound and smell of the drill or having a bunch of dental tools in our mouths. We go to the doctor even though we may not love having blood drawn or the feel of a cold stethoscope. We bring our cars to be serviced even though we may dread seeing the bill. The point is that we do many things we are not thrilled to do because it leads to something we like, want, or need. If we wish to help people reach their full potential and to be part of our organization's success, we know at some point we may want to be speaking to groups. Even though it is not blatantly obvious that we will go from being a so-so public speaker to becoming a confident and competent one over time, watching other leaders and hearing their stories shows us that it can be done.

Take on the leadership role because you want to make a difference and help others to do the same. This skill, along with most others that you will want to develop, can be learned, and once learned it will make you more confident in your ability to become a more effective leader.

19. A few of my staff members copy me on every email they send out and constantly send me updates regarding what they are working on. There are just too many things going on for me to read all of these. How do I nicely tell them to stop?

To do this effectively, it is important to understand why some of your staff engage in this behavior, and as importantly, why some do not. What differentiates the "carbon copiers" (CCers) from the others?

At the start of any supervisory or leadership relationship, it is helpful to spend time discussing expectations. A supervisor may say they expect the staff to arrive on time for meetings and to meet deadlines unless they have discussed an extension with you in advance. An employee may say that they expect their supervisor to prioritize their emergencies and to help them problem solve through challenging situations. One expectation that should also be discussed pertains to communication. With email often being such an important component of communication between you and your staff, it is helpful to clarify when you, as supervisor, want to be copied on emails sent to other people. Likewise, it is helpful for your staff to know when you do not need or want to be copied, so your inbox can be manageable.

Staff who report to you need to get a sense of the volume of communications you receive in a day and the amount to which you need to respond. They can be helpful in determining how they can keep you informed of significant issues and communications with specific people of interest (to you). Likewise, you must understand their need to keep you informed of their progress on projects or their conflicts so you can be aware of them and be helpful.

Sometimes, this need to overshare can be alleviated using timely one-on-one meetings, where each staff member can provide updates and challenges regarding the goals and projects they are pursuing.

Additionally, it is often helpful to discuss what it may mean to the person they emailed when you were copied. To some people, having a supervisor copied on an email indicates a possible mistrust issue (i.e., they will not act on something unless someone higher up is involved), which leads to supervisors being copied throughout the organization and ultimately to what we affectionately call "email diarrhea." With a bit of reinforcement and alterations over time, both your and your staff's communication needs can be met.

20. I am a supervisor who just started a job in a new organization. I really want my staff to enjoy coming to work every day, but many of them seem to be so negative about the department and division leaders. They see anyone who is not in the union as not being on their side. How can I help heal the wounds that have developed over the years?

Inheriting old wounds as a leader/supervisor can be challenging. Despite you being new to the organization and to your leadership role, many of the employees within your leadership responsibilities are not new and their negative views of past incidents do not fade away just because you are here now. Part of emotional intelligence is having empathy for others' challenges and views of the workplace. An important action to take is to allow time for a frank and honest discussion about the concerns of staff and their and your hopes for the future.

While the first step is naming the problems, the second step is to make sure that a new path is established through your actions and theirs. If the previous leader was not effective with following up on promises, they will be carefully watching to see if you make good on your intention to follow up on their needs in a timely way. If you do this, perhaps their guard can be lowered and their trust of you to keep your word will increase.

It would be wonderful to erase all the negative incidents of the past, but the injuries caused by each disappointment take time to heal. Regarding the injuries for which you have control, you can make a large dent in negative attitudes each time you follow through as promised. This becomes more challenging when there's a situation happening that is not in your control. Those issues may require your willingness to intervene with other supervisors across the organization.

Over time, as the healing occurs, it will be important for you to not allow a "we-they" situation to develop. You may become seen as part of the "we," which means the trust in you is high, but if you allow the staff to view disappointing results as "their" (the organization's) fault, the negativity will remain, albeit with a different target. Negativity can be relieved when trust is developed. Communication helps develop better understanding, particularly when employees have a voice in improving situations they perceive to be unhealthy for the organization. It is a sizable challenge, but when you begin to see folks smiling as they arrive to work, your extra efforts will most certainly feel worth the cost.

AUTHOR'S NOTE

As a thank you for reading this book and to support your future role of being "the leadership we need" and helping others to do so as well, I welcome the chance to connect with you to discuss leadership challenges you are currently experiencing or ones you experience in the future.

Please feel free to reach out at BANOquestions@gmail.com. I would be honored to engage in discussion and/or offer my thoughts on any leadership questions you choose to submit.

Best wishes for your successful and effective leadership.

ACKNOWLEDGEMENTS

Writing a book on any topic is rarely an individual effort and this book is certainly no exception. Seeing the decline in leadership effectiveness up close and personal, and then spending the past two and a half years researching and putting a myriad of thoughts on paper, there were many times that I thought an end would never be in sight. I owe a large debt of thanks to many people for pushing and pulling me, challenging and supporting me, listening to me, allowing me to listen to them, demonstrating that there is a better way through leadership, and contributing their thoughts, ideas, and expertise to this effort.

I would like to give special thanks to my family for their support and patience. I also thanked them 15 years ago after I completed my doctoral dissertation with their help, but this time was different. My daughter, Alexandra, was an amazing editor of my work and told me honestly when it was too verbose, sounded like a very old person wrote it (I am old!), and that I needed to get rid of most of the 76 exclamation marks. She really was exceptional! (Exclamation mark intended.) My son, Matthew, helped me to keep this task in perspective by making me laugh out loud on a daily basis and my saint-like spouse, Sherri, was once again a ray of sunshine for me when I felt in the dark. My mother passed away during this process. She was the incredible reader in the family and pushed me to get my thoughts onto paper so others might find value from my experiences. My dad is approaching the century mark and has always been a great role model for persisting through challenges. During this process, every time we talked, he asked me when he could get a copy of the book, and he was never satisfied with my "soon, Dad" response.

I want to acknowledge a group of very special individuals who have dedicated themselves to being the most ethical and effective leaders my world has ever known, and who, in their own unique and powerful ways, have influenced me to appreciate the importance and influence of effective leadership: Jeff Augustine, Jim Collins, Dr. Susan Costa, Paula Cruz, Joshua Encarnacion, Dr. Fran Hoffman, Dr. Sandra Kanter, Dr. Anita Miller, Jacob Miller, Mike Morrill, Sherri Nickel-Milstone, Dr. Mona Olds, Joe O'Neill, and Dr. Marcie Williams. An extra special thank you to four of these people: Jim Collins, Joshua Encarnacion, Paula Cruz, and Jacob Miller for contributing their thoughts to make Chapter VII a reality.

I appreciate all the wonderful individuals who took time to respond to my Facebook/LinkedIn survey requests to help me better understand the climate of current leadership and the need for this book.

I thank Dr. Linda Kent Davis for being an "early reader" who offered wonderful suggestions, Dr. Eugene Kogan for encouraging me to go a step further than I would normally have gone, Elan Turcotte-Shamski and Chris Laib for helping me retrieve critical data, and Matthew LeBlanc and the Marketing department at the University of Massachusetts Dartmouth for granting me use of the author photo.

In my professional life, I have been able to practice and study leadership supported by four amazing assistants: Marie Samuelson, Lisa Mills, Monica Jenkins, and Ann Valentino. Due to their commitment to those we served and served with, we were able to think deeply about how the leadership in our organizations worked and did not work. I can never thank them enough.

I have been extremely fortunate to work with and learn from so many professionals who have influenced my leadership views and practice during my career and in my personal life. No professors had a more profound impact on my learning about leadership than Dr. Jay Dee and

Dr. Sandra Kanter, and I hope they know that. I want to also acknowledge some of the numerous colleagues who served as leadership role models to me – some supervised me, some I supervised, some were peers, and all are amazing: Lucinda Poudrier-Aaronson, Mary Beckwith, Court Booth, Tina Bruen, Wendi Chaka, Dr. Carolyn Cohen, Heidi Rosenthal Cox, Paul Cox, Dr. Betsy Cracco, Dr. Linda Kent Davis, NP Sheila Dorgan, Dr. Tony Garro, Dr. Anne Hopkins Gross, Beth-Anne Guthrie, Dr. Royal Hartigan, Derek Heim, Carole Johnson, Dr. Mohammad Karim, Chris Laib, Dr. Richard Panofsky, Larry Robinson, Dr. Robin Robinson, Shelly Metivier Scott, Dr. Jamie Washington, Keith Wilder, and Nicole Williams. Again, some may not realize how much I learned from them, which demonstrates a pattern I need to fix.

Teaching in a leadership classroom and working as a student affairs administrator for several decades afforded me the privilege of getting to witness extraordinary faculty, staff, and student leadership. Some of my best teachers were student government officers, graduate student senate officers, faculty senate presidents, class officers, resident assistants, orientation leaders, club and organization heads, student-athletes, camp counselors, interns, and community educators and organizers. Some were single parents and some were first-generation students. Some found their voices through leadership and others used theirs to improve the lives of others. Each of these people filled me with awe and continue to do so.

During my fascination with leadership that began many years ago, numerous extraordinary student leaders and professional colleagues were integral to my learning: Swarna Basu, Craig Berquist, Alyse Bukowski, Chris Card, Bhairav Desai, Susan Dubord, Rick Gropper, Donna Santacroce Henderson, Fluney Hutchinson, Drago Kassabov, Jasmine Kaur, Lydia Tai Kim, Jack Foley, Mark Frank, Steve Goulet, Julie O'Hara, Mark O'Hara, Steven Ostendorf, Rachel Nenner Payton, Marcus Poulin, Nancy Raymond, and Markie Smith. They developed my blueprints from which future leaders would be measured.

Contrary to what I recommended in Chapter II about naming names, I need to mention some other amazing student leaders who demonstrated their hearts and impact over the past 15 years, ending up forever situated in the "Donald C. Howard Leadership Corner" as Pillars of their Community, Leadership, and Unsung Hero award recipients: Carlos Aguilera, Collin Allen, Michael S. Andrade II, Nicole Arruda, George Henry Aulson IV, Lance Bard, George Barnes, Genesis Barrlentos, Brandi Bass, Charlens Beneche, Johanna (Hobin) Bielawski, Phillip Blais, Jacqueline Boardman, Amy Boateng, Sephora Borges, Desiree Bradford, Barret Bradley, Kelsey Briggs, Allison Browning, Angela Cadet, Edward Callahan, Justin Carleton, Jayashree Chakravarty, Kharlita Chambers-Walker, Cassandra Charles, Retha Charette, Ngo Sze Chen, Matthew Cicero, Samantha Coffin, Alix Coletta, Jaime Conlon, Zachary Connolly, Veronica Cooley, Jesse Correia, Joseph Costa, Jack Crowell, Jennifer Crowley, Paula Cruz, Maurice Cyr, Erin Dacey, Deborah Dele-Oni, Jeremy Dias, Christopher Dinan, Christopher Donovan, Deborah Dorcelus, Donald Dow, Laura (King) Dunham, Joshua Encarnacion, Charlemya Erasme, Laodecia Fevrier, Jacqulyn (Sardina) Fitzpatrick, David Garth, A.G. Garthaus, Nicole Gelinas, Anthony Geller, Stephanie Gibson, Zachary Grant, Mikayla Harris, Rola Hassoun, Jacob Hibbert, Matthew Higgins, Felishia Holmes, Austin Hoyt, Matthew Hoyt, Marven Rhode-Hyppolite, Kerri Ibbitson, Eric James, Imad Jbara, Myriam Jeannis, Eve Kuzmech, Connor Joyce, Heather (Fatcheric) Joyce, Sophal Kea, Jona Koka, Anna-Rae LeClaire, Hannah LaPlante, Chris LaPorte, Brandon Lozeau, Stephanie Luz, Duncan MacLeod, Amanda Magalhaes, Hamza Malik, Ashlee Mastrangelo, Kristi Matsumoto, Trevor Mattos, Lamar McClinton, Christopher McCrimmons, Daniel McSweeney, Sigute Meilus, Joey S. Mello IV, Melissa Mello, Guerline Menard, Todd Migliacci, Jacob Miller, Stacey Miner, Andrea Moore, Colin Murphy, Joseph Murphy, Courtney Nunes, Callie Nunez, Zachary O'Brien, Oyindamola Ogunjobi, Barbara Okafor, Emike Okhipo, Malcolm Pace II, Kendra Pereira, Ausubel Pichardo, Gabriella Pires, Nicholas Prizio, Mark Realbuto, Samantha Reid, Sophia Reppucci, Brandon Roberts, Albert Roberson, Elizabeth (Janson)

Rollins, Courtney Roy, Elaine Sanchez, Kebeh Sando, Kathryn Scanlon, Peter Schock, Natasha Shiku, Danielle St. Pierre, Nicholas Prizio, David Santilli, Stephen Small, Sade Smith, Schmidt St. Fleur, Danielle St. Pierre, Jason Strojny, Mabel Tejada, Hubert Thevenin, Jr., Michael Thomas, Brian Towne, Stavroula (Sheila) Tsiakalos, Adam Turner, Lauren Underwood, Kimberly Urena, Brendon Valencia, Tyler Varda, Tayla Vincent, Ronald Voltz, Anna Lisa Vust, Moriah Wiggins, Katey Wright.

Additionally, the following student leaders demonstrated the kind of leadership they may believe was unnoticed, but I can assure them it was not: Fatima Alvarez, Kelsey Briggs, Jayashree Chakravarty, Kevin Delaney, Ann DeMattia, Rafael Glod, Remynelle Espinola Horton, Eric Leonard, Caitlyn Moakley, Francis Ndicu, Jared Nickerson, Ashley Nunez, Thomas Oakley, Sapna Jawid Piracha, Silavong Phimmasone, Ann-Melissa Pongnon, Matt Quincy, Deana Sanford, Katy Shoemaker, Joy Southworth, and A.J. Vincelli.

These leaders, past and present, young and less young, have always given me great hope for the future of our institutions, country, and our world. A great many have become mentors to thousands of young, impressionable leaders – and continue to do so day after day. The common thread that courses through every one of these leaders is humility. All who have crossed their paths are certainly better for those experiences.

BIBLIOGRAPHY

Bennis, Warren. *On Becoming a Leader: The Leadership Classic.* Perseus Books, 2003.

Cabral, Amber. *Allies and Advocates: Creating an Inclusive and Equitable Culture.* Wiley, 2020.

Cain, Susan. *Quiet: The Power of Introverts in a World That Can't Stop Talking.* Crown, 2013.

Carnegie, Dale. *The Quick and Easy Way to Effective Speaking: Modern Techniques For Dynamic Communication.* Pocket Books, 1990.

Collins, Jim. *Good to Great: Why Some Companies Make the Leap...and Others Don't.* Harper Business, 2001.

Cottrell, David. *Monday Morning Leadership.* Cornerstone Leadership Institute, 2002.

Esposito, Janet E. *In the Spotlight: Overcome Your Fear of Public Speaking and Performing.* Self-published, 2005.

Fisher, Roger, and Ury, William. *Getting to Yes: Negotiating Agreement Without Giving In.* Houghton Mifflin, 1992.

Fuller, Pamela, Murphy, Mark, and Chow, Anne. *The Leader's Guide to Unconscious Bias: How to Reframe Bias, Cultivate Connection, and Create High Performing Teams.* Simon & Schuster, 2020.

Goleman, Daniel. *Emotional Intelligence: Why It Can Matter More Than I.Q.* Random House Publishing Group, 2005.

Goleman, Daniel. *Working with Emotional Intelligence.* Bantam, 2000.

Goodwin, Doris Kearns. *Leadership in Turbulent Times.* Simon & Schuster, 2019.

Harts, Minda. *The Memo: What Women of Color Need to Know to Secure a Seat at the Table.* Seal Press, 2019.

Huffington, Arianna. *Thrive: The Third Metric to Redefining Success and Creating a Happier Life.* W. H. Allen, 2014.

Huffington, Arianna. *Thrive: The Third Metric to Redefining Success and Creating a Life of Well-Being, Wisdom, and Wonder.* New York, US: Harmony, 2015.

Iacocca, Lee. *Where Have All the Leaders Gone?* Scribner, 2008.

Kotter, John P. *Leading Change.* Harvard Business Review, 2012.

Kouzes, John and Posner, Barry. *The Leadership Challenge: How to Make Extraordinary Things Happen in Organizations.* San Francisco: Jossey-Bass, 2017.

Laskowski, Lenny. *10 Days to More Confident Public Speaking: Say Goodbye to Stage Fright Forever!* Grand Central Publishing, 2001.

Maccoby, Michael. *The Productive Narcissist: The Promise and Peril of Visionary Leadership.* New York: Broadway Books, 2003.

Banaji, Mahzarin R. and Greenwald, Anthony G. *Blind Spot: Hidden Biases of Good People.* Bantam, 2016.

Maxwell, John C. *The 21 Irrefutable Laws of Leadership: Follow Them and People Will Follow You.* Nelson Business, 2007.

Maxwell, John. *Developing the Leaders Around You: How to Help Others Reach Their Full Potential.* Nelson Business, 2005.

Northouse, Peter G., *Leadership: Theory and Practice.* 4th ed. Sage Publications, Inc., 2006.

Northouse, Peter G., *Leadership: Theory and Practice.* 3rd ed. Thousand Oaks, CA: Sage, 2004.

Pandya, Mukul and Shell, Robbie. *Lasting Leadership: What You Can Learn From the Top 25 Business People of Our Times.* Warton School Publishing, 2004.

Reynolds, Garr, *Presentation Zen: Simple Ideas on Presentation Design and Delivery.* New Riders, 2019.

Thomas Peters, J. and Waterman, Robert H. *In Search of Excellence: Lessons from America's Best-Run Companies.* New York: HarperTrade, 1982.

Sandberg, Sheryl. *Lean In: Women, Work, and the Will to Lead.* Knoff, 2013.

Ury, William. *Getting Past No: Negotiating in Difficult Situations.* Bantam, 1993.

Useem, Michael. *The Leadership Moment: Nine True Stories of Triumph and Disaster and Their Lessons for Us All.* Crown Business, 1998.

Walton, David. *Introducing Emotional Intelligence: A Practical Guide.* MJF Books, 2012.

Welch, Jack and Byrne, John A. *Straight from the Gut.* Grand Central Publishing, 2003.

Welch, Jack and Welch, Suzy. *Winning.* HarperCollins, 2005.

Woodward, Bob. *Rage.* Simon Schuster, 2020.

NOTES

Names and identifying details have been altered throughout the book's "real-life examples" to protect the anonymity of individuals and organizations.

INTRODUCTION

1 "Americans' Views of Government: Low Trust, but Some Positive Performance Ratings," *Pew Research Center*, September 14, 2020, https://www.pewresearch. org/politics/2020/09/14/americans-views-of-government-low-trust-but-some-positive-performance-ratings/.

2 Lee Iacocca, *Where Have All the Leaders Gone?* (Scribner, 2008).

3 "Operation Iraqi Freedom U.S. Casualty Status," *U.S. Department of Defense*, September 17, 2019, https://www.defense.gov/Newsroom/Casualty-Status/%EF%BB%BF/.

4 Tina Susman,"Civilian Deaths May Top 1 Million, Poll Data Indicate," *Los Angeles Times*, September 14, 2007, https://www.latimes.com/archives/la-xpm-2007-sep-14-fg-iraq14-story. html.

5 Report studied 2.5 million manager-led teams in 195 countries and included 27 million employees. Concluded, "Manager talent is rare, and organizations have a hard time finding it (7)." "Only one in ten have the talent to manage a team of people" (3) and organizations should "grow, not promote" leaders (9). Jim Clifton, "State of the American Manager: Analytics and Advice for Leaders," *Gallup* 2017, https://www.gallup.com/services/182138/state-american-manager.aspx.

CHAPTER I: THE CURRENT STATE OF LEADERSHIP

6 Over 38,400 people asked the primary reason they sought employment outside their current organization - 25 percent responded, "I want higher pay." "Why They Quit You: Top Reasons an Employee Leaves," *Payscale*, November 2017- January 2019, https://www.globenewswire.com/news-release/2019/05/14/1823096/0/en/PayScale-Research-Shows-the-1-Reason-Employees-Quit-is-Pursuit-of-Higher-Pay-but-Money-Alone-May-Not-be-Enough-to-Attract-Talent.html.

7 "It is not enough to simply label a manager as 'bad' or 'good.' Organizations need to understand what managers are doing in the workplace to create or destroy engagement." The study involved 7,272 U.S. adults. Jim Harter and Amy Adkins, "Employees

Want a Lot More from Their Managers," *Gallup Business Journal: Workplace*, April 8, 2017, https://www.gallup.com/workplace/236570/employees-lot-managers.aspx.

8 Survey of 1,000 managers and leaders. "Frontline Leader Project," *DDI*, December 9, 2019, https://www.prnewswire.com/news-releases/new-ddi-research-57-percent-of-employees-quit-because-of-their-boss-300971506.html.

9 Poll sent to approximately 500 *Facebook* and 1500 *LinkedIn* associates. Asked respondents to rate current and past supervisors as either 1) excellent/good, 2) fair/between good and not-good, or 3) not-good/poor. From March 13-30, 2021, 135 respondents rated 1412 supervisors and senior leaders as: excellent/good – 523 (37 percent), fair/between good and not-good – 569 (40 percent), and not-good/poor – 320 (23 percent).

10 Amazon: leadership books, https://www. amazon. com/s?k=leaderships+-books&gclid=EAIaIQobChMI4-be2ZPF8QIVh5WzCh0vkAm_EAAYAiAAEgIs-q_D_BwE&hvadid=323064213744&hvdev=c&hvlocphy=9002161&hvnetw=s&hv qmt=b&hvrand=17205292941325830144&hvtargid=kwd-351829086127&hydad-cr=24378_11048775&tag=googhydr-20&ref=pd_sl_7rc894f1jg_b.

11 The three-second rule applies, which tells drivers to "pick an object in front of you, like a signpost or tree. When the vehicle in front of you reaches the object, count out one one-thousand, two one-thousand, three one-thousand. If you reach the object before you count to three, you are too close. Slow down until you've put enough distance between you and the other vehicle." Retrieved July 2, 2021. Massachusetts RMV Driver's Manual, *Mass. DMV*, 70-71, https://dmv-permit-test.com/massachusetts/drivers-handbook.

12 "Employee Job Satisfaction and Engagement : The Doors of Opportunity are Open," *SHRM*, April 24, 2017, https://www.shrm.org/hr-today/trends-and-forecasting/research-and-surveys/pages/2017-job-satisfaction-and-engagement-doors-of-opportunity-are-open. aspx.

13 Oleg Vishnepolsky, *LinkedIn*, June 4, 2018, https://www.linkedin.com/pulse/train-people-well-enough-so-can-leave-treat-them-dont-vishnepolsky.

14 Saturday Night Live - The Whiners were a married couple played by Robin Duke (Wendy) and Joe Piscopo (Doug). The couple often mentioned that they had diverticulitis, usually whining this in unison. Retrieved July 2, 2021, https://snl.fandom.com/wiki/The_Whiners.

15 "More than Half of Employees Have Worked for a Micromanager," *CISION PR Newswire*, July 1, 2014, https://www.prnewswire.com/news-releases/survey-more-than-half-of-employees-have-worked-for-a-micromanager-265359491.html.

16 Sean Achor et al., "9 Out of 10 People are Willing to Earn Less Money to Do More Meaningful Work," *Harvard Business Review*, November 6, 2018, https://hbr.org/2018/11/9-out-of-10-people-are-willing-to-earn-less-money-to-do-more-meaningful- work.

17 Warren Bennis quote. Retrieved July 2, 2021, https://www.brainyquote.com/quotes/warren_bennis_121713.

18 Margaret Thatcher quote. Retrieved July 2, 2021, https://www.goodreads.com/quotes/401090-don-t-follow-the-crowd-let-the-crowd-follow-you.

19 Peter G. Northouse, *Leadership: Theory and Practice* (Thousand Oaks, California: Sage, 2004), 3.

20 Kouzes and Posner quote. Retrieved July 2, 2021, https://grace4success.com/wp-content/uploads/2019/08/Drafting-a-Personal-Definition-of-Leadership. pdf.

21 Maxwell quote. Matt Rocco, *LinkedIn*, October 28, 2019, https://www.linkedin.com/pulse/leadership-influence-nothing-more-less-matt-rocco?articleId=6594567871295217664.

22 Tonya Love, "3 Tips for Being a Truly Great Leader," *Fortune*, November 16, 2016, https://fortune.com/2016/11/16/xerox-key-to-great-leadership/.

23 Sandberg quote. Retrieved July 2, 2021, https://www.goo dreads.com/quotes/785876-leadership-is- about-making-others-better-as-a-result-of.

24 Shep Hyken, "Treat Employees Like They ARE the Customer," *Social Media Today*, January 19, 2011, https://www.socialmediatoday.com/content/treat-employees-they-are-customer.

CHAPTER: II: WHY ARE SO MANY OF TODAY'S LEADERS INEFFECTIVE?

25 "Dr. Sheldon Cooper BS, MS, MA, PhD, and ScD," The Big Bang Theory Fansite," *CBS*, Producers Chuck Lorre and Bill Prady. Retrieved July 2, 2021, https://the-big-bang-theory.com/characters.Sheldon/.

26 Peter G. Northouse, *Leadership: Theory and Practice* (Sage Publications, Inc., 2006), 111.

27 Chester Buckenmaier III, "The More You Know About the Past, the Better You Are for the Future," *U.S. Medicine*, June 8, 2020, https://www.usmedicine.com/editor-in-chief/the-more-you-know-about-the-past-the-better-prepared-you-are-for-the-future/.

28 Dallon Christensen, *WhiteBoard Business Partners*. Retrieved July 2, 2021, http://www.whiteboardbusiness.com/those-who-fail-to-learn-from-history-are-doomed-to-repeat-it-sir-winston-churchill/.

29 Jim Collins, *Good to Great: Why Some Companies Make the Leap…and Others Don't* (Harper Business, 2001).

30 Thomas J. Peters. and Robert H. Waterman, *In Search of Excellence: Lessons from America's Best-Run Companies (New York:* HarperTrade, 1982).

31 Michael Useem, *The Leadership Moment: Nine True Stories of Triumph and Disaster and Their Lessons for Us All* (Crown Business, 1998).

32 Mukul Pandya and Robbie Shell, *Lasting Leadership: What You Can Learn From the Top 25 Business People of Our Times* (Warton School Publishing, 2004).

33 Bill Latshaw and Matthew Shannon, "Leadership Development Solutions: Market Primer," *Deloitte Development LLC.*, 2020, https://www2.deloitte.com/content/dam/Deloitte/us/Documents/human-capital/us-leadership-development-solutions-market-primer. pdf.

34 Rasmus Hougaard, "The Real Crisis in Leadership," *Forbes*, September 9, 2018, https://www.forbes.com/sites/rasmushougaard/2018/09/09/the-real-crisis-in-leadership/?sh=750a4c603ee4.

35 Tori Fica, "What People Really Want from Onboarding," *BambooHR*, October 3, 2018, https://www.bamboohr.com/blog/onboarding-infographic/.

36 Saul McLeod, "Maslow's Hierarchy of Needs," *Simply Psychology*, December 29, 2020: https://www.simplypsychology.org/maslow.html.

37 John F. Kennedy, "Executive Order 10925 – Establishing the President's Committee on Equal Employment Opportunity," *The American Presidency Project*, March 6, 1961, https://www.presidency.ucsb.edu/documents/executive-order-10925-establishing-the-presidents-committee-equal-employment-opportunity.

38 Kathleen Martinez, "More History of Affirmative Action Policies From the 1960s, Executive Order 11246," *American Association for Access, Equity , and Diversity (AAAED)*, 1965, 1967, 1971, retrieved July 2, 2021, https://www.aaaed.org/aaaed/History_of_Affirmative_Action. asp.

39 David Ortiz played 1997-2016. Career statistics - 541 home runs, 1768 RBIs., *Major League Baseball*. Retrieved July 2, 2021, https://www.mlb.com/player/david-ortiz-120074.

40 "The Buck Stops Here," Harry S. Truman National Archives Library and Museum. Retrieved July 2, 2021, https://www.trumanlibrary.gov/education/trivia/buck-stops-here-sign.

41 "Board Leadership and Governance Best Practices," *YMCA of the USA*, retrieved July 2, 2021, http://www.csaymca.org/uploads/3/4/6/6/3466162/board-leadership-governance-best-practices. pdf.

42 Michael Maccoby, "Narcissistic Leaders: The Incredible Pros, the Inevitable Cons," *Harvard Business Review*, January 2004, 2, https://hbr.org/2004/01/narcissistic-leaders-the-incredible-pros-the-inevitable-cons.

43 "What is Narcissistic Leadership," *HRZone*, retrieved July 2, 2021, https://www.hrzone.com/hr-glossary/what-is-narcissistic-leadership.

44 Maccoby, "Narcissistic Leaders," 3, https://hbr.org/2004/01/narcissistic-leaders-the-incredible-pros-the-inevitable-cons.

45 Steve Heroux, "Narcissism Isn't a Form of Leadership," *Victory Selling*, May 1, 2020. https://www.victoryselling.com/424-2/.

46 Maccoby, "Narcissistic Leaders," 4, https://hbr.org/2004/01/narcissistic-leaders-the-incredible-pros-the-inevitable-cons.

47 David Remnick, "Trump and the Enemies of the People," *The New Yorker: Daily Com-*

ment, August 15, 2018, https://www.newyorker.com/news/daily-comment/trump-and-the-enemies-of-the-people.

48 "Power and Authority," *Acton Institute: Lord Acton Quote Archive*, retrieved July 2, 2021, https://www.acton.org/research/lord-acton-quote-archive.

49 Aaric Hale, "20 Worst Leaders in History," *ListSigma*, updated December 7, 2020, https://listsigma.com/worst-leaders-in-history/.

50 "10 Unethical Famous Examples," *K. M. Trust and Partners*. Retrieved July 2, 2021, https://www.kmtrust.com/10-unethical-famous-examples/.

51 Dakin Andone and Ray Sanchez, "Jerry Sandusky Resentenced to Same Prison Term," *CNN*, November 22, 2019, https://www.cnn.com/2019/11/22/us/jerry-sandusky-sentencing/index. html.

52 Taylor Romine, "Michigan Attorney General Closes Investigation into Larry Nassar's Abuses After Saying University Was Unhelpful," *CNN*, March 26, 2021, https://edition.cnn.com/2021/03/26/us/michigan-nassar-university-investigation-closed/index. html.

53 Stephanie Pagones, "Who is College Admissions Scandal Mastermind William 'Rick' Singer?" *FOX Business,* June 1, 2020, https://www.foxbusiness.com/lifestyle/who-is-college-admissions-scandal-mastermind-william-rick-singer.

54 Sara M. Moniuszko and Cara Kelly, "Harvey Weinstein Scandal: A Complete List of the 87 Accusers," *USA Today*, June 1, 2018, https://www.usatoday.com/story/life/people/2017/10/27/weinstein-scandal-complete-list-accusers/804663001/.

55 Steve Kovach, "Apple Apologizes for Slowing Down iPhones with Older Batteries, *Insider*, December 28, 2017, https://www. businessinsider. com/apple-apologizes-for-iphone-slowdowns-2017-12.

56 Shefali Luthra, "Pharma Bro Shkreli is in Prison, but Daraprim's Price is Still High." *Kaiser Health News (KHN)*, 2018, https://khn.org/news/for-shame-pharma-bro-shkreli-is-in-prison-but-daraprims-price-is-still-high/.

57 Arthur Schwartz, "The 5 Most Common Unethical Behaviors in the Workplace," *Career and Workplace*, January 26, 2015, https://www.bizjournals.com/philadelphia/blog/guest-comment/2015/01/most-common-unethical-behaviors-in-the.html.

58 Kim Parker, Juliana Menasce Horowitz, and Molly Rohal, "Women and Leadership: Public Says Women are Equally Qualified, but Barriers Persist," *Pew Research Center*. Retrieved July 2, 2021, https://www.pewresearch.org/social-trends/2015/01/14/women-and-leadership/.

59 "Whistleblower Protection Act: An Overview," *Findlaw*, revised March 16, 2017, https://www.findlaw.com/employment/whistleblowers/whistleblower-protection-act-an-overview.html.

60 Glenn Kessler et al., "Trump's False or Misleading Claims Total 30,573 Over 4 Years," *The Washington Post*, January 24, 2021, https://www.washingtonpost.com/politics/2021/01/24/trumps-false-or-misleading-claims-total-30573-over-four-years/.

CHAPTER III: IS THIS PERSON LEADERSHIP MATERIAL?

61 Courtney Connley, "A Record 41 Women are Fortune 500 CEOs – and for the First Time, Two Black Women Made the List," *Make it: CNBC, Division of NBC Universal,* June 2, 2021, https://www.cnbc.com/2021/06/02/fortune-500-now-has-a-record-41-women-running-companies. html.

62 Aaron O'Neill, "Number of Countries with Women in Highest Position of Executive Power 1960-2021," *Statista,* June 4, 2021, https://www.statista.com/statistics/1058345/countries-with-women-highest-position-executive-power-since-1960/.

63 "Demographics of the U.S. Military," *Council on Foreign Relations,* July 13, 2020, https://www.cfr.org/backgrounder/demographics-us-military.

64 "Undergraduate Enrollment," *National Center for Educational Statistics 2019,* updated May 2021, https://nces.ed.gov/programs/coe/indicator/cha.

65 Lee Gardner, "What Happens When Women Run Colleges?" *Chronicle of Higher Education,* June 30, 2019, https://www.chronicle.com/article/what-happens-when-women-run-colleges/.

66 Swarna Venugopal Ramaswamy, "School Superintendents are Overwhelmingly Male: What's Holding Women Back from the Top Job?" *USA Today,* February 20, 2020, https://www.usatoday.com/story/news/education/2020/02/20/female-school-district-superintendents-westchester-rockland/4798754002/.

67 "Women in the U.S. Congress 2021," *Center for American Women and Politics (CAWP),* https://cawp.rutgers.edu/women-us-congress-2021.

68 Kenyon quote. Retrieved July 2, 2021, https://www.goodreads.com/quotes/3215674-just-because-you-can-doesn-t-mean-you-should---acheron.

69 Fred Johnson, "Build Relational Skills to Improve your Leadership," *Initiative One Leadership Institute,* July 13, 2015, https://www.initiativeone.com/insights/blog/build-relational-skills-to-improve-your-leadership/.

70 "10 John C. Maxwell Quotes Every Leader Should Know," *Lifeway Leadership.* Retrieved July 2, 2021, https://leadership.lifeway.com/2017/04/24/10-john-c-maxwell-quotes-every-leader-should-know/.

71 Hayden Bird, "Tom Brady's Philosophical Antonio Response and 3 Other Takeaways from His WEEI Interview," *Boston.com,* September 23, 2019, https://www.boston.com/sports/new-england-patriots/2019/09/23/tom-brady-antonio-brown-weei-interview/.

CHAPTER IV: WHAT QUALITIES/SKILLS DO EFFECTIVE LEADERS NEED?

72 Barbara Kate Repa, "Your Right to a Reasonable Accommodations Under the American with Disabilities Act (ADA)," *NOLO*, retrieved July 2, 2021, https://www.nolo.com/legal-encyclopedia/free-books/employee-rights-book/chapter7-8. html.

73 Ray Bradbury quote. Retrieved July 2, 2021, https://www.goodreads.com/quotes/547018-love-what-you-do-and-do-what-you-love-don-t.

74 "Seinfeld: The Nap," Season 8, episode 18, *NBC*, Created by Larry David and Jerry Seinfeld. Retrieved July 2, 2021, Seinfeld, season 8, episode 18 - the nap - Bing.

75 Dana Sparks, "Stop Negative Self-Talk to Reduce Stress," *Mayo Clinic News Network*, August 18, 2020, https://newsnetwork.mayoclinic.org/discussion/stop-negative-self-talk-to-reduce-stress/.

76 Lou Solomon, "Two-Thirds of Managers Are Uncomfortable Communicating with Employees," *Harvard Business Review*, March 9, 2016, https://hbr.org/2016/03/two-thirds-of-managers-are-uncomfortable-communicating-with-employees.

77 Jose Maria Rodriguez Garcia, coined in 1597, "Scientia Potestas Est – Knowledge is Power: Francis Bacon to Michel Foucault," *Springer Link*, January 2001, https://link.springer.com/article/10.1023/A:1011901104984?utm_medium=affiliate&utm_source=commission_junction&utm_campaign=3_nsn6445_brand_PID100357191&utm_content=de_textlink.

78 Glenn Croston, "The Thing We Fear More Than Death," *Psychology Today*, November 29, 2012, https://www. psychologytoday. com/us/blog/the-real-story-risk/201211/the-thing-we-fear-more-death.

79 Toastmasters International: https://www.toastmasters.org.

80 Ginger: https://www.gingerleadershipcomms.com.

81 TED Talks: https://www.ted.com/talks.

82 *The Public Speaking Project*, https://publicspeakingproject.org.

83 "Mehrabian's Communication Theory: Verbal, Non-Verbal, Body Language," *Businessballs*, June 9, 2017, https://www.businessballs.com/communication-skills/mehrabians-communication-theory-verbal-non-verbal-body-language/.

84 "The Egan Model and SOLER," *Counseling Central*, November 8, 2018, https://www.counsellingcentral.com/the-egan-model-and-soler/.

85 "Ray Tomlinson, Who Sent the First E-Mail, Has Died," *The Economist*, March 7, 2016, https://www.economist.com/science-and-technology/2016/03/07/ray-tomlinson-who-sent-the-first-e-mail-has-died.

86 Paul Goodman, "12 Disadvantages of Texting," *TurboFuture*, May 27, 2021, https://turbofuture.com/cell-phones/Disadvantages-of-Texting.

87 Allana Aktar and Marguerite Ward, "15 Email Etiquette Rules Every Professional Should Follow," *Business Insider*, September 4, 2020, https://www.businessinsider.com/

email-etiquette-rules-every-professional-needs-to-know-2016-1.

88 Arielle Pardes, "The Wired Guide to Emoji," *WIRED*, February 1, 2018, https://www. wired.com/story/guide-emoji/.

89 Adam Geller, "Half a Million Dead in US, Confirming Virus's Tragic Reach," *AP NEWS*, February 22, 2021, https://apnews.com/article/us-deaths-over-500k-coronavi-rus-acab3cc916330a3f068b7589350a18cd.

90 "Social Darwinism," *History*, April 6, 2018, https://www.history.com/topics/ear-ly-20th-century-us/social-darwinism.

91 William Ury, "Getting Past No – The Five Steps of Breakthrough Negotiation," *WilliamUry*, September 20, 2000, https://www.williamury.com/the-five-steps-of-break-through-negotiation/.

92 "Alternative Dispute Resolution at the Department of Justice," *The United States Department of Justice Archives*, updated July 24, 2020, https://www.justice.gov/archives/olp/alternative-dispute-resolution-department-justice.

93 Charles Green, "Five Approaches to Dealing with Conflict," *Chron*, January 29, 2019, https://smallbusiness.chron.com/five-approaches-dealing-conflict-894. html.

94 Roger Fisher and William Ury, *Getting to Yes: Negotiating Agreement Without Giving In* (Houghton Mifflin, 1992).

95 William Ury, *Getting Past No: Negotiating in Difficult Situations* (Bantam 1993).

96 "About William Ury," *Amazon*. Retrieved July 2, 2021, https://www.amazon.com/William-Ury/e/B000AQ6KZ8%3Fref=dbs_a_mng_rwt_scns_share. "About Roger Fisher," *Amazon*. Retrieved July 2, 2021, https://www.amazon.com/Roger-Fisher/e/B000AQ1S-RI%3Fref=dbs_a_mng_rwt_scns_share.

97 Jack Zenger and Joseph Folkman, "The Skills Leaders Need at Every Level," *Harvard Business Review*, July 30, 2014, https://hbr.org/2014/07/the-skills-leaders-need-at-ev-ery-level.

98 Amy Mitchell and Rachel Weisel, "Political Polarization & Media Habits," *Pew Research Center*, October 21, 2014, https://www.pewresearch.org/wp-content/uploads/sites/8/2014/10/Political-Polarization-and-Media-Habits-FINAL-RE-PORT-11-10-14-2. pdf.

99 David Milstone, "Leadership Theory and Civic Engagement Class Syllabus: Leadership and Ethics Seminar," *University of Massachusetts Dartmouth*, Fall 2019.

100 David Milstone, "Leadership Week Seminar," *Westwood High School*, May 2018.

101 Frank Sonnenberg, "Times May Change but Your Core Values Don't," *Frank Sonnenberg Online*, August 12, 2014, https://www.franksonnenbergonline.com/blog/times-may-change-but-your-core-values-dont/.

102 "New DDI Research: 57 Percent of Employees Quit Because of Their Boss," *AP News*, December 9, 2019, https://apnews. com/press-release/pr-newswire/d9af58456901b44039d248dc602d1567.

103 Heather Craig, "The Theories of Emotional Intelligence Explained," *Positive Psychology*, February 23, 2021, https://positivepsychology.com/emotional-intelligence-theories/.

104 Daniel Goleman, *Emotional Intelligence: Why It Can Matter More Than I.Q.* (Random House Publishing Group, 2005) and Daniel Goleman, *Working with Emotional Intelligence* (Bantam, 2000).

105 "Six Benefits of Emotional Intelligence in the Workplace," *Pacific Prime*, February 14, 2020, https://www.pacificprime.com/blog/six-benefits-of-emotional-intelligence-at-the-workplace.html.

106 David Walton, *Introducing Emotional Intelligence: A Practical Guide.* (MJF Books, 2012).

107 Myers-Briggs Type Indicator (MBTI): https://www.myersbriggs.org/my-mbti-personality-type/mbti-basics/the-16-mbti-types.htm.

108 Jacqueline Hinds, "Emotional Intelligence: Do You Know the Four Basic Components?" *Hinds Consulting Ltd*, December 18, 2017 (first published October 1, 2017, *HRZone.com*), https://www.wilsonhindsconsulting.com/post/emotional-intelligence-do-you-know-the-four-basic-components.

109 "Friends: The One Where Ross and Rachel Take A Break, ('We Were On a Break')," Season 3, Episode 15, *NBC*, Creators David Crane, Marta Kauffman. Retrieved July2, 2021, Friends episode "We were on a break" September 16, 2019 - Bing.

110 Jim Schleckser, "The Myth of Motivating People: Either They've Got It or They Don't – But There Is Something We Can Do," *INC.*, September 18, 2018, https://www.inc.com/jim-schleckser/the-myth-of-motivating-people.html.

111 "The Big Bang Theory: The Empathy Optimization," Season 9, Episode 13, *CBS* (2007-2019), Creators Chuck Lorre and Bill Prady, "The Big Bang Theory " The Empathy Optimization (TV Episode 2016) - IMDb.

112 Andrea Brandt, "Learn Empathy in Just 5 Steps," *Psychology Today*, September 6, 2018, https://www.psychologytoday.com/intl/blog/mindful-anger/201809/learn-empathy-in-just-5-steps.

CHAPTER V: HOW CAN WE HIRE THE LEADERS WE NEED?

113 Pamela Fuller, Mark Murphy, and Anne Chow, *The Leader's Guide to Unconscious Bias: How to Reframe Bias, Cultivate Connection, and Create High Performing Teams* (Simon & Schuster, 2020).

114 Banaji R. Mahzarin and Anthony G. Greenwald, *Blind Spot: Hidden Biases of Good People* (Bantam, 2016).

115 Minda Harts, *The Memo: What Women of Color Need to Know to Secure a Seat at the Table* (Seal Press, 2019).

116 Amber Cabral, *Allies and Advocates: Creating an Inclusive and Equitable Culture* (Wiley, 2020).

117 Will Kenton, "What is a Headhunter?" *Investopedia*, July 17, 2020, https://www.investopedia.com/terms/h/headhunter.asp.

118 "First Impressions: Nearly Half of Employers Know if a Candidate is a Good Fit Within the First 5 Minutes," *HR Daily Advisor*, March 9, 2018, https://hrdailyadvisor.blr.com/2018/03/09/first-impressions-nearly-half-employers-know-candidate-good-fit-within-first-5-minutes/.

119 Mehrabian's Communication Theory: Verbal, Non-Verbal, Body Language, *Businessballs*, June 9, 2017, https://www.businessballs.com/communication-skills/mehrabians-communication theory-verbal-non-verbal-body-language/.

120 "Friends: The One With The Cooking Class, (*Chandler's Job Interview*)," Season 8, Episode 21, *NBC*, Creators David Crane, Marta Kauffman. Retrieved July 2, 2021, Chandler's Job Interview (Friends) - Bing video.

121 "Friends: The One With Princess Consuela, (Rachel's Interview with Gucci)," Season 10, Episode 14, *NBC*, Creators David Crane, Marta Kauffman. Retrieved July 2, 2021, Rachel's Interview with Gucci - Friends - Bing video.

122 Richard Taverner proverb in 1539: "Better the Devil You Know." *Idioms Online*, August 4, 2018, https://www.idioms.online/better-the-devil-you-know/.

123 Courtney Connley, "A Record 41 Women are Fortune 500 CEOs – and for the First Time, Two Black Women Made the List," *Make it: CNBC, Division of NBC Universal*, June 2, 2021, https://www.cnbc.com/2021/06/02/fortune-500-now-has-a-record-41-women-running-companies. html.

124 Poll sent to approximately 500 *Facebook* and 1500 *LinkedIn* associates. Asked respondents to rate current and past supervisors as either 1) excellent/good, 2) fair/between good and not-good, or 3) not-good/poor. From March 13-30, 2021, 135 respondents rated 1412 supervisors and senior leaders as: excellent/good – 523 (37 percent), fair/between good and not-good – 569 (40 percent), and not-good/poor – 320 (23 percent).

125 Heather Craig, "The Theories of Emotional Intelligence Explained," *Positive Psychology*, February 23, 2021, https://positivepsychology.com/emotional-intelligence-theories/.

126 Peter G. Northouse, *Leadership: Theory and Practice* (Sage Publications, Inc., 2006).

127 Travis Bradberry, "Why do CEOs Have Such Low Scores in Emotional Intelligence?" *World Economic Forum*, July 2, 2019, https://www.weforum.org/agenda/2019/07/the-real-reason-your-boss-lacks-emotional-intelligence.

CHAPTER VI: WHEN IS IT TIME FOR A LEADER TO LEAVE?

128 Susan Cain, *Quiet: The Power of Introverts in a World That Can't Stop Talking* (Crown, 2013).

129 Saul McLeod, "Maslow's Hierarchy of Needs," *Simply Psychology*, December 29, 2020, https://www.simplypsychology.org/maslow.html.

130 "Seinfeld: The Wig Master (Jerry returns clothing for spite)," Season 7, Episode 19. *NBC*, Created by Larry David and Jerry Seinfeld. Retrieved July 2, 2021, Seinfeld - The Wigmaster, Jerry tries to return a jacket out of spite - Bing video.

131 Victoria Sarne, "Living Well is the Best Revenge," *The Tribune*, June 25, 2019, http://www.tribune242.com/news/2019/jun/25/life-lines-living-well-best-revenge/. "Living well is the best revenge" is a quote from George Herbert, a 16th century poet.

132 Christina Sterbenz, "12 Famous Quotes That Always Get Attributed," *Business Insider*, October 7, 2013, https://www.businessinsider.com/misattributed-quotes-2013-10.

CHAPTER VII: WHAT CAN WE LEARN FROM EXPERIENCED LEADERS?

133 Janet Kierstead, "Montessori and Dewey: A Comparison of their Theory and Practice," *ERIC*, 1980, https://eric.ed.gov/?id=ED198506.

134 "Endeavor Scholars Program at UMass Dartmouth Receives $75K Grant," *The Herald News*, December 9, 2013, https://www.heraldnews.com/article/20131209/NEWS/312099861.

135 Arianna Huffington, *Thrive: The Third Metric to Redefining Success and Creating a Life of Well-Being, Wisdom, and Wonder* (Harmony, 2015).

136 "A conversation with Arianna Huffington on redefining success." *The Forum at Harvard School of Public Health*, 2014, https://theforum.sph.harvard.edu/events/thrive.

137 Jim Rohn, "What happens, happens to us all," LifeShiftNow, September 4, 2013. The full quote from Rohn is "It's not what happens in the world that determines the major part of your future. What happens, happens to us all. The key is what you do about it," https://lifeshiftnow.wordpress.com/2013/09/04/what-happens-happens-to-us-all/.

138 Voltaire quote. Retrieved July 2, 2021, https://jonathansouter.com/2021/06/27/on-cultivating-ones-own-garden-first/.

CHAPTER VIII: HOW CAN WE CHANGE THE LEADERS WE HAVE TO THE LEADERS WE NEED?

139 Peter Parker (Spiderman), "With great power comes great responsibility." *Fandom*. Retrieved July 2, 2021, https://spiderman-animated.fandom.com/wiki/With great power comes great responsibility.

140 "The Simpsons: You Only Move Twice (Um, Are You Guys Working?)," Season 8, Episode 2, *FOX*, Creator, Matt Groening. Retrieved July 2, 2021, https://www.youtube. com/watch?v=r8miwsWtzRw.

141 "Kotter's 8-Step Change Model," *SanzuBusiness Training*, October 1, 2020, https:// sanzubusinesstraining.com/kotters-8-step-change-model/.

142 Ryan Williams, "10 Best David Letterman Top 10 Lists (2021)," *BounceMojo*. Retrieved July 2, 2021, https://bouncemojo.com/letterman-top-10-lists/.

143 Jon Archer, "If It Ain't Broke, Don't Fix It vs. Continuous Improvement," *DZone*, March 18, 2011, https://dzone.com/articles/if-it-aint-broke-dont-fix-it.

CHAPTER IX: 20 QUESTIONS (AND ANSWERS) WITH THE AUTHOR

144 Susan Cain, *Quiet: The Power of Introverts in a World That Can't Stop Talking* (Crown, 2013).

145 "Power and Authority," *Acton Institute: Lord Acton Quote Archive*. Retrieved July 2, 2021, https://www.acton.org/research/lord-acton-quote-archive.

146 Poll sent to approximately 500 *Facebook* and 1500 *LinkedIn* associates. Asked respondents to rate current and past supervisors as either 1) excellent/good, 2) fair/between good and not-good, or 3) not-good/poor. From March 13-30, 2021, 135 respondents rated 1412 supervisors and senior leaders as: excellent/good – 523 (37 percent), fair/ between good and not-good – 569 (40 percent), and not-good/poor – 320 (23 percent).

147 Michelle Adams, "What are the Essential Components of an I-Message?" *Gordon Training International*, May 31, 2012, https://www.gordontraining.com/leadership/ what-are-the-essential-components-of-an-i-message/.

148 Melissa Kelly, "Wait Time in Education: Giving Students a Chance to Think Before Responding Can Boost Learning." *ThoughtCo.*, April 4, 2020, https://www. thoughtco. com/importance-of-wait-time-8405.

149 "Robert's Rules of Order: Cheat Sheet," *BoardEffect*, retrieved July 2, 2021, https:// www.boardeffect.com/wp-content/uploads/2020/07/Roberts-Rules-of-Order-Toolkit-Refreshed. pdf.

150 David Cottrell, *Monday Morning Leadership* (Cornerstone Leadership Institute, 2002).

151 "Seinfeld: The Raincoats (The Close Talker)," Season 5, Episodes 18 and 19, "The Puffy Shirt (The Low Talker)," Season 5, Episode 2, "The Pledge Drive (The High Talker)," Season 6, Episode 3, *NBC*, Created by Larry David and Jerry Seinfeld, The Close Talker - Seinfeld - Bing video. The Puffy Shirt | TBS. com, Seinfeld Dan the high talker - YouTube. https://www.youtube.com/watch?v=pXlp0EVmxik.

Index

A

Accountemps, 171
active listening
  examples, 93
  impact, 103
  mediation subset, 111
  supervisory skill, 158
Acton, Lord Baron, 56, 59, 238, 269, 276
Affirmative Action, 41, 43
Amazon, 9, 125, 239, 266, 272
Americans with Disabilities Act (ADA), 81, 82, 271
Amin, Idi, 59, 124
Aramark, 200
arbitration, 108, 109, 111, 112
authentic, 224

B

Bacon, Sir Francis, 90
BambooHR survey, 39, 171, 268
Banaji, Mahzarin, 138
BANO, 236
Bennis, Warren, 17, 18, 266
best practices, 49, 150, 161
BetterUp Labs, 16, 171, 233
bias
  decisions, 221, 242
  hiring process, 44
  resources, 138
  societal/sexism, 65, 66, 238
  unconscious, 169, 170
Biden, Joe, 3
Big Bang Theory tv show, 24, 134, 267, 273
Board of Directors/Trustees
  challenges, 50, 177
  communication, 51
  hiring, 51, 52, 174

role, 48
Boston Children's Hospital (BCH), 208
Boston Marathon, 215
Bradbury, Ray, 83, 271
Brady, Tom, 70, 270
Branson, Richard, 12
Braven, 216
Burger King, 3, 4
Bush, George W., 2
Business Insider, 99, 233, 271, 275

C

Cabral, Amber, 139, 274
Cain, Susan, 186, 238, 275, 276
Career and Workplace Survey, 61, 171, 269
Carnegie, Dale, 92
Center for Analysis and Behavioral Research (CABER), 126
Change Theory, 232
Chara, Zdeno, 143
Chief Financial Officer (CFO), 79, 204
circular toxicity, 15, 21, 48, 140, 180, 240
Citizens School, 215, 216
Clark University, 194, 199, 202
coalition, 234
college students, 118, 119
Collins, Jim
  author, 36
  experienced leader, 194
commissioned officer, 66
communication skills, 24, 31, 66, 91, 94, 241
conflict resolution
  development, 113, 114
  primary types, 106

277

super-skill, 103
Congress, 61, 63, 66, 270
Constitution, 2, 172
Contingency Theory of Leadership, 175
Cook, Tim, 60, 124
Cooper, Sheldon, 24, 134, 267
Coronavirus/COVID-19, 3
Corporate Leadership Council, 38
Costanza, George, 83
Cottrell, David, 247, 276
counseling, 35, 73, 131, 145, 284
cover letter, 138, 150, 151
credibility, 25, 26, 88, 191
Crowe, Russell, 17
Cruz, Paula, 206, 258, 260

D

Daraprim, 60, 269
Darwin/Darwinian, 105
DDI/Frontline Leader Project, 6, 126, 171, 266, 272
Deloitte Report, 36
Department of Justice (DOJ), 112
Dewey, John, 191
Dream Scholarship/Gala, 211, 215
drivers
   highway leadership, 10
   MA Registry of Motor Vehicles, 10
   Progressive Drivers, 10, 11
   road rage, 4, 234
   rules of the road, 4, 234
   Same-Ole, Same-Ole Drivers, 11
   Win at All Cost Drivers, 10, 11, 13

E

Einstein, Albert, 233
Ellison, Larry, 53
email
   disadvantages, 99, 101
   history, 98, 99
   problematic examples, 101, 102
   tips on usage, 99, 100, 130, 131, 253

email diarrhea, 253
emoji, 98, 102, 272
emotional intelligence
   benefits, 126, 134
   roadblocks, 209
   self-awareness, 71, 117, 130
empathy
   emotional intelligence, 126, 127, 134
   leadership quality, 216
   learned skill, 74, 135
   narcissists, 53
Employee Assistance Program (EAP), 47
Employee Golden Rule, 19
Encarnacion, Joshua, 213, 258, 260
Endeavor Scholars, 207, 275
engagement, 4, 265, 266
Enron, 59
equality/equity, 42, 224
Esposito, Janet, 92
ethics, 61, 63, 114, 118, 125
executive leader (EL)
   accountability, 49, 56
   board of directors, 177
   decision-making, 27
   position legitimacy, 144
   professional development, 75, 188
   search process, 52, 146, 171, 172, 174, 175
   staff attrition, 40, 50
Executive Order, 41, 42, 268
executive recruiter, 145
executive search firm/ESF/headhunter, 145, 146, 147, 274
eye contact, 75, 97, 153, 160

F

Facebook
   poll, 7, 13, 149, 171
   social media, 97
faculty development, 41
first impressions, 40, 150, 151, 160, 161, 166
Fisher, Roger, 114, 272

ABOUT THE AUTHOR

Dr. David Milstone worked in higher education for four decades, most recently serving as the chief student affairs officer responsible for student development, leadership, and support offices at a large New England university. He has served as a Dean of Students at three colleges and universities, taught academic classes on Leadership Theory, Civic Engagement, and Social Justice, and has been a leadership development consultant and conference presenter throughout the United States. Dr. Milstone has served on university assessment and accreditation teams across New England and abroad, chaired community boards, and is a certified community mediator. He earned a bachelor's degree in education, a master's degree in counseling, and a doctorate in educational leadership, and lives in Massachusetts.

A portion of the proceeds from this book will be donated to Sharing the Harvest, a nonprofit, volunteer-driven community farm run by the Southcoast Massachusetts YMCA. The farm's mission is to alleviate hunger, promote volunteerism, and provide agricultural education to Southcoast residents of Massachusetts. Since 2006, volunteers have made it possible for the YMCA to donate 547,000 pounds of fresh produce to those in need across the cities and towns of Massachusetts.